Cognitive Behavioural Therapy in Primary Care

Cognitive Behavioural Therapy in Primary Care

A Practical Guide

Richard France and Meredith Robson

Jessica Kingsley Publishers
London and Philadelphia

We believe that there is no entirely satisfactory solution to the problem of gender pronouns in this type of material. Reluctantly we have adopted the traditional convention of using the masculine except where the majority of those under consideration are female. We felt that to use 'she' all the time would appear contrived to many of our readers and might also under certain circumstances be percieved as showing a sexist bias. We would like to apologise to any reader who may be offended by this solution.

First published in the United Kingdom in 1997 by
by Jessica Kingsley Publishers
116 Pentonville Road
London N1 9JB, UK
and
400 Market Street, Suite 400
Philadelphia, PA 19106, USA

www.jkp.com

First published in paperback in 1995

Copyright © 1994 Richard France and Meredith Robson

Library of Congress Cataloging in Publication Data
A CIP catalog record for this book is available from the Library of Congress

British Library Cataloguing in Publication Data
A CIP catalogue record for this book is available from the British Library

ISBN-13: 978 1 85302 410 8
ISBN-10: 1 85302 410 4

Contents

List of Tables

List of Figures

To the late Merlin and Paddy who continued to defy our
best efforts to the end

Part One

METHODS

Chapter One

Introduction

A sense of dissatisfaction with the established, largely pharmacological, methods of treating emotional and social problems was probably evident amongst general practitioners (GPs) and their fellow members of the primary health care team even before the news media and academic medicine took up the topic with crusading enthusiasm. It has, however, proved difficult to find an alternative that provides effective treatment producing reasonably rapid results within the short consulting time possible in general practice, when the majority of patients present with both physical and psychological problems.

Over the years various forms of psychotherapy have none the less had their influence on primary care. The most important of these has been the Balint movement which took its name from a Hungarian psychoanalyst who came to England World War II. He became interested in the dynamics of the doctor–patient relationship (Balint 1974). The groups that he started with GPs after the war profoundly influenced the modern view of the consultation, and their successors and the society and Journal (*Journal of the Balint Society*) founded in his name still flourish. The Balint philosophy and psychotherapeutic approach has been adopted enthusiastically by some GPs but never appealed to the majority, for even in its later modification, with increased emphasis on brief focal techniques, it does not conform to the realities of today's general practice. The same may be true of the client centred counselling of Carl Rogers (Rogers 1951) and the transactional analysis model of Eric Berne (Berne 1966) which also have their advocates and their uses. Compared with all these, drug therapy, despite its manifest drawbacks, is often quickly effective, easy to administer, accessible and relatively cheap. Indeed there are those who would argue that the six-minute consultation permits nothing more. These objections, however, are more often raised by those outside general practice than by GPs themselves. It is probably the case that few doctors stick rigidly to six minutes when faced with a newly presenting emotional problem. Most will give more time to this type of patient in the hope that it can be made up later by savings on simple cases such as sore throats and certificates. Surgery time is, however, always short and must be used economically. By using the cognitive behavioural approach, for example, the patient can make use of his own resources outside the consultation.

History

As with so many modern disciplines, sporadic references to the concepts later incorporated in cognitive and behavioural therapy can be traced back to antiquity. In spite of these it has essentially developed during the twentieth century, for example in the treatment of hysteria and shell shock in World War I (W.H.R. Rivers in Barker 1991) and largely within the last 30 years.

The work of Pavlov on the conditioned reflex (Pavlov 1927) and Thorndike (1913) on the psychology of learning in the earlier part of this century laid the theoretical foundations. Both worked with animals and Pavlov's dogs salivated to the production of meat and the sound of a bell, subsequently producing the conditioned response of salivating to the bell alone. This is still quoted as the typical example of classical (antecedent induced) conditioning.

Watson in 1920 produced the first clinical application of treatment based on learning theory when he tried to overcome the conditioned fear of Little Albert to a white rat and other furry objects (Watson and Rayner 1920). This must be one of the most famous incomplete experiments as Little Albert left the hospital before any conclusions could be reached. Later work by Jones (1924), Watson, Mowrer (Mowrer and Mowrer 1938) and others was more successful in the treatment of neuroses. By World War II a trickle of reports of early behavioural treatments was appearing. After the war this trickle grew steadily into a torrent.

In the 1950s Wolpe introduced systematic desensitisation in the treatment of phobias (Wolpe 1954). The subject learned to relax (the response incompatible with anxiety) and was then gradually exposed to the feared stimulus with resultant reduction of fear. In 1953 Skinner (q.v.) published *Science and Human Behaviour*, introducing the concept of operant (consequence induced) conditioning to explain many aspects of human behaviour. The novel *Walden Two* (Skinner 1976), based upon these ideas, had appeared some years previously. This must be an almost unique example of a work of fiction introducing a major advance in scientific thinking. In the 1960s the Maudsley Hospital group of Marks (1969), Gelder (Gelder, Marks and Wolff 1967) and Rachman (1966) extended the use of behavioural therapy to sexual disorders and were responsible for the introduction and use of flooding, i.e. rapid exposure as opposed to gradual exposure, into the treatment of phobias, and Ellis (1962) laid the foundations for the cognitive additions.

The 1970s saw a massive expansion of behaviour therapy into previously unexplored areas such as the management of depression and marital therapy. A considerable increase in the associations and scientific journals connected with the approach followed. Equally important, however, was the introduction of the cognitive or information processing element into the model. According to the original workers, behaviour had to be externally observable and measurable in order to have significance and the human subject was controlled by a 'black box' programmed to give a specific response to a given stimulus. Workers such as Mahoney (1974) and Seligman (1975) recognised and expressed the inadequacy of this concept. They began to study and modify internal or information processing behaviour leading directly to the rapid development of the cognitive therapy movement led by Beck (1976) and Meichenbaum (1977) and influenced by the work of Ellis (1962) back in the 1960s. It is this movement that dominated clinical therapy in the late 1980s and continues to expand, although the cognitive model on its own without the behavioural component has its limitations. At the same time as the post-war developments described above were taking place, the emerging profession of clinical psychology was looking for a role in treatment to supplement the one that it had already acquired in assessment. It was soon clear that behaviour therapy promised to meet that need and, ever since, clinical psychologists have been the foremost practitioners of this method of treatment and the cognitive behavioural approach has, in turn, provided the framework for a great deal of psychologists' treatment methods and research. Some early work was rather too dependent on the research psychologist's laboratory approach and some types of aversion therapy which were neither particularly attractive nor effective gave the model a dubious reputation which it took some time to live down. Gradually, clinical psychologists provided services which were based at district departments of child and adult psychiatry. Milestones in Britain were the founding of a separate Division of Clinical Psychology by the British Psychological Society in 1966, the founding of the British Association for Behavioural Psychotherapy (now British Association for Behavioural and Cognitive Psychotherapies) in 1972 (Hackmann 1993) and in 1995 a Special Interest Group in Primary Care. Clinical psychologists have become increasingly involved in primary care since 1972 and in many instances have been responsible for introducing cognitive behaviour therapy into surgeries and health centres. Here the principles and methods have attracted the attention of other workers, notably health visitors, social workers, counsellors and GPs themselves. In the last 15 years many behaviourally trained nurse therapists and some community psychiatric nurses with appropriate experience have offered cognitive behaviour therapy in the community in the UK, thus improving the availability of treatment. Resources of all kinds remain very scarce and dependent on local policy and funding priorities.

The Principles of Cognitive Behaviour Therapy

Cognitive behaviour therapy does not provide a panacea for all the difficulties faced by the GP or other primary health care worker when coping with psychological problems. There are, however, many ways in which the model fits the existing methods of working in primary care quite closely, in that problems can be defined and conceptualised in operational and functional terms.

The principles may be summarised as follows:

(1) Whilst originating from theories of learning, present-day methods are based mainly on empirical studies and are not slavishly derived from any one theory of function.

(2) Problems appropriate for management in this way must be current, repetitive and recordable. Treatment regimens are aimed at explicit, clearly defined goals. Progress is carefully monitored and discussed with the patient.

(3) Current controlling factors are paramount in both assessment and treatment. Past history is of value in functional analysis, formulation and choosing management strategy.

(4) An individual 'tailor made' description is used rather than fitting the problem into diagnostic categories which may be at best unhelpful or at worst misleading.

(5) Treatment plans should always emphasise the increase of the positive rather than the suppression of the negative.

(6) The patient collaborates as fully as possible in assessment, hypothesis creation and treatment.

(7) Reliable and objective measurements should always be made and the treatment plan modified if necessary in the light of these measurements.

The Place of Behaviour Therapy in Primary Health Care

The GP and other primary health care workers see a lot of short term psychological disturbance related to life events and transitions which nonetheless may be extremely disturbing and disabling while they last (Mann 1992). Second, they cope with periodic acute manifestations of long term problems, often starting in childhood. Third, they are often called upon to help people having to deal with unalterable stressful living conditions, material or personal. They are accustomed to using a practical, problem-solving approach with limited time available although many are aware of their lack of technical training in mental health (Turton, Tylee and Kerry 1995). A knowledge of cognitive behaviour therapy sets this practical approach within a framework and allows the experience of others to extend its scope (Strohsahl 1996). They do not have to rediscover everything for themselves as they go along but can tap into existing experience and methods. Primary care workers at behavioural workshops have often remarked that much of what they are learning is applied common sense which they use instinctively in consultations anyway. We do not see this as a criticism but believe that the nearer a behavioural intervention can be made to common sense and everyday life the more likely it is to be successful. In order to modify problems, however, change must be achieved. If the required change were completely obvious and easy the sufferer would probably have made it himself anyway and would not be seeking professional advice. Some additional knowledge and skill are required and the cognitive-behavioural approach can provide these.

Cognitive behaviour therapy can operate at three levels in primary care. With the most complex problems an understanding of what is possible enables the GP, nurse or health visitor confidently to refer a patient with a difficult problem, which they feel is beyond their personal resources, to the appropriate professional agency. In most cases this will be a clinical psychologist, or possibly psychiatrist, based in the community or in a local hospital department. At the second level the primary care worker decides to undertake an intervention himself. This will often involve more time in the early stages than the six-minute consultation allows. It is important that as accurate and complete analysis of the problem as possible is carried out. It need not, however, require a great deal more time and the later continuing sessions can be fitted back into normal surgery hours. At the third level it will be found that a knowledge of the cognitive behavioural approach is constantly useful when giving advice on everyday problems, be they physical, psychological or more commonly a combination of the two. For example, conditions and their antecedents and consequences are clarified by the use of a diary record and to be able to fit a problem such as childhood tantrums into an operant conditioning framework clears the thinking and improves the quality of advice given.

Suitable Problems

The principles of the cognitive behavioural approach and functional analysis can be applied to any situation if only to formulate the problem. If therapeutic techniques are applied, these should be monitored and evaluated and reference made to any recent research findings.

Suitable problems may, however, be fitted into three main groups:

Specific Psychological Disorders

(1) Anxiety states, phobic conditions and obsessive compulsive disorders.

(2) Depression – often combined in the primary care setting with antidepressant drug therapy.

Problems of Living

(1) Family, marital and sexual relationships.

(2) Self-damaging habits, such as smoking or excessive eating or drinking.

(3) Problems in childhood, such as enuresis, encopresis, eating problems, sleep disorders and tantrums.

(4) Failure to cope at school or work.

(5) Difficulties in adjusting to handicap or disability.

Problems Associated with Physical Illness

(1) Adherence to treatment.

(2) Preparation for surgery and recovery from illness and surgery.

(3) Chronic pain, hypertension, asthma and migraine.

(4) Illness and disability in old age including dementia.

This is by no means an exclusive list but is included simply to give some idea of the field covered. More information is given in the second part of the book where individual problem groups are considered.

References

Balint, M. (1974) *The Doctor, his Patient and the Illness.* London: Pitman.

Barker, P. (1991) *Regeneration.* Harmondsworth: Penguin.

Beck, A.T. (1976) *Cognitive Therapy and the Emotional Disorders.* New York: International Universities Press.

Berne, E. (1966) *Games People Play: The Psychology of Human Relationships.* London: Andre Deutsch.

Ellis, A. (1962) *Reason and Emotion in Psychotherapy.* New York: Lyle Stuart.

Gelder. M.G., Marks, I.M. and Wolff, H.H. (1967) 'Desensitisation and psychotherapy in the treatment of phobic states: A controlled enquiry.' *British Journal of Psychiatry 113*, 53–73.

Hackman, A. (1993) 'Behavioural and cognitive psychotherapies: Past history, current applications and future registration issues.' *Behavioural and Cognitive Psychotherapy Supplement 1*, (Passim).

Jones, M.C. (1924) 'Elimination of children's fears.' *Journal of Experimental Psychology 7*, 382.

Mahoney, M.J. (1974) *Cognition and Behaviour Modification.* Cambridge: Ballinger.

Mann, A. (1992) 'Depression and anxiety in primary care: The epidemiological evidence.' In R. Jenkins, J. Newton and R. Young. *The Prevention of Depression and Anxiety: The Role of the Primary Care Team.* London: Her Majesty's Stationary Office.

Marks, L.M. (1969) *Fears and Phobias.* London: Heinemann Medical.

Meichenbaum, D. (1977) *Cognitive Behavior Modification.* New York: Plenum.

Mowrer, O.H. and Mowrer, W.M. (1938) 'Enuresis: A method for its study and treatment.' *American Journal of Orthopsychiatry 8*, 436–59.

Pavlov, I.P. (1927) *Conditioned Reflexes: An Investigation of the Physiological Activity of the Cerebral Cortex* (trans. by G. V. Anrep) London and New York: Oxford University Press.

Rachman, S. (1966) 'Studies in desensitisation: II Flooding.' *Behaviour Research and Therapy 4*, 1–15.

Rogers, C.R. (1951) *Client Centred Therapy: Its Current Practice, Implications and Theory.* Boston: Houghton Mifflin.

Seligman, M.E.P. (1975) *Helplessness: On Depression, Development and Death.* San Francisco: Freeman.

Skinner, B.F. (1953) *Science and Human Behaviour.* New York. Macmillan.

Skinner, B.F. (1976) *Walden Two.* New York: Macmillan (New Edition).

Strosahl, K. (1996) 'Confessions of a behaviour therapist in primary care: The Odyssey and the Ecstasy.' *Cognitive and Behavioral Practice 3*, 1–28.

Thorndike, E.L. (1913) *The Psychology of Learning* (Educational Psychology 11) New York: Teachers' College.

Turton, P., Tylee, A. and Kerry, S. (1995) 'Mental health training needs in general practice.' *Primary Care Psychiatry 1*, 197–199.

Watson, J.B. and Rayner, P. (1920) 'Conditioned emotional reactions.' *Journal of Experimental Psychology 3*, 1.

Wolpe, J. (1954) 'Reciprocal inhibition as the main basis of psychotherapeutic effects.' *Archives of Neurology and Psychiatry 72*, 205.

Wolpe J. (1969) *The Practice of Behaviour Therapy.* Pergamon Press.

Useful Addresses

Association for the Advancement of Behavior Therapy, Membership Chairperson, 15 West 36th Street, New York, NY10018. The AABT publishes Behaviour Therapy five times per year. It also holds an annual convention, has an active committee structure and provides discounts on journal subscriptions.

British Association for Behavioural and Cognitive Psychotherapies, Harrow Psychological Health Services, Harrow, Middlesex HA1 3JV Tel: 0181 869 2326 Fax: 0181 977 1017.

Membership Secretary, Social Services Department, Craig House, Bank Street, Bury, Lancashire BL9 0BA. Journal: Behavioural and Cognitive Psychotherapy (Wisepress). The Association holds an annual conference and workshop conventions. It also has active regional branches and provides discounts on journals.

Other Journals

Behaviour Research and Therapy .Elsevier Science Ltd, Exeter.
Journal of Behavioral Medicine. Plenum Press: New York.

Chapter Two

Services and Organisation

Special Characteristics of Primary Care

Primary care is the ideal setting for the application of cognitive behavioural techniques to psychological and organisational problems. The functional and behavioural analysis of problems is suitable for psychological problems related to both physical and mental illness and the transitions and problems of everyday life.

The dictionary definition of primary is that which holds first place in time, importance and development. It precedes that which is secondary. The primary health care team are at the cutting edge and are accessible in both time and location to meet patients' needs without the stigma, real or imagined, attached to the mental health services. Cognitive behaviour therapy can be a useful tool in the help offered by all members of the team, even if it only consists of an assessment of a patient's problem in order to refer within the team or on to secondary services.

Primary care differs from other settings in that patients choose whether or not to use the service in response to their own needs. The clinician deals with any problem that the patient chooses to bring. The help required for the problem is a matter of negotiation, not of guidelines and tight adherence to the therapeutic models. No problem is 'inappropriate' as by definition either the patent or the referrer perceives the situation as a 'problem' in need of clarification or solution. Similarly, if one consultation is all that the patient thinks he requires it is often because he has derived benefit. It is not necessarily non-compliance in the derogatory sense (as is often assumed) if he fails to return or to fulfil the prescribed tasks at that particular time.

The 'General Psychological Practitioner'

A clinical psychologist working as a 'general psychological practitioner' in the primary health care team should be available to patients in the same way as the medical general practitioner (Cummings 1991a). Appointments should be available quickly. The concept of a waiting list is anathema to primary care as much misery is caused by serious short term problems and some of these, if neglected, will become long term problems causing more distress and consuming more resources. Appointments with the patients can be of differing lengths, available at various times of day and allow flexibility in terms of number, spacing and location. If patients can opt in and out of the service then there may be no need for contracts, acceptance 'into therapy' or discharge, but there should be open communication and liaison with other members of the team who may be involved. There has been recent enthusiasm for short contact therapy with rigid formats, most notably the 'two plus one' protocol introduced by Barkham and Shapiro (1988). These represent an alternative to the structure outlined above but appear less flexible.

Flexible Interventions

In primary care work it is difficult and disadvantageous to separate assessment and therapy in the conventional sense (Cummings 1991a). It can result in a lot of time being spent collecting excessive information and for some patients this may be unnecessarily intrusive at this stage of intervention. Informed intuition by the patient and professional may be the preferred starting point but such flexibility requires experience and it may be useful for the less experienced to work with some form of analysis check list (see Chapter Three).

A service which is responsive to patients' needs, however well organised, cannot open all the pathways or break down all the barriers which exist between experience of discomfort or symptoms and their relief.

Socio-economic and demographic factors influence health and consult-ation rates, as do individual psychological characteristics, coping abilities and locus of control. Patients of different ages and sex or ethnicity may have very different views on the acceptability of asking for help via the surgery or health centre. It is important to keep a close eye on barriers to access and try to be both flexible and innovative in what is offered and how it is offered. At this early stage help-seeking behaviour is extremely fragile, particularly when sensitive problems are involved. Comments such as:

'I do not want to go into therapy.'

'It seems like a sledge hammer to crack a nut.'

'I am not mental – why do I have to go to a mental health team.'

'I can't get to the hospital and I don't want to be seen there.'

are commonly heard and indicate the ambivalence of many people of seeking help and also the discrepancy between their perception of their problems and those of professionals. These remarks also highlight the anxiety aroused by the stereotypes and myths still surrounding psychological therapies, mental health and psychiatry.

Structure of Care

For the non-mental health professional the use of cognitive behaviour therapy (CBT) in primary care can be defined at three levels, determined by the resources, knowledge, skills and interest of the providers.

(1) At the basic level the clinician should have enough knowledge of the appropriate applications of CBT to liaise with available specialists and be able to refer patients for assessment, advice or specific therapy. Ideally, such users of resources would know enough of assessment, functional and operational analysis of problems so that more accurate targeting of help can be achieved than is possible using a diagnostic label based on the medical model.

(2) The second level is to use selected methods derived from CBT in everyday clinical situations for example the use of self-monitoring diaries, simple anxiety management with the help of a patient leaflet (see Chapter Six) and help with sleeping problems. Groups, for example for stress management or child behavioural problems, can also be incorporated in the practice programme.

(3) The enthusiast can incorporate CBT theory and practice into the core work of a profession. Many therapeutic or organisational interventions can be based on a sound functional analysis, hypothesis testing and monitoring of the particular situation. Initially this might involve extra time and effort, but this diminishes somewhat as expertise develops. Often if time is spent initially in analysis and setting up a programme, later monitoring can be re-incorporated in normal surgery work.

Provision of Services

A difficult part of the task of the clinician when wanting to refer a patient for cognitive behaviour therapy (CBT) is understanding the resources and skills available in his locality both inside and beyond the primary health care team. In the current structure of the NHS, resources vary greatly between different trusts, teams, and departments and access is often limited by policy restrictions, waiting lists and strategies of commissioning agencies. The need for neat (on paper) referral pathways and neat financial management and neat or right models of therapy has tended to dictate the local planning of primary care services in five main ways:

(1) It has produced a *shifted outpatient service.* That is, the main therapy service is offered by individuals from secondary care who work in GP surgeries but do not incorporate the advantages of this setting into their service structure and impose a model of service delivery lifted directly from a hospital setting.

(2) Patients with mental health problems are referred from primary care direct to a *community mental health team.* This is clearly inappropriate and often unacceptable for the majority of patients who visit the GP with a psychological problem and this is particularly true if the problem has a substantial physical component.

(3) Consultants in mental health impose a *primary care 'triage' system.* This may be efficient but is unreliable. Many patients, especially those presenting somatic symptoms, need time and the opportunity to reveal the psychological nature of the problem and the right moment may well be missed. Similarly, many problems in primary care can be resolved with one or two sessions of specialist CBT intervention and this opportunity would be lost for at least a third of the patients.

(4) *Independently appointed counsellors and psychologists* have been employed in primary care, especially by fundholders. This may be cost effective but limits networking, the liaison with, and development of secondary care services.

(5) Clinical psychologists, counsellors and nurses may work in surgeries on *contract arrangements* from local trusts. This can provide for the patients a non-threatening and flexible access to CBT provision and from there to other specialist services in the PHCT (Primary Health Care Team), secondary care or the voluntary sector (Cummings 1991b).

Response in the Community

The first goal of a CBT practitioner working in primary care is to try to understand the needs of the patient by accepting that by consulting, the patient, by definition, wants some help and the term 'inappropriate referral' should be used extremely sparingly if at all. The attendance may have been self-initiated or have been encouraged by the doctor, health visitor, nurse or any other member of the ever increasing team. There is no gold standard used by the community to judge the severity of a problem. Severity is a multi-dimensional concept and includes the real and perceived characteristics of the problem. The important starting point is to find out what has led to an attendance at this particular time and hence what response in terms of assessment, intervention and coping methods may be appropriate. It follows that a first appointment should be available to a patient in the practice at the earliest opportunity and at worst within a week or two of requesting it. Analysis and intervention can progress hand in hand thereafter and therefore be picked up and dropped as need arises and be incorporated into the patient's own way of life. It also follows that a flexible time scale and opportunity for appointments is necessary for maximum benefit. It is unhelpful to have a rigid number or length of sessions. If several members of the team work in a cognitive behavioural way, then by liaising rather than working separately or even in opposition to each other, valuable ideas, information and support will be available. Where medication is used in conjunction with 'talking therapy,' side effects of drugs, different ways of prescribing the drug taking, the use of placebo and one off prescriptions for certain events may all be important for planning a patient's therapeutic programme and defining realistic goals.

Summary of the Special Characteristics of CBT Services in Primary Care

(1) Patient lead service.

(2) Patients opt in and out of the service as required.

(3) Knowledge of local services, both statutory and voluntary, is easily available, for example, employment, recreational, advisory and educational.

(4) Appropriate timetables for patients.

(5) Local setting involving less travel, less time and less child minding.

(6) Availability of life-span knowledge of the patient in the PHCT.

(7) Waiting lists can be avoided.

(8) Easy liaison between members of the PCHT.

(9) Relatives and friends can co-operate in consultations or therapeutic programmes.

(10) Secondary care can be available.

(11) Reduction of stigma.

(12) More acceptable to those with physical health problems.

References

Barkham, M. and Shapiro, D. (1988) 'Psychotherapy in 2 sessions: a research protocol.' *Social and Applied Psychology Unit Memo No 891*. University of Sheffield, Dept. of Psychology.

Cummings, N.A. (1991a) 'Brief intermittent therapy throughout the life cycle.' In C.S. Austrad and W.H. Berman (eds) *Psychotherapy in Managed Health Care – The Optimal Use of Resources*. Washington: American Medical Association.

Cummings, N.A. (1991b) 'Arguments for the financial efficacy of psychological services in health care settings.' In J.J. Sweet, R.G. Rozensky and S.M. Tovian. *Handbook of Clinical Psychology in Medical Settings*. New York: Plenum.

Recommended for Further Reading

Resnick, R.J. and Rozensky, R.H. (eds) (1996) *Health Psychology Through the Life Span*. New York and London: American Psychological Association.

Chapter Three

Assessment

We now come to consider the order and content of the initial interview. There is no need to carry out the scheme presented here in its entirety on every occasion. Often time will not permit this in primary care, sometimes much more detail will be required about certain parts of the scheme at the expense of others. Assessment should be regarded as more of a problem solving exercise than an effort to find a diagnosis and its matching treatment. Disorders in primary care often do not lend themselves easily to DSM IV (American Psychiatric Association 1994) classification and for this reason an attempt has been made under the International Classification of Diseases (10th revision) (ICD 10) to include a classification of mental disorders including management guidelines (Üstün *et al.* 1995). The value of this has yet to be proved, as has the value of management guidelines in psycho-social disorders in primary care in general. It is rather depressing to find that this proposed classification *with management guidelines* was constructed by three psychiatrists and two epidemiologists. The authors do not include either a GP or a clinical psychologist with primary care expertise which may, we fear, limit its usefulness. The concept of a once and for all assessment can be misleading in primary care and lead to a false distinction between assessment and therapy.

One of the special characteristics of offering a cognitive behavioural approach in this setting is that any session will be a mixture of assessment, education in the model and 'treatment'. There is therefore no need to complete this interview schedule at one sitting. Some of the background information may already be known to primary care workers and the rest may be built up over several shorter contacts and through diaries and question-naires. In this way the system is particularly suitable for use in short clinic sessions and within normal surgery appointment systems with whichever professional is involved.

The more prescriptive nature of cognitive behavioural work means that assessment is more multi-dimensional than with other types of psychotherapy. Problems, and hence, interventions, vary with symptoms, maintaining factors, aetiology and patient characteristics. Different aspects of one problem may require several techniques and conversely multi-problem cases may require the creative application of only one technique as the problems may all arise from the same root. Often the initial contact serves to define or structure the problem into the behavioural, cognitive, and physiological components and their interactions. This process is often sufficient for the patient to see how to apply their own coping methods and release themselves from what may have seemed overwhelming and insoluble distress.

A checklist of the various assessment stages which follow is included at the end of this chapter for easy reference.

Presenting Problem(s)

Some statement of the presenting problem will have been made before the decision to adopt the cognitive behavioural approach has been taken. A much more detailed description is likely to be necessary as most patients present their problems in vague general terms such as 'I feel awful', 'I can't cope', or 'I'm always so tense'. Sometimes problems are described from the outset in terms of possible solutions, for example, 'I think I need a tonic', 'something to make me sleep' or even 'I must have something for my nerves'. None of these descriptions really tells us very much and the first task is a gentle but searching clarification of the problem. It may turn out, for example, that feeling awful or needing tranquillisers is related to a recent episode of shouting at a child who repeatedly asks questions. This is followed by guilty thoughts related to 'having lost control as a mother' which has in turn produced a depressed feeling 'because mothers shouldn't behave like that therefore I am an inadequate mother'.

The patient should be asked to describe precisely the frequency and intensity of the problem and give an idea of why they have come for help at this time. The history and development of the condition and previous episodes of difficulty are helpful in as much as they clarify the surrounding circumstances. Those circumstances which lead to the problem behaviour are the antecedents and those which occur as a result of the behaviour are the consequences. It is generally the consequences that reinforce the thoughts and behaviour, maintain it and thus make it difficult for the patient to overcome the problem themselves.

This detailed description of the facts and how they have affected the patient's thinking allows the clinician to get to grips with the problem. Once a clear description has been obtained it is worth summarising this with the patient who will thus be able to confirm that it is correct and will probably also be reassured that his or her difficulty has been understood. Patients often agonise for a long time before seeking professional services on personal and psychological matters. Uppermost in their minds during this time is the fear that their problems may be misunderstood and inappropriately treated. Some reassurance, therefore, that the clinician is on the right track and they are not wasting your time is extremely welcome at this early stage.

None of this should imply that a problem or problem list cannot be revised later. Often patients are themselves only dimly aware of the real nature of a problem at a first interview and the picture may change radically as time goes on. There is therefore a limit to what can be gained from lengthy assessments and more emphasis can be given to designing good data collection diaries and monitoring devices.

Other Problems or Problem Areas

A balance has to be struck between allowing the interview to drift off into irrelevant topics and missing some other essential ingredient of the patient's distress. Usually a few open questions will uncover other important problems and these may then be clarified by limited direct questioning. Suitable questions might be 'If this problem were put right would anything else be bothering you?' or quite simply 'Do you have any troubles in other parts of life?' The patient may not always see these as relevant to the chief reason for his seeking help. They may none the less be important in their own right, substantially affect the persistence of the presenting problems or alter the possible channels of intervention. A patient suffering from panic attacks in shops is not likely to get much help from her spouse as co-therapist if there is a pre-existing marital problem and the panic is exacerbated by anxiety. A mother of five small children living at the top of a tower block with a broken lift is unlikely to do homework tasks outside the home or attend appointments at a specialist clinics.

Positive Characteristics of the Patient (Client Assets)

The patient's strengths and skills can usefully be discussed at this point for three reasons. First, it is useful to note how aware he is of his good points and how ready he is to talk about them. Second, a short time spent on the things he does well may relieve the gloom of the discussion of difficulties.

Third, the discovered assets will often be used in a subsequent treatment plan. As well as the things he currently does well and enjoys doing, it is useful to enquire about past activities which have now been discontinued. This often serves to demonstrate how changes in life style have contributed to the current difficulties, and the re-introduction of these, or related activities will often be a goal in treatment of certain types of disorder. Exercise is often abandoned with disastrous consequences on physical and mental health but this can easily be reversed.

Functional Analysis of the Problem(s)

This is the core of the whole interview. The object is to discover the factors currently maintaining the problem, in what way it is interfering with the patient's life and also whether its persistence is serving any useful purpose for him or for others. The object of the functional analysis is to look at the target problem or *behaviour* in relation to its *antecedents* and *consequences*, conveniently memorised as the A-B-C model. Each of these factors may *increase* or *decrease* the behaviour, making it more or less likely and they may occur either *externally* (overtly) in the outside world or *internally* (covertly) in the internal thoughts and feelings of the patient.

When referring to and analysing the problem there are three aspects which require consideration each in terms of the antecedents, behaviour and consequences of the problem (the ABC).

(1) The overt external behaviour itself (always observable).

(2) The physical or bodily reactions (either observable, recordable, measurable, or reported).

(3) The associated internal factors, the thoughts, images and feelings (as reported by the patient).

Antecedents are the cues or triggers which lead to the behaviours (as exemplified by the bell in Pavlov's experiment to produce salivation in dogs (see Chapter One). In a current clinical situation the end-of-meal cup of coffee serving as a stimulus for lighting a cigarette would be a typical example. Certain therapy programmes, particularly those designed to cope with habit disorders, rely on interrupting the link between cue and response. Cues rarely operate in isolation but lead from one to the other in a chain before finally producing a response. Each cue produces its own intermediate response which in turn acts as a cue for the next response and so on until the final behaviour which is causing a problem. The length of this chain will determine how easy it is to reach the final behaviour and how easy it is to alter the final behaviour by interrupting the chain. Let us consider the man who wants to smoke with his after-lunch coffee. He may simply be offered a cigarette and a light by a fellow diner. This constitutes a very short chain and the links are easily forged. If, however, he needs to fetch his debit card from his locked car, go to the bank, stand in a queue, get money from the cash point, go to the tobacconist, buy cigarettes and lighter fuel, refill his lighter and finally light the cigarette, the chain is long and the final response only reached after considerable effort. The differences can be used advantageously when designing a programme to modify an unwanted response.

Behaviour—a precise description of the problem is required. It can be useful to ask the patient to describe a recent example of the distressing situation.

The background and general environment in which a problem occurs are also important. Technically, these contextual factors may be cues of a sort but if important elements are not to be overlooked it is wise to consider them separately. For example, panic attacks may occur in a tube train but not in an overground train and sexual difficulties may present themselves in a bedroom but not on a rug in the living room. This is an example of a situational variable. Others may be cognitive, behavioural or physiological.

The third element of the A-B-C model, the *consequences*, is generally the most important of all. The effects that the patient's problem are having on himself and those around him must be considered. These may be either good or bad, positive or negative, and by a feedback mechanism may have a strong effect on the frequency or severity of the problem.

The effect that consequences have upon an event producing them is the result of *operant conditioning* which, although first described in detail by Skinner (1953) (see Chapter One), has probably been a feature of human behaviour since the beginning of the race. Put very simply, we do those things more intensely and more often which we know from experience are likely to be rewarded or have a positive consequence. For example, we go to work with the reasonable expectation that we will get paid. Actions may, however, have other results or consequences; for instance, stopping a particular behaviour may produce a reward, the behaviour may be punished or it may achieve no results at all.

Behaviour can therefore be changed by altering the consequences, as removal of the reinforcers will cause extinction of the behaviour. Punishment will tend to reduce the frequency of a behaviour unless the punishment holds reward value itself, such as providing attention for the person being punished who might otherwise be ignored.

The use of operant techniques in therapy will be discussed in Chapter Five, but supporting factors must be understood in the assessment before they can be modified in treatment.

Most of the discussion so far has involved the externally observable (overt) first and second aspects of the A-B-C model. The internal information processing systems, however, can be involved at any point producing cognitive (covert) cues, background factors and consequences. It is important to note that negative thoughts can be powerful in initiating and maintaining maladaptive behaviour. Thus statements such as 'I wonder if I'm going to panic', 'I'll never get a girlfriend again', 'I know I won't get to sleep', 'I've failed again' all help to feed fear and anticipatory anxiety, or reinforce the feelings of failure and inability to cope. The meaning of the problem to the patient should also be considered at this point. For example, he is unlikely to respond well to biofeedback treatment of his tension headaches if he believes these to be due to hypertension or a brain tumour and these possibilities have not been discussed nor his blood pressure measured.

Finally, under this section an enquiry should be made about any incompatible behaviours which could be of use in management. It is virtually impossible to pull out hair while wearing thick gloves, or to tense the mouth and neck while chewing gum. Patients generate their own incompatible behaviours with a little guidance and it is as well to let them do so without the prejudices and values of the therapist intruding! Incompatible behaviours also have their cognitive aspect, for example blocking thoughts by singing or reciting poetry aloud. These are used in certain distraction techniques which will be discussed later under their appropriate sections.

Development of the Problem

Information on the origins and development of the problem may reveal important additional facts and can be used to test the data obtained from the functional analysis. A problem may have occurred for the first time in connection with job change, marriage, childbirth or some other significant transition. A significant life event in a parent, spouse or friend may give rise to a problem. All GPs will be familiar with the man who develops chest pain following sudden death from a heart attack of a colleague at work. The mediating mechanism in this case might well include; (1) an overestimate of the risk of coronary heart disease in his age group, (2) selective attention to otherwise unimportant chest sensations, and (3) a gloomy estimate of the stress produced by the job. These three together combine to initiate worrying thoughts about heart attacks with a subsequent increase of the bodily symptoms.

It is valuable to see how people have responded to stress or crisis in the past, as this can become a prototype for the way they will attempt to solve future crises or transitions. This may result in an adaptive means of self help or a defensive response such as depression, dissociation or somatisation. For instance, a child who is under stress at school may find that a 'tummy ache' serves to relieve the problem although replacing it with another. By incorporating this information in the formulation, therapeutic interventions can be better adapted to help the individual learn new ways of responding and to understand the reason for the required change.

Some enquiry about changed circumstances can also be made at this point. A wife's returning to work may have quite profound effects on both partners, as may a change from employed to self-employed or unemployed status. It is worth finding out if previously valued activities have been gradually lost due to life changes or abandoned because of physical or psychological problems. It is common to find rewarding activities becoming more and more infrequent with depression and other problems. If this is the case, is it because of lack of time, interest or money or because they are no longer eagerly anticipated? What would need to happen for them to be reinstated or what new activities or ambitions could be initiated?

Previous Coping Attempts

Although many patients attending GP surgeries have a psychological component to their distress, the majority do not and they manage to 'cope' most of the time. In spite of this, 'I can't cope' is a frequent presenting statement in the consultation and may signal psychological problems more often than the presentation of a clear symptom suggesting a formal diagnosis.

In assessing a person's coping effort and ability, it is necessary to define which particular aspects of the person or situation is creating the 'threat' to their well-being and whether their coping is adaptive and successful or maladaptive and failing. Lazarus (1993) outlines two kinds of coping.

(1) *Problem focused* – endeavouring to create change by altering oneself, the environment or the interaction between them.

(2) *Emotion focused* – endeavouring to change the meaning of, and ways of focusing on, the environment to reduce the stress even though the conditions cannot or may not be changed.

Because both types of coping are relevant to primary care consultations which encompass physical and psychological problems, it is relevant to consider coping style as part of the assessment before embarking on an intervention with certain categories of patients.

Difficulties arise where people have psycho-social problems, chronic ill health or long term threats (e.g. of redundancy, terminal illness of a relative or an alcoholic family member), where there is a limit as to what can be done to change the situation.

In these cases more emotion focused effort, using cognitive methods, is the preferred choice as rational problem solving could be counter-productive and actually increase stress.

However, as well as coping style, the functional analysis will reveal to what extent there is room for change in spite of what appears to be an overwhelming stressor. There is usually some room for manoeuvre to alleviate stress but this may be more successful following or accompanying some cognitive change rather than as a first line of attack.

Coping processes can be assessed using the Ways of Coping Questionnaire (Folkman and Lazarus 1988). This highlights the use of *problem focused strategies* – aimed at trying to solve a situational problem and *emotion focused strategies* which aim to reduce the internal distress caused by a situation.

Sub-strategies measured in the Questionnaire will give more detail as to what respondents actually do and hence how to intervene therapeutically. Researchers who assessed coping in chronic fatigue syndrome sufferers and their carers stress the importance of looking at the coping and illness adjustment in both carers and sufferers where this relationship exists (Ax, Greg and Jones 1996).

There have almost always been some previous attempts to cope with the problem. The ones that the patient has thought it worthwhile to use himself are particularly important. Any intervention should, where possible, be based on the satisfactory elements of the person's repertoire of coping skills. This will increase the chance of success, boost the person's self esteem and minimise the scale of intervention needed. Many people, for example, use distraction techniques or positive self talk, but may need help to target these techniques more appropriately at the current problem. In other cases their own techniques may be out of date, inadequate, or overburdened by the current problems. In these cases a more radical change of direction may be called for. A common reaction to anxiety is progressively to avoid places where anxiety occurs until even leaving the house is a problem or reliance on alcohol is adopted for the relief of tension. Relatives and friends may have made some attempt to help or other attempts may have been made to get professional help from other sources.

Finally, if it is not already available, the nature and effect of any medication which has been prescribed for the problem should be noted and the patient's attitude to medication taken or offered. Benzodiazepines should rarely be prescribed now for indications apart from crisis anxiety but are still used as sleeping pills and can cause problems if prescribed regularly for any length of time. Anxiolytics or beta blocking drugs can be useful if a patient is required to enter a one-off situation while still early in treatment and where a severe panic would be a risk. For example: an agoraphohic having to attend a wedding reception while still struggling to get to the corner shop, or a business man or woman needing to give a presentation at a client's firm while still finding it difficult to speak at meetings. Fear of flying still affects a large number of people but there are good courses, tapes and books which can be recommended rather than medication (see end of Chapter Six).

Expectations of Outcome

The importance of the patient's own interpretation of his problem has been mentioned earlier. It follows, therefore, that it is also necessary to discover what sort of management the patient is expecting and whether he believes that it can help. He may have come expecting a prescription for some sort of medication and some preparation, perhaps with the help of a booklet, may be necessary before he is prepared to accept another approach or the possibility of a combined treatment of drugs and psychological therapy. In this situation the short consultation can prove useful, as the seeds of an idea can be sown at one visit and time for consideration and perhaps home reading allowed before the next. This is particularly valuable when the clinician is thinking of using an approach which may be unfamiliar to and unexpected by the patient. Previous attempts at treatment should be described and possible reasons for failure discussed. When the current treatments and rationale for them are explained, differences from previous attempts may be highlighted. For example, the current treatment may offer more regular appointments, partner co-operation, consideration of cognitive factors or a complete change of direction from drug treatment to a behavioural approach.

Effects of Change

Assessment also requires an investigation of the limits that have been placed on a person's life as a result of the problem. Situations which directly provoke or exacerbate a problem may gradually be avoided and this avoidance often spreads at an alarming rate until the patient's life is very restricted. These facts can be elicited from a discussion of how life used to be and how this pattern has changed. Some patients have always avoided certain situations because they feel incapable of handling them. The assessment should discover what they want life to be like. As well as considering whether the patient thinks change is possible, it is important to consider the effect of change, for better or worse, upon the patient, his family and the environment.

Some will have unrealistic expectations of the effect of a desired change. The fat girl who loses weight will not necessarily find the world a Utopia – rather she may have difficulties with her female friends who now perceive in her a threat which was not present previously. The agoraphobic who manages to get a job and have her own money to spend has seemingly benefited, but how is this going to affect her husband who has devoted his life to enabling her to stay at home and not have to go out? Is he going to be able to adjust to her increased assertiveness, competence and, by extension, to his changed role?

Forming an Hypothesis

From the information gathered in the interview it should now be possible for patient and therapist in co-operation to form an hypothesis of the rationale and maintenance of the problem. In one sense this takes the place of a diagnosis but it should always be provisional, flexible and subject to modification in the light of further information. A medical diagnosis usually leads to a standard form of treatment. A cognitive behavioural hypothesis, on the other hand, is first further tested by means of baseline measurements followed by the setting of goals and the formation of a mutually agreed individual treatment plan, all of which may be modified as time goes on.

Cognitive Behavioural Checklist for the Interview Assessment

(1) Exact description of the *presenting problem(s)* or *pattern of behaviour.*

(2) Outline of *other problem areas.*

(3) Obtain information about skills, pleasures and positive characteristics of the patient (*client assets*).

(4) *Functional analysis of the problem(s), with regard to both behaviour and cognitions.*

    (a) *Antecedents* producing increase or decrease.

    (b) *Background* contextual factors producing increase or decrease.

    (c) *Consequences* of behaviour either positive or negative on patient/spouse/others.

    (d) *Incompatible thoughts, images and behaviours* – physical or functional.

(5) Obtain a short description of the *development* of the problem.

(6) Obtain information about the *previous coping attempts* of the patient/spouse/others.

(7) Discuss the patient's *expectation of treatment* and whether change is possible.

(8) Obtain information about the likely *effect of change* on patient/spouse/others.

References

Ax, S., Greg, V.H. and Jones, D. (1966) 'Coping with chronic fatigue syndrome'. Paper presented at BPS Annual Conference, Brighton, April 1966.

Folkman, S. and Lazarus, R.S. (1988) ' If it changes it must be a process: study of emotion and coping during three stages of a college examination.' *Journal of Personality and Social Psychology 48*, 150–170.

Lazarus, R.S. (1993) 'Coping Theory and Research: Past, Present and Future.' *Psychosomatic Medicine 55*, 234–247.

Sturmey, P. (1995) *Functional Analysis in Clinical Psychology*. Chichester: Wiley.

Recommended for Further Reading

American Psychiatric Association (1994) *Diagnostic and Statistical Manual of Mental Disorders*. Washington: American Psychiatric Association.

Barlow, D.H., Hayes S.C. and Nelson R.O. (1984) *The Scientist Practitioner*. Oxford: Pergamon.

Bellack, A.S. and Hersen, M. (1988) *Behavioral Assessment· A Practical Handbook*. Oxford and New York: Pergamon Press.

Hawton, K., Salkovskis, P.M., Kirk, J. and Clark, D.M. (eds) (1989) *Cognitive Behaviour Therapy for Psychiatric Problems. A Practical Guide*. Oxford: Oxford University Press.

Üstün, T.B., Goldberg, D., Cooper J., Simon, G.E. and Sartorius, N. (1995) 'New classification for mental disorders with management guidelines for use in primary care: ICD-10 PHC.' Chapter Five. *British Journal of General Practice 45*, 211–213.

Chapter Four

Data Collection and Monitoring

It is sometimes difficult to obtain precise antecedents and consequences but these can often be disentangled with the help of charts, questionnaires and diaries. The problem itself may be ill-defined and it is useful to ask the patient to keep a record of a typical episode of a problem or some relevant factors on a typical day or week after the initial appointment. For example, patients may complain that they 'never sleep a wink' or are 'never without a headache'. It is often informative and therapeutic to discover, by keeping a precise record, that their problem follows some pattern or is not quite as severe as they describe. The fact that they do sleep an hour or two or have the odd hour without a headache on Sundays provides a glimmer of hope. It also helps motivation and makes sense of the problem by searching for the pertinent factors controlling it before embarking on a regime of therapy.

All stages of a programme require the collection of data for the purposes of monitoring. It is necessary to arrive at baseline measurements, to show change during a programme and to assess outcome. The data collected during the baseline period serve to clarify and confirm the initial hypothesis which in its turn has indicated what sort of data may be required. At this stage a preliminary contract may be agreed with the patient. This should include:

(1) Tentative goals of treatment.

(2) Agreement on methods to be used.

(3) Responsibilities of both parties.

(4) Time limit for this particular intervention if necessary to the patient or therapist.

Once agreement on the methods to be used has been reached the details of baseline recording can be decided. Theoretically this recording may be of four kinds:

(1) Mechanical recording of physiological variables such as heart rate, blood pressure, electro-myographic studies and galvanic skin response.

(2) Measurement of a permanent product such as pages of work written, numbers of wet beds or activity schedules.

(3) Observational recording such as the number of hours out of bed, number of tics, number of social interactions etc.

(4) Thought and feeling record.

Observational Recording

In the primary care setting this the most frequently used method. Before any piece of observational recording is attempted a number of questions must be considered. These are:

(1) What precisely is to be observed and recorded?

(2) Who is to do it?

(3) When is it to be done?

(4) For how long is it to be done?

(5) What is to happen if problems are encountered?

All of these require some further consideration.

What precisely is to be observed and recorded?

Many problems are initially expressed in terms far too vague to permit accurate measurement. 'Bad behaviour' in a child and 'failing to help in the house' by a partner or flatmate are subject to many differing interpretations and not amenable to proper measurement. The number of times Jack punches Tracy would be an exact and measurable refinement of 'bad behaviour'. Even so, problems of definition may occur. For example, does a nudge during tea-time count as a punch? It does not matter greatly what the decision is, as long as it is clearly understood by all involved and the same definition is consistently applied.

When considering what is to be measured it should be borne in mind that only a few specified behaviours can be recorded at any one time without inaccuracies creeping into the results.

Who is to do it?

Most commonly it will be the patient himself and there will be no problem. If a child is the subject and the parents are to do the recording it must be decided how the task is to be shared or else confusion will result. Whenever possible the child should be included at some level.

When is it to be done?

This often requires the most judgement and must be decided according to the expected nature and frequency of the problem. If Jack punches Tracy only intermittently then a simple count of punches, similar to a boxing referee's score sheet, may suffice, noting the time of each punch. This is called *event frequency recording*. If however the rate of punching is increased then this type of recording may be too time-consuming and we may have to be satisfied with counting the punches in the first ten minutes of each hour or on a car journey to school – a technique called *time sampling*. An alternative way of limiting the number of observations to be made is *interval recording* where the day is divided into a number of equal periods and a record made of whether any punches occur during each interval. More continuous behaviour such as dribbling or studying may require a *duration record* to yield adequate information. Where the incidents to be studied are more complex, such as panic attacks or depressive episodes, a diary record of several aspects of the same event may be necessary.

For how long is it to be done?

This must be decided in advance and will be determined by such factors as the expected frequency of the problem and the timing of the next appointment. Too long a baseline recording period may alienate the patient, whereas too short a one may not yield adequate information.

What is to happen if difficulties arise?

It is wise to foresee the unforeseen and include an agreed mechanism for dealing with difficulties. The easiest is to offer some way of making contact before the next appointment – generally a brief telephone call will suffice to sort the problem out. Alternatively, a sample recording can be dropped off at the surgery to be checked and the patient contacted if there appears to be a difficulty.

The Diary

The 'diary' is the most universal assessment tool for this approach. It can be made simple or complicated and adapted to changing requirements as therapy progresses and different information is required.

Many patients are at first unable to specify when a problem occurs or to describe the events surrounding the problem or their thoughts and feelings about it. Similarly they may have lost awareness of avoidance behaviour and can use the diary to pinpoint what they are *not* doing as well as what they *are* doing.

The diary can also serve to put the problem in perspective and allow the patient to see a trend of progress over time even though there may be setbacks or plateau phases in the course of treatment. Some crude overall rating over a period of time may also highlight the possible cyclical nature of problems. Detailed counts of specific behaviours or behavioural deficits can be made and these can be rated and related to changes in mood.

The diary is often used to monitor thoughts, images and emotions (see Chapter Six for an example of a record) as well as external behaviour. Like avoidance, thoughts and mood changes can be so automatic that this type of recording is essential to make the patient aware of them. The association between certain activities and moods and the thoughts which provoke or accompany them may become apparent only with the help of a diary.

Physiological reactions, if recorded in a consistent way, can be used to challenge cognitions. A patient who panics because he thinks the tightness in his chest is a sign of an imminent heart attack can see that it occurs at times of emotional stress but is absent when he plays squash or runs up stairs. This information can then be linked to coping strategies like muscle relaxation and positive self talk for the early stages of panic.

It is useful to design a very simple diary to start with and add more if the patient feels this can be managed. Easily observable behaviours and feelings may be recorded first and more complex thoughts and images added later. It is possible to design charts (especially useful for children) where only a tick, cross or star is needed to complete the chart.

The diary is flexible and can be appropriately modified to self-monitor in any type of problem. If there is a real danger of a private or particularly personal or embarrassing record being found or seen by other people it is advisable to invent a code or shorthand which is only comprehensible to the patient. This diary can usually be designed to fit in a small notebook so that it can be carried around at all times and filled in when thoughts and situations arise. Ratings made in hindsight are inaccurate and thoughts become abbreviated summaries. Sometimes practice is required to record personal details on paper or, at the other extreme, some patients are prone to write a full scale autobiography each week. Diaries can be modified in these cases and care be taken that the patient, especially if depressed, does not feel a failure or be labelled uncooperative just because they are unable to think or record in those terms. Despite being a journalist, one patient had a writers block when it came to his own emotions and could only describe images for the first stages of treatment. Diaries are commonly 'forgotten' when coming to the next appointment and this should act as a reminder for the clinician to explore possible blocks. It should also be remembered that even today illiteracy is still common and the possibility that the patient may be educationally rather than psychologically incapable of writing must be borne in mind.

When the concern is with cognitions rather than external events, the diary is used both to identify thoughts and feelings and to record alternatives generated in the course of therapy. Tables 4.1–3 show examples of typical diaries.

Table 4.1. Urgency and frequency of micturition

Date	Time	Where	Anxiety (0–10)	Urgency (0–10)	Amount (0–10)	Drinks
Wed.14	7.15	Home	4	7	8/10	1 cup hot water 2 cups coffee
	7.50	Home	4	4	4	
	8.10	Leaving	6	4	1	
	11.45	Office	3	8	10	2 cups coffee
	1.00	Office	3	4	6	1 cup coffee
	5.00	Office	3	6	10	1 glass sherry
	10.30	Home	2	4	10	1 cup coffee
Thurs.15	6.35	Home	2	2	8	1 cup water
	7.15	Home	2	3	4	2 cups coffee
	7.55	Home	2	7	1	
	8.10	Home	4	6	1	
	11.35	Office before dictation	5	8	5	2 cups coffee
	2.00	Office	3	5	6	1 cup coffee
	7.00	Theatre	7	9	5	1 glass wine
	9.00	Theatre	7	9	2	1 cup coffee
	11.30	Home	2	6	8	1 mug milk

Note: The aim of the diary is to discriminate cues for urgency with and without need to urinate.

Table 4.2. Record of sleep

Date	Time to bed	Approx. time to sleeping	Number times awake	Action	Feelings next day (Rate 0–10)
18.	11.00	1.30–2	3–4	Moved to spare room	6–7
19.	11.00	11.30ish	3–4	Husband to other room	6
20.	11.45	12.30	2	No probs.	7–8
21.	11.30	3.30	many	Went to spare room	6–7
22.	11.30	3.00	3–4	Ditto	5–6
23.	10.30	11.00	2 (one long)	Got up made drink	6
24.	9.30–11.00	1.00	many (noise outside)	(1) to spare room (2) ear plugs	7–8
25.	11.00	3.00	3–4	To spare room with drink and snack	5
26.	11.15	11.30	2–3	Husband in other bed	6–7
27.	12.00	12.30	3	Ditto	7–8
28.	11.00	11.20 12.45	several	took sleep pill because bladder over-sensitive	7

Table 4.3. Baseline diary relating relevance of cigars to beer consumption

Day	No.Cigars before 17.30	No.Cigars after 17.30	Pints of Beer	Total Cigars
Tues.	2	9	7	11
Wed.	3	5	3	8
Thurs.	2	7	7	9
Fri.	2	4	5	6
Sat.	1	8	6	5
Sun.	2	0	0	0

Rating Scales

These can be considered in two groups: home-made scales tailored for individual problems and used in conjunction with diaries, and formal questionnaires and schedules usually addressed to a particular type of problem or problem group.

Home-made Scales

These can be infinitely adapted to suit individual situations. They are used to impose a measurement system on something such as a symptom which is not usually subjected to measurement. This in turn has several uses:

(1) It serves to clarify the pattern of the problem in the patient's own mind.

(2) It enables him to describe that pattern more easily to the therapist.

(3) It enables change and outcome to be measured and recorded.

(4) It shows up the relationship with other variables which may need modification.

Such scales may seem contrived and unfamiliar to some patients. Their use should be explained and the patient involved in the design of the scale and some preliminary practice in completing it, using as an example a recent occurrence of the problem, before leaving the surgery. Once they are familiar with the idea fewer hurdles usually arise as patients discover that rating their problem gives them some additional control over it (see Table 4.1). The diary records the pattern of the patients problem of urgency and frequency of micturition which was becoming very disabling and limiting the patients life. The patient was also drastically reducing her liquid intake. The diary therefore highlighted the fact that the anxiety type feeling of urgency did not correlate with amount of urine produced and could be discriminated from a real need to urinate in response to a full bladder. She could also see that increasing her liquid intake to her previous level did not affect the 'anxiety urgency' which tended to occur when access to a toilet was difficult. Problem solving was also introduced and the wearing of incontinence pads was suggested for a time to tackle avoidance situations such as long bus journeys. Table 4.2 demonstrates how keeping a diary helped the patient establish a base line of sleep and see if any particular factors or actions affected the number of waking times. Such diaries often demonstrate that how a person feels the next day does not always correlate with what they consider to be a good nights sleep.

Whilst systems such as the above can be used, there are two other systems that may be applied in a number of diverse situations:

(1) The *visual analogue scale* (VAS) is usually a 10cm line with verbal tags at certain points, as shown below. This type of scale is used in a number of formal assessment instruments but it is only a matter of labelling the points meaningfully to adapt it for individual use in other situations. There can be any number of points on the scale but there is evidence that nine or five points is, in most cases, optimal as fewer do not allow sufficient discrimination and more do not increase sensitivity.

Table 4.4. Visual analogue scale

0	1	2	3	4	5	6	7	8
Calm		Slightly anxious		Definitely anxious		Markedly anxious		The most anxious you could be

(2) *Subjective units of disturbance* or SUDS (Wolpe 1973 p.120); a system used mainly in the context of anxiety, which uses a rating out of a hundred with the result expressed as a percentage. Beck (Beck *et al.* 1979) uses percentages to express degrees of emotion and beliefs in thoughts.

These artificial scales are used alone if there is a single dimension to measure but are more meaningful if used during a session of graded exposure or cognitive therapy to monitor immediate change. They can be used in conjunction with other diaries or formal questionnaires. It is important to find out how far an agoraphobic can go from home and what situations she avoids as well as the subjective degree of anxiety about it.

Formal Questionnaires and Schedules

These are less important in the context of primary care but it is worth being aware of them; the advantages and disadvantages can then be assessed for a particular patient, therapist or problem. There are those to be completed by the patient, which can often be done in the waiting room to save time, and those used by the therapist to quantify a problem or results of a clinical interview. Their disadvantages are:

(1) They are not designed for the individual problem.

(2) The clinician using them must fully understand the usefulness and limitations of each instrument and in many cases this requires special training.

(3) A stock of forms and in some cases score sheets must be readily available.

(4) Many originate in the USA and there may be some cross-cultural wording difficulties in their use in other countries.

(5) There is a tendency to rely too much on a score which may be misleading, or accurate only for a limited time (state-dependent).

(6) They may be seen as mechanistic, and may adversely affect the clinician–patient relationship if used insensitively.

There are a number of compensatory advantages:

(1) They provide additional information about severity and progress.

(2) This information is in a form in which comparison is possible with that of other workers for research purposes.

(3) For the most part they have been designed by authorities with a great deal of care and thus may be better expressed and balanced than home-made alternatives.

(4) They are usually comprehensive in their subject and may pick up important points which can be missed at interview.

Vast numbers of questionnaires exist covering every conceivable topic and problem area. Even full-time professionals can not know more than a limited number selected for appropriateness for their field of work. The best advice for the primary care worker is to get to know reasonably well a few that are appropriate for problems which frequently occur in that setting and which serve the dual purpose of monitoring and providing useful additional assessment. Reference should be made to the literature when deciding which questionnaires to use for a research study, however small in scale, so that results can be assessed in relation to other studies.

Details of several questionnaires which have been found useful are:

○ General Health Questionnaire (Goldberg 1972)

○ Beck Depression Inventory (Beck *et al.* 1979, pp.398–399) (reprinted in full)

○ Beck Anxiety Inventory (MH needs ref RF)

○ Marks and Mathews Fear Inventory (Marks and Mathews 1979)

○ Hospital Anxiety and Depression Scale (Zigmond and Snaith 1983)

Other more specialised ones are mentioned in their appropriate chapters.

Assignments and Homework Tasks

Homework is a core feature of cognitive behaviour therapy for a number of reasons. First, the behaviour and cognitions are observed first-hand by the patient himself which increases the clarity with which he sees and understands the factors maintaining the problem. Second, doing the recording may increase the sense of control over the problem itself, often alleviating the problem and the feelings of helplessness somewhat. Third, the fact that this part of the work is done by the patient himself confirms the self-management philosophy of this form of treatment. Fourth, it reduces the requirement for expensive and limited therapist time. It is strange that GPs have always been aware of time pressures in their job but have been largely reluctant to allow the patient to take control of at least part of his treatment himself, be it medical or psychological. Specifically homework assignments may be used:

(1) To assign the monitoring tasks. To record behavioural and cognitive factors, initially for baseline, and then for therapeutic or measurement reasons. For example, the activity schedule.

(2) To observe and record a live situation and thus test a hypothesis formed previously in the session. For example, it appears that panic attacks occur in the supermarket when there is a long queue and when the patient has a full trolley of urgently needed shopping. She may be asked to test out her reaction when the shop is quiet and she has just picked two items to buy.

(3) To learn and practice a new skill for use in therapy. For example: learning to challenge irrational beliefs, learning relaxation, distraction or massed practice.

(4) To apply a technique or skill to test its effect in a controlled situation. For example: contributing once to a conversation in a group situation such as the pub or seminar. Asking for help from a friend or using relaxation and controlled breathing when beginning to feel bad on a train or bus.

(5) To test the validity of some belief or opinion. For example, if the patient believes she is a failure because her child wakes at night and other children do not, enquiries may be made to other mothers as to how their children do in fact behave.

Clarification of Goals

After the collection of baseline data the treatment goals are clarified, modified if necessary and restated, and the treatment contract adjusted in any other way indicated by the new information.

Goal Setting

In the initial stages of assessment when the patients are considerably distressed by their problem, it may be difficult to concentrate on long term goals and they may decide on fairly modest changes. Other patients suffer considerable anticipatory anxiety if too much emphasis is put on defining goals high on their hierarchy of difficulty. It may be better in these cases to concentrate on more immediate tasks and renegotiate further goals as treatment progresses. One useful technique is to ask them to project them- selves well away from the current problems and think what they would ideally like to be doing in five years time, one year or one month. It may then be possible to find some life plan or ambitions and hence a hierarchical path to achieve these ends. At least this will allow the patient to feel that his efforts are heading in the right direction, however long the path. This time projection technique is helpful with patients whose response to tasks is 'yes but' and those who feel they have already 'wasted years' or feel it's 'too late to start'.

Some patients, particularly the 'perfectionists', set unrealistically high goals and see any intermediate steps as an unacceptable compromise. An attempt at cognitive restructuring should be made or failure at these goals will demoralise both patient and therapist.

Goals should always be defined in clear operational terms. For example, in the case of someone who is socially anxious:

- to enter a pub at lunchtime and have one soft drink
- to buy a sandwich in the work canteen and sit with colleagues for at least five minutes before returning to his desk.

Statements such as 'feeling confident', 'able to cope', 'be sociable' must be translated into workable targets.

Allied to the agreement on goals is the need for discussion and agreement on the type and methods of treatment to be tried. A brief outline of the main features of cognitive therapy for depression, or a description of the difference between desensitisation and flooding for treatment of a specific phobia, enable the patient to decide and judge if it 'fits' with his view of the problem and his coping capabilities.

The Contract

This is really a matter of personal preference and philosophy.

A contract is usually unnecessary when CBT is used in the day-to-day surgery consultation. In fact by imposing such restrictions on patients you may inadvertently sabotage their efforts at self-help and personal responsibility which you are trying to encourage.

However, contracts may be an advantage to the 'therapist' where:

(1) a patient makes unreasonable use of open access through surgery and clinic appointments

(2) time for appointments has to be specially set aside by the clinician

(3) evidence exists that fixed spacing or a contracted number of sessions improves potential outcome, for example; sex therapy or cognitive therapy for severe depression

(4) it is helpful for the patient and or therapist to be clear about what is expected of them.

A contract is always open to re-negotiation. An agreement can be made to review progress after a fixed number of sessions and decide whether further work would be beneficial.

Scheme of Intervention

The type of treatment programme is the joint decision of the patient and therapist. The decision depends on the preferences and motivation of the patient, the abilities of the therapist, the factors to be modified and other available treatment resources. Early success is important, therefore more simple problems or stages should be tackled first. The monitoring will indicate the usefulness of any intervention and what changes need to be made to the programme if progress is unsatisfactory. It may be that the best move at this stage is to refer on for more specialist help or a second assessment. This should be done in such a way that neither patient or therapist feels they have failed but merely moved on to another stage. Problems are compounded when patients come for therapy with histories of all the other therapies they have tried and failed when they may only have had an introduction interview and not 'had the therapy'.

References

Beck, A.T., Rush, A.J., Shaw, B.F. and Emery, G. (1979) *Cognitive Therapy of Depression.* New York: Guilford.

Beck A.T. and Matthews (1985) *Anxiety Disorders and Phobias.* New York: Basics Books Passim.

Goldberg, D.P. (1972) *The Detection of Psychiatric Illness by Questionnaire.* London: Oxford University Press.

Marks, I. and Mathews, A.M. (1979) 'A brief standardised self-rating scale for phobic patients.' *Behaviour Research and Therapy 17,* 263–267.

Wolpe J. (1969) *The Practice of Behaviour Therapy.* Pergamon Press.

Zigmond, A.S. and Snaith R.P. 1983) 'Hospital anxiety and depression scale.' *Acta Psychiatrica Scandinavica 67,* 361–370.

Useful Material Source

Powell, T. (1992) *The Mental Health Handbook.* Bicester: The Winslow Press.
(This spirally bound book contains questionnaires, including several mentioned in this chapter, and a wealth of patient handouts designed to be copied for therapeutic use.)

Chapter Five

The Basic Concepts of Intervention

The purpose of this chapter is to give an idea of the range of techniques used in cognitive behavioural treatments. The main concepts are covered in outline, leaving the practical applications and more specialised techniques to be considered in the second part of the book under the chapters devoted to individual groups of problems.

Because they are simpler and serve to illustrate the general scientist–practitioner approach, the behavioural techniques are described before the cognitive ones. This is not meant to imply that they are more important, in fact the reverse is probably true. Cognitive theory and practice is advancing all the time with new fields, theories and techniques being expounded (Salkovskis 1996).

Behavioural Interventions

It is convenient to consider two classes of measures; those designed to increase and those designed to decrease particular behaviours. This distinction is, however, by no means clearcut, as certain techniques can be used in different ways to obtain change in either direction. The first part of each section will deal with basic techniques leading to a description of more complex compound methods later.

Measures to Increase Behaviour

Reinforcement

This is probably the most important behavioural tool with large numbers of applications over many problem areas. It derives from the basic operant principle that behaviour is maintained by its consequences. The reinforcer is defined as that consequence (or the C part of the A-B-C model mentioned in Chapter Three) which, when following a behaviour, increases the likelihood or frequency of that behaviour occurring in the future. It is thus almost identical to a reward in ordinary language but the latter has rather more limited, less universal, connotations. It is a truism that reinforcers are not the prerogative of behaviour therapy. Everyone who passes an exam, gets a smile or collects a pay packet has received a reinforcer. A reinforcer may be supplied directly such as food or a toy for a child, or indirectly by means of a star on a chart or a nod of approval. Money is really an indirect reinforcer but has come to occupy an intermediate position because its value is universally apparent and acknowledged. Many indirect reinforcers have widely differing values from person to person – a smile from a particular person may have a powerful reinforcing value to one recipient but none at all to another. As with other behavioural concepts, reinforcement may be from outside (overt) or from within the person himself (covert) and methods of covert reinforcement will be considered under the cognitive section. The effects of a particular reinforcer will depend upon how it is applied and this applies equally to negative or unpleasant consequences – see Table 5.1.

Table 5.1 Application of reinforcers

Consequence	Administered	Withdrawn
Positive (Reward)	Behaviour increases (Positive reinforcement)	Behaviour decreases (Response cost)
Negative (Punishment)	Behaviour decreases (Punishment)	Behaviour increases (Negative reinforcement)

Specific situations where reinforcement is used in therapy will be considered individually in their appropriate sections in Part 2. Positive reinforcement may be applied continuously or intermittently. If intermittently the ratio may be fixed or variable. The type of schedule selected will vary the effect on the behaviour.

A reward after every performance results in a behaviour pattern being acquired quickly but if the reinforcer is withdrawn the behaviour ceases (extinguishes) equally quickly.

Fixed intermittent ratio schedules can be learned so that the response pattern increases when the reinforcer is expected. This is shown by the increased queue for the fruit machine when the next jackpot is thought to be due. The players assume that the machine operates on a fixed schedule and a certain amount of time or number of pulls must elapse between one jackpot and the next. They may, however, be wrong and the machine may operate on a variable schedule with no fixed interval between reinforcers.

Variable schedules promote the slowest but most permanent learning. Many unrewarded trials have to take place before the respondent becomes sure that no reinforcer is forthcoming and the response is extinguished. There are many examples of different reinforcement schedules in everyday life; investing in the stock market, doing piece work, waiting for buses or doing scientific research may be quoted as just a few. The behaviour therapist looks at the schedules of reinforcement operating in his subject's life and sees if they can be changed or modified to produce improvement in the target problem.

In order to promote reinforcement of changed behaviour certain rules have to be observed for maximum effectiveness. Reinforcement must be *immediate* – delayed reinforcement is greatly weakened (few will wait an extra month for their pay).

It must be *consistent* – great damage is done if the expected reinforcer doesn't materialise. This of course only applies to continuous and fixed ratio schedules.

It must be *significant* to the subject – ice creams are not reinforcers if you don't like ice creams even if your parents and therapist do.

It must be *appropriate* – too small a reinforcer is ineffective, too large a one unmanageable. We know that Richard III in Shakespeare's play offered his kingdom for a horse but his value system was modified by extreme circumstances. Some parents involved in behavioural programmes are a little like Richard III. They suggest reinforcers out of proportion to the task such as a bicycle if Sam takes his tablets for a week. If too valuable a reinforcer is used it distorts the value of the behaviour being reinforced and makes it difficult to design a continuing programme. There is a danger that the supply of reinforcers will become quickly exhausted. It is often possible to work towards a valuable terminal material reinforcer by using a points system as token reinforcement. For example, if Sam takes his tablets he gets one point per day recorded on a chart towards the 100 points needed for a bicycle. Small tangible intermediate reinforcers such as marbles or toys may be used in addition to points.

It must be *frequent* – whether a continuous or intermittent schedule is used the reinforcer has to be available often enough to have some effect.

It must be *specific* – 'some money', 'a treat' or 'be nice to you' are not specific. They might be replaced by 'give you 5p', 'allow you to watch TV half an hour longer' or 'take you out to dinner at the Chinese restaurant'.

It must be *unmixed with criticisms* – 'thank you very much for doing the washing up but why didn't you start doing it 10 years ago' will not serve as a positive reinforcement. If possible reinforcers of *variable kinds* should be used rather than a single system. This applies particularly in families where praise from mother, father, granny and older sister will be more effective than just mother alone. It is also important to be specific about the action that has earned the reward and reiterating this to others, may also serve as a positive support. For example Kirk, a diabetic aged 10, is told: 'You earned your points for preparing your syringe, cleaning the skin, filling the syringe with the right dose of insulin and giving your injection correctly!' When father appears for breakfast, mother repeats the same statement in front of father and son in the hope of gaining some back-up of approval from father thus increasing the reinforcement. It also makes clear exactly what has to be done to earn the reinforcement.

The examples quoted have concerned children and adolescents but the same principles apply to adults being reinforced by themselves or others. In the main, such programmes are somewhat easier for children as it is simpler to gain control over the potential reinforcers.

Under certain circumstances it may be difficult to find sufficient desirable behaviour to reinforce. With, for example, a disruptive child, it may be necessary to engineer a situation where the child does something that can be reinforced and start the process of shaping (see p.46) from there.

From Table 5.1 it will be noted that negative reinforcement also acts as a reward and thus increases behaviour. It works in the same way as the old saying about banging your head against a brick wall – it's nice when it stops. A classic clinical example of both positive and negative reinforcement is the child that cries at night and is taken into bed with his mother to get him to stop. The child receives positive reinforcement from the mother's warm bed. The mother gets negative reinforcement as the crying stops and she can get back to sleep. The result of this sequence is that both the crying and the taking into bed are likely to be repeated. The short-term negative reinforcement of mother may become a long term punishment for her (and father) when the child in bed becomes a nuisance.

Prompting, modelling and shaping are all used to create new behavioural patterns.

Prompting or Cueing

These belong to the A or antecedent end of the A-B-C model (Chapter Three) and occur in a number of different forms. A prompt may be a set of verbal instructions to cope with a particular social or business situation, such as initiating a conversation or asking for a rise, or it may also be a therapy manual or instructions for a set of homework tasks. With children, prompting will often take the form of physical guidance through a task, by holding the child's hand, for example. Once this has been done a number of times the therapist gradually fades his involvement by allowing the child to undertake progressively more steps by himself. Quite complicated chains of behaviour can be taught even to children with learning disabilities if these are first broken down into a series of smaller and simpler steps. The final steps in the chain, such as actually putting the food in the mouth or pulling up the pants and flushing the toilet, are usually taught first by vigorous reinforcement. In this way the achieving of the final target can also be used as an additional reinforcer (backward chaining).

Many child and adult programmes also involve the use of cues in the form of prompt cards or self instruction, which introduces a cognitive component, using positive statements like 'I did it last time so I can do it again now' or 'It won't be easy but I'm sure I can make it because I know what to do' written on them. Cues for relaxation sequences may be provided by the patient saying a key word such as 'calm' to himself or looking at a red spot or the date on a watch. Cue discrimination is taught by teaching the patient to spot the earliest physical sensations produced by hyperventilation or those leading to panic so that an appropriate alternative, more helpful, response can be put into operation. In the cognitive treatment of depression the identification of worrying thoughts serves as a cue to generate more rational alternatives which will be discussed in more detail in Chapter Nine.

Modelling

The presentation of an appropriate model is a useful way of forming new behaviour patterns. The model may either be the therapist or a competent performer observed in real life. A member of a peer group, if feasible, is likely to be a more effective model than someone who appears remote or authoritarian. This has been found to be particularly important with problems such as smoking in school children. Someone who performs the task with a struggle (the coping model) will be more effective than a perfectly accomplished performer (the mastery model) (Meichenbaum 1971). A suitable setting may be found in role play, films or videos, or in real life. A short role play of situations like interviews or asking for a date is perfectly feasible in the consulting room and the rehearsal may prove invaluable for the real life attempt. For modelling to be successful a system of small individual steps may have to be used so that the eventual goal is reached gradually. Judgement, experience and negotiation are required to assess how much is achievable at each step. The power of modelling in changing behaviour is seen in populations at war or in a crisis when panic or courage can be transmitted by the behaviour of a few prominent individuals (Rachman 1980).

A problematic form of modelling is frequently seen in the consulting room when children of headache sufferers themselves complain of the same symptom or express other forms of distress in terms which they have learnt from common family usage. More useful is the apprenticeship type of craft training formerly used in many professions and trades and still found in medical education. The medical student is expected to develop his or her diagnostic skills by emulating the eminent consultant on his teaching round. Later the GP registrar is provided with a model in the form of the trainer. A traditional but effective form of modelling is the examination of the doll or the teddy bear's chest so that the young patient can learn what to expect before his turn comes and at the same time be persuaded that 'Teddy didn't mind so he won't either'.

There are many further practical uses of modelling. Demonstrations to the newly diagnosed diabetic of a competent performer giving his own injections are helpful. Films of similar children coping with an operation are shown to children about to undergo surgery to accustom them to the sights, sounds and stages of the procedures they will experience. The widespread use of video taped material has provided a useful tool to extend the scope of modelling.

Shaping

This is the third and most complex method of developing new behaviour. Essentially the steps followed are:

(1) Deciding the eventual goal.

(2) Breaking down the change required to achieve the goal into small steps.

(3) Either finding or engineering something in the subject's current repertory which is in the direction of the first step. This is then reinforced so that its frequency increases.

(4) Choosing the next approximate step in the right direction from the new range of behaviour. This is then reinforced, at the same time extinguishing those variations not in the direction of the goal. This process is continued until the goal is reached.

In practice, shaping is often carried out by starting near the goal and working backwards through the behaviour chain, as with prompting. For example, if the goal is to get Julie to put all the clothes away in her bedroom, she may initially be rewarded for putting the final sock away in a bedroom which has been tidied by her mother. This has the advantage that not only does she get praise and points (or whatever reinforcer has previously been arranged) but also the neat tidy bedroom may have reinforcing value of its own.

Shaping is therefore a system of successive approximation towards a new pattern by differential reinforcement of selected behaviour. Inevitably it often requires patience and a lot of time. Parents, however, will often be prepared to spend time if the problems are severe and support and supervision are forthcoming from a health visitor, nurse or doctor. Shaping programmes fail if:

- the steps are too great or
- the next step is tackled before the previous one has been properly learned.

In the first case an attempt must be made to find smaller steps and in the second a return must be made to relearn an earlier step.

Measures to Decrease Behaviour

Extinction

Any action which produces no reward of any kind, either internal or external, is likely to cease in time. If the monthly pay cheque stops arriving you will not continue doing that job for long. When the cheque first fails to arrive the natural reaction is to inquire from the pay office, grumble to the boss and make a fuss. When it is clear that there really is no more pay you stop doing the job and look for some other way of earning your living. In exactly the same way, extinction schedules work in behaviour therapy.

Philip may be getting a great deal of attention by throwing the tea cups at the cat and screaming. It is decided to extinguish this behaviour whilst reinforcing the drawing of cats and teacups in his drawing book. Initially when he stops getting attention, he will try hard to find tea cups and a cat in order to continue the behaviour pattern which he knows has gained him the centre of the stage in the past. Once he realises that this is futile he will give up and seek alternatives, at which point picture drawing can more easily be shaped and reinforced.

This example introduces two important points about reducing behaviour by means of extinction. The first is that the unwanted behaviour will always increase in a desperate attempt to gain the withdrawn reinforcement before it finally begins to lessen (extinction burst). The second is that extinction should wherever possible be used in such a fashion that there is a positive as well as a negative dimension to the programme. Both these points can lead to difficulties in practice as spouses, care-givers for the elderly and parents often get discouraged at the point of upsurge in an unwanted behaviour and despondently abandon the programme. The professional can help by warning that this problem will occur and giving support when it does.

Parents sometimes launch themselves into extinction programmes with punitive vigour but without thought of anything positive to replace the

behaviour being extinguished. Extinction, of course, should never be punitive – the goal being to withdraw attention of any sort either favourable or
unfavourable. Parents often need to be reminded that attention, not praise or
pleasure, is the reward the child is seeking. A parent 'blowing his or her top'
may be highly reinforcing to a child who has previously noted that quiet
constructive play results in being ignored while the adults get on with their
own activities.

It should be noted that the rapidity with which extinction is effective
depends on the previous schedule of reinforcement. If the behaviour has
been continuously reinforced it will be extinguished the more rapidly.
Equally, inconsistent extinction with occasional 'giving in' is in fact identical
to a variable reinforcement schedule. This will prove ineffective in reducing
behaviour – rather, the latter will slowly but strongly increase. The child that
gets its request for sweets refused ten times but granted on the eleventh has
not been taught that sweets cannot be obtained by pestering, rather that
sweets are only obtained by pestering persistently. From the practical point
of view, therefore, it is very important that extinction schedules are not used
unless the user has the resources to use them consistently. It is perfectly true
that night-time waking and crying in a young child can be extinguished if
the mother possesses the resolution and perhaps lack of normal maternal
feelings to be able to carry it through but few mothers can do this.

Punishment

Early and much publicised behavioural work made considerable use of
punishment in the form of aversion therapy. In this, an attempt was made to
reduce undesirable behaviours by pairing them with an unpleasant event such
as an electric shock. Such attempts met with only limited success and a
number of theoretical and practical snags became apparent. Aversion therapy
is often found to be specific to the treatment situation and does not generalise
into outside life. Even when successful, it does nothing to replace the
suppressed behaviour with desirable behaviour – the negative may be
removed leaving an awkward vacuum rather than anything positive. The
exhibitionist may cease to flash but is no nearer achieving an appropriate
sexual performance. The model may be an unfortunate one in that the child
that is slapped by its parents may be taught that violence is needed to control
others. He may then try out this lesson in his dealings with smaller children
at school or in the family.

The subject, whether child or adult, may try to escape the punishment in
unforeseen and undesirable ways by cheating, lying or avoiding being
caught. Lastly, there is the temptation for the punisher to use the technique

inappropriately through the sequence behaviour/punishment/forgiveness in which, for example, pulling the cat's tail is followed by a modest slap and then a kiss and a cuddle from mother. It may happen that kisses and cuddles are only available when 'naughtiness' is to be forgiven. The pattern of 'making it up' after punishment is particularly seductive as the child receives strong terminal positive reinforcement and the mother is negatively reinforced by the calming of her feelings of guilt at having been unkind to her child. In spite of its superficial attraction, as a way of changing behaviour it is useless, as there are no clear signals as to what is expected next time. Parallel examples exist in adult life; it is not uncommon to come across couples who have sexual intercourse only at the end of a major row.

When all these factors have been taken into account, punishment has been and is likely to continue to be frequently used in everyday life. It has occasional applications in behavioural management and it is worth listing the rules for its effective use which are:

(1) It should be decisive and not subject to negotiation.

(2) It should be of appropriate intensity, neither too severe, producing anxiety or too mild, having no effect.

(3) It should be immediate.

(4) It should be consistent: intermittent punishment lacks effect and may induce anxiety more rapidly.

(5) The reason for it should be made clear.

(6) An appropriate alternative behaviour should be available and achievable.

Response Cost

This involves the loss of positive reinforcement under certain contract conditions. In the case of a teenager an agreement might be reached that making his bed in the morning permits going out in the evening after supper. Failure to make his bed in the morning entails the response cost of loss of the evening reinforcer.

Natural contracts may replace artificial ones. For example the response of smoking 40 cigarettes a day for many years may entail the cost of loss of the reward of normal pulmonary function. This cost is, sadly, irreversible but the principle is used when giving medical advice about smoking. The technique is also used in a variety of points or token programmes where certain actions entail a loss of points. It has been extensively employed as part of programmes for the management of obesity or smoking in the form of money deposits which are forfeited if goals are not met. Results were variable and modern techniques take more account of the decision making process and the importance of relapse prevention.

Attempts are sometimes made to strengthen the cost involved in these programmes by stipulating that the money, if lost, goes to some agency strongly disliked by the subject. For example a churchman might agree to his forfeit going to a left-wing atheist organisation or vice-versa. One of the problems with response cost programmes is that they may unwittingly contribute to a belief by the subject that once the reinforcer has been lost he has failed totally and there is no point in trying any more. This abstinence violation effect can be avoided by careful programme design and will be discussed in more detail in Chapter Eight.

Time-Out[1]

This can for practical purposes be regarded as a special form of response cost. There is, however, an important theoretical difference as the latter is removal of reinforcers already earned whereas Time-Out (short for 'time out from positive reinforcement') involves the use of an environment in which no reinforcement is available. The common practice of sending a child to his bedroom without his supper is an attempt to use Time-Out in everyday family life. Used in this way it is often ineffective as there is no consistent planning in its use, and sources of reinforcement such as toys, books and household plumbing may still be available. This technique is probably most effectively used in institutions where it is possible to provide a special setting, i.e. a small, bare, dull room and staff trained in its use. Paradoxically it is in these settings that it has come in for criticisms from the media; where it is easily and frequently misrepresented. Correctly used, however, whether in home or school, it is an effective and humane way of reducing unwanted behaviour and to be preferred to conventional punishment in almost every way.

The object of the technique is that following unwanted behaviour the child is temporarily removed from all reinforcers that are currently available to him. In order to do this several decisions have to be taken (McAuley and McAuley 1977):

(1) Where? Bedrooms and bathrooms are not recommended as they are too vulnerable and cannot be observed. Equally, dark cupboards are frightening and should not be used. The corner of a hall, kitchen or living room 'to let you calm down' is probably to be preferred.

---

1   See also Chapter 12

(2) How long? Two to three minutes after becoming quiet is enough for a very young child. Five to six minutes may be used for an older child and ten minutes for an eleven-year-old.

(3) How? It is important that the whole procedure is explained to the child in advance.

The sequence is then as follows:

(1) Parent commands. If child complies reward is given.

If child does not comply;

(2) parent repeats command with the threat of Time-Out. If child complies reward is given.

If child does not comply;

(3) child is sent to Time-Out for the predetermined time 'to calm down'.

The whole sequence is repeated as required and a later opportunity is taken to explain again when and why time out is used.

It should be noted that properly applied Time-Out is a humane and educational way of setting limits for a child. It has nothing to do with the highly publicised 'pin-down' system used in certain children's institutions which was rightly criticised as cruel and criminal.

Differential Reinforcement of Other Behaviour (DRO)

From the above sections it will be apparent that if an alternative is reinforced the original behaviour is likely to reduce. This principle, therefore must be considered amongst the ways of reducing unwanted behaviour. In practice the use of physically or functionally incompatible behaviours is frequently included in both purely behavioural and cognitive treatment plans. The smoker may be encouraged to fight his craving by going for a run or a swim and the anxious patient to visualise scenes or make self statements about coping competently with the situation which makes him anxious. This will be discussed in more detail in the sections dealing with strategies for individual problems.

Stimulus Control

With this technique we return to the A end of the A-B-C model. Certain behaviours are classically conditioned and occur in response to a recurrent stimulus. For example, a panicky patient may have an attack in a supermarket queue as she knows by the last experience that this is 'when it will start'. In this case the stimulus is the situation aided by negative thinking which will be discussed later under Cognitive Methods. For the smoker who always wants a cigarette at the end of a meal it may be appropriate to try and change the circumstances surrounding the end of the meal by having it in a different place or getting up and going for a walk straight after the last mouthful. In this way the expected conditioned response of wanting a cigarette may be avoided. Many everyday actions occur as a result of a response chain which can potentially be interrupted at several different points. It has been observed that the terminal response is less likely to occur if the chain is lengthened. Let us take our smoker mentioned in Chapter Eight. In order to have his cigarette he needs normally to pull out the packet and his lighter, operate the lighter and take the first puff. Supposing, however, he needs to buy cigarettes and in order to do that he needs to go to the cashpoint and get money, and his debit card is locked in the boot of the car in a car park ten minutes' walk away. The whole chain is now considerably longer. The likelihood of his resisting the urge to smoke is in itself greater and there are more links in the chain which might be modified by alternative behaviour. This lengthened response chain also provides an opportunity for various cognitive techniques to be employed (see later in this Chapter). Various methods of controlling stimuli and lengthening response chains can be built into a number of treatment programmes.

Compound and Complex Techniques

A number of commonly used behavioural techniques include several of the elements described under the appropriate problem sections; some occur often enough to be worth considering here.

Exposure

Fears are reduced by repeated or continuous exposure to the stimulus producing the fear. This is a commonplace truism incorporated in such everyday remarks as 'it's always worse at first' and 'it will be better when you get used to it'. Anybody who doubts the truth of this should try to remember their first day at a new school. In spite of this, many patients respond to fearful situations by avoiding them, thus making the problem worse. Various techniques for encouraging exposure have thus been devised in behaviour therapy to overcome this problem. These will be described in detail in Chapter Six which is devoted to anxiety related problems. Theoretically, exposure may be considered a mixed technique as, consequent upon it, fear is extinguished. This diminution of fear, however, acts as negative reinforcement of the previously avoided behaviour which now increases in frequency and extent.

Systematic Desensitisation

This is one of the oldest behavioural interventions which is still extremely useful for phobic anxiety when in vivo exposure is impossible or inappropriate (Wolpe 1954). The patient learns deep muscle relaxation at first with a training session or taped instructions. If a tape is used one made by the clinician is preferable to the commercial ones.

A hierarchy of carefully arranged scenes graded in difficulty by the patient is then drawn up. For example:

Social Phobia Hierarchy

(1) Getting a sandwich to take away from a snack-bar.

(2) Having a drink in a quiet pub.

(3) Having a drink in a busy pub.

(4) A pub meal.

(5) Going out motor racing, meeting with friends.

(6) A sit-down Chinese meal.

(7) A meal in a London restaurant.

(8) A formal business dinner with speeches (by others).

(9) A formal business dinner with patient giving a vote of thanks.

A further example of a hierarchy is given on page 81 in Chapter Six.

The concept of the Fear or Anxiety Thermometer, which measures these emotions on a scale of 0 to 100 Subjective Units of Disturbance (SUDs), is then introduced. Subsequent sessions consist of presenting scenes from the hierarchy repeatedly to the relaxed patient starting from the least threatening until fear or anxiety drops to an acceptable level. Then the next scene is tackled. The classic form of systematic desensitisation has been described but in practice the hierarchy can be made more dynamic and fluid and the relaxation can be less formal.

Massed Practice

This is a technique used to reduce or eliminate minor problems such as tics and habit spasms. The patient is encouraged to perform deliberately the tic for a certain length of time each day, which contrasts strongly with the usual reaction of 'Do stop doing that, William!'. This may be regarded as a method of reducing unwanted behaviour but it probably depends for its effectiveness on several different elements. First, the practising of the habit produces fatigue and boredom. Second, it teaches control over the elements making up the tic. Third, relief occurs when the practice is stopped, and finally, the reaction of the family, which although probably unfavourable, may reinforce through providing attention, is removed. Massed practice can be used very simply in primary care as these kinds of problems are relatively simple to define, supervision is not time-consuming and the results are often extremely worthwhile.

Contingency Contracts

These are agreements, ideally in written form, made between two or more people specifying relationships between behaviour and its consequences. They provide a framework for mutual reinforcement and fulfil much the same function as commercial contracts. For example, the job to be performed is clearly stated and is to be rewarded in a specified way. A personal contract may also be used. For example, a smoker who gives up may make a contract with himself that after six months abstinence he will treat himself to a week's holiday in Spain. The intermediate reinforcer might be watching the saved money accumulate in a Dimple Haig bottle on the mantelshelf.

Interpersonal contracts are of use with family and marital problems where both the task and the reward may be broken down into intermediate stages. For example, if a bicycle is to be the terminal reward for making the bed and tidying the bedroom each morning for six months, a points system could be arranged in which Bicycle = 1,000 points. Early points may be awarded against a sub-contract which states that, for the first two weeks, one point may be earned for having no clothes on the floor at morning inspection. This is introduced in order to shape the required room tidying in small steps.

There are a number of rules which are helpful in arranging any contract (Stuart 1971):

(1) Contract reinforcement should he earned, not given, as a right and when earned it should be granted immediately.

(2) The arrangement should be reciprocal so that reinforcing others earns reinforcement from them.

(3) The value of the reinforcers exchanged must be seen to be equal from the point of view of value and frequency in the estimation of the contracting parties nor just in the estimation of the therapist or contract manager. Scales of values amongst individuals are very different. For example, going to a party may be a reinforcer for one

person but a punishment for another. Ideally the reinforcers exchanged should be small enough to be earned frequently.

(4) Reinforcers should always follow, never precede, the task. 'If I give you a cuddle now, will you go to bed at once afterwards?' is the wrong way round and doomed to failure.

(5) The terms of the contract must be clear and carried out systematically. In this way freedom of decision and action is actually increased as each party knows where they are. They know what the choices are and what the consequent rewards or costs will be.

When suggesting a contract to parents some attitude change is frequently necessary on their part. They must abandon the 'because I say so' approach in favour of a much more equal relationship. Marriage partners also frequently feel that they have a right to expect the other party to change in response to a criticism without the criticiser conceding anything in return. These attitudes must be explored and modified before a contract will be successful.

Assertion and Social Skills

These topics will be discussed in Chapter Six. Some aspects of them, however, form an integral part of many behavioural programmes so it is not out of place to make some mention here of the general principles involved. Without adequate assertive behaviour many of the normal reinforcers of everyday life are simply out of reach. No man will arrive at a sexually fulfilled relationship unless he is able to hold a conversation with a woman. Social skill may be described as an ability to behave in a way that is likely to be rewarded by others around you and is unlikely to be punished, ignored or met with disapproval. Social behaviour may be divided into three types. The *aggressive* which is hostile and criticises and attempts to coerce the other person. The *submissive* where the person is unable to express his rights and aspirations and allows himself to be trampled over, often with hidden resentment. The *assertive* where the subject, without attacking or attempting to coerce the other, expresses clearly what he thinks, wants and has a right to receive. Establishing the differences among the three is often central to management in parenthood, education, working life and marriage. It is also important in dealing with the medical profession either as a colleague or a patient.

Cognitive Techniques

The work of Ellis (1974) and Meichenbaum (1971) but above all Beck (Beck *et al.* 1979) has caused a revolution in methods of therapy which now often concentrate on the role of maladaptive thinking and cognitive distortions in the genesis and maintenance of many psychological problems. Although these interventions can become very sophisticated and complex many of the principles can be used in short term interventions in primary care by professional therapists and some techniques are easily adapted for use in the consulting room.

Beck's Cognitive Therapy

Beck (Beck *et al.* 1979) sees the problem of depression and anxiety in terms of the way the patient looks gloomily at himself, the world and the future whilst at the same time engaging in an internal dialogue in which he talks himself down and minimises his achievements.

The first part of cognitive therapy consists of an enquiry into the nature of the problem followed by an explanation of the approach and the role of thinking in maintaining mood. This may be aided by written material appropriate to the type of problem presented. Suitable examples of patient leaflets are given under the various problem-orientated chapters in Part 2. A simple example showing how thinking and interpretation can effect mood and feelings may usefully be given at this point. For example, the mood created by seeing a letter from the tax authority in the morning post is critically influenced by whether you are expecting a rebate, a form to fill in or a demand for payment.

This general rationale is followed by a detailed and sensitive analysis of the individual problem. This may be aided by role play or the instant replay technique. In the latter the patient is asked to shut his eyes and re-play the critical event in his mind describing it, in the present tense, as he does so. this may be explained as being like the replaying of an important incident in a televised football match. This analysis enables the therapist to arrive at a formulation of the current problem and its maintaining factors which is discussed fully and openly with the patient. The approach is fully collaborative and often the patient will modify or add to the formulation. The formulation may be extremely simple and often involves a feed-back cycle for example:

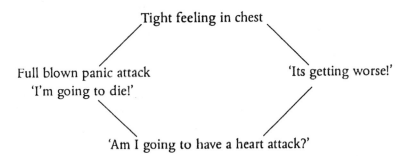

This initial phase of therapy serves two essential purposes. First it provides the therapist with the opportunity of obtaining the information he needs and second it gives the patient an explanation of what may be happening to him and puts him back in a position of perceived control over some aspects of his difficulties.

Control is also helped by diary keeping which is included in the next stage. The first diary may record activities together with a record of the pleasure and achievement associated with each (Weekly Activity Schedule). The patient then begins to spot, count and record negative automatic thoughts which he does by means of an ongoing record, for example:

Date/ Time	Emotion(s) *What do you feel? How bad is it (0–100)?*	Situation *What were you doing or thinking about?*	Automatic thoughts *What exactly were your thoughts? How far do you believe them (0–100)?*
13/2	Sadness 90%	Received job refusal letter	I will never get another job 80%
15/2	Guilt 100%	Unable to give money for children's new blazers	I'm hopeless as a father 70% They should be able to depend on me 80%

The next stage is to challenge and answer these distorted thoughts by questioning their logic and usefulness trying to find a more flexible, less negative way of thinking about it. This involves learning about common types of distorted thinking and how to frame questions to challenge these (see Chapter Nine).

The final stage of therapy looks at the underlying assumptions or schemata which govern our thinking and behaviour. These are the life rules which are learnt in childhood, often from our parents. Such rules are necessary but if they are too rigid or absolute they impose a black and white or perfectionist pattern on a patients thinking which can be extremely destructive or defeating.

Beck's Cognitive Therapy, which was originally introduced as a treatment for depression, has now been extended into many other areas such as anxiety, panic, relationship problems and personality disorders with considerable success. Much more detailed accounts of its use are include in appropriate chapters in Part 2, particularly Chapter Nine on depression.

Motivational Interviewing

Rollnick and Miller (1995) define motivational interviewing as 'a directive client-centred counselling style for eliciting behaviour change by helping clients to explore and resolve ambivalence'. The main elements are:

(1) Motivation for change is elicited from the client, not imposed from outside.

(2) It is the client's task not the clinician's to articulate and resolve ambivalence.

(3) Direct persuasion is not an effective method for resolving ambivalence.

(4) The counselling style is a quiet and eliciting one.

(5) The clinician is directive in helping the client to examine and resolve ambivalence.

(6) Readiness to change is not a client trait but a fluctuating product of interpersonal interaction.

(7) The therapeutic relationship is more like a partnership or companionship than expert/recipient roles.

The therapist should:

(1) Seek to understand the client's frame of reference.

(2) Express acceptance and affirmation.

(3) Selectively reinforce the clients own self-motivating statements.

(4) Monitor the client's degree of readiness to change.

(5) Affirm the client's freedom of choice and self-direction.

Mixed Programmes

Many of the methods described in the first part of this chapter dealing with external behaviour have internal parallels which can be used for work with thoughts, feelings and information processing aspects of problems. For example, exposure techniques can be used either *in vivo* or in imagination. Appetite disorders (q.v.) are best treated by a combined package which addresses both the body weight itself and overvalued and distorted ideas of body image (dysmorphophobia). Anxiety management uses relaxation, exposure and at the same time tries to modify worrying thoughts. Management of habit disorders addresses decision making and relapse prevention as well as addressing the direct control of the habit itself.

Some older techniques may be useful in primary care, for example:

Thought Stopping

This was the earliest cognitive technique to be widely used and is applied very simply. A patient is asked to concentrate on the thoughts that worry him. The therapist then shouts 'Stop' and the patient, often to his surprise, notices that the thoughts do actually cease, at least for a time. The second and third stages of the technique involve the patient saying 'Stop'; first out loud and then to himself. A variation is to get the patient to visualise the word 'Stop' on a TV screen in front of him gradually moving like a programme credit. The technique, although it has its uses, can be a rather transient and crude one. It is more effective if the unwanted thought is immediately replaced by a prepared pleasant or relaxing image (see Chapter Six).

Distraction

This may be regarded as a development of thought stopping, as the attention is switched off the worrying thoughts but this switched time onto another activity. This may involve focusing the attention on some aspect of the surroundings such as birds singing, counting bald men in the train or focusing for 30 seconds on a red spot stuck on a watch. Alternatively one can engage in some distracting physical activity, like doing a crossword, or mental activity like reciting poetry or doing mental arithmetic. It is often used in the early stages of cognitive therapy but should be regarded with caution in the long term as it often comes perilously close to cognitive avoidance which can be a major obstruction to success in therapy.

References

Beck A.T., Rush, A.J., Shaw. B.F. and Emery, G. (1979) *Cognitive Therapy of Depression*. New York: Guilford Press and Chichester: John Wiley.

Ellis, A. (1974) *Humanistic Psychotherapy: the Rational Emotive Approach*. New York: McGraw Hill.

McAuley, R. and McAuley, P. (1977) *Child Behaviour Problems*. London: Macmillan.

Meichenbaum, D. (1971) 'Examination of model characteristics in reducing avoidance behavior.' *Journal of Personality and Social Psychology 17*, 298–307.

Rachman, S.J. (1980) *Fear and Courage*. San Francisco: W.H. Freeman.

Rollnick, S. and Miller, W.R. (1995) 'What is motivational interviewing?' *Behaviour and Cognitive Therapy 23*, 325–334.

Salkovskis, P.M. (1996) (ed) *The Frontiers of Cognitive Therapy: The State of the Art and Beyond*. Hove: Guilford.

Stuart, R.B. (1971) 'Behavioral contracting with the families of delinquents.' *Journal of Behavior Therapy and Experimental Psychiatry 2*, 11.

Wolpe, J. (1954) 'Reciprocal inhibition as the main basis for psycho therapeutic effects.' *Archives of Neurology and Psychiatry 72*, 205.

Wolpe, J. (1973) *The Practice of Behavior Therapy*. New York: Pergamon.

Recommended for Further Reading

Hawton, K., Salkovskis, P.M., Kirk, J. and Clark, D.M. (eds) (1989) *Cognitive Behaviour Therapy for Psychiatric Problems. A Practical Guide*. Oxford: Oxford University Press.

Trower, P., Casey, A. and Dryden, W. (1988) *Cognitive–Behavioural Counselling in Action*. London: Sage.

Useful Material Source

Powell, T. (1992) *The Mental Health Handbook*. Bicester: The Wimslow Press.

(This spirally-bound book contains questionnaires, including several mentioned in this chapter, and a wealth of patient handouts designed to be copied for therapeutic use.)

Part Two

PROBLEMS

Chapter Six

Anxiety and Related Disorders

The Nature of Anxiety

It is difficult to produce satisfactory definitions for anxiety, fear and stress. There is considerable overlap between the three concepts. Each can be helpful as well as problematic. In each case the correct recognition of the origin of symptoms is important in management. Anxiety may be regarded as pivotal in this group of disorders and a working definition of anxiety is that it is a state of body and mind produced by the perception of threat or danger – real or imagined. This state includes three main components:

Apprehensive Thoughts and Feelings

These are subjective and are therefore the most easily described, recognised and correctly attributed to anxiety.

Bodily Changes

Muscle tension, palpitations, headaches and related physical symptoms may all be produced by anxiety. The sensations may be correctly recognised but their cause misattributed to some physical mishap such as a heart attack or brain tumour or a precursor of such a disaster.

Behaviour Changes

Anxiety may cause the sufferer to escape from disturbing situations and to learn to avoid those which he fears. Both escape and avoidance make it more difficult to face a similar situation next time around and confidence is lost.

Phobic anxiety occurs when the feared situation is external and usually readily identifiable, whereas general anxiety disorder describes a condition where worrying thoughts and images are the usual prime causes. Table 6.1 outlines the channels through which anxiety is expressed.

Table 6.1 The three channels of anxiety
(often not synchronous)

Disturbing Thoughts and Feelings	Bodily Responses	Behaviour Changes
Fearful thoughts and panic associated with an external cause Anxiety asscoiated with internal worrying thoughts & images Memory and concentration defects associated with intrusive thoughts or castastrophic images Performance deterioration due to inadequate problem solving, detachment or derealisation	Sympathetic nervous system overactivity resulting in hyperventilation, tachycardia. raised BP, dyspepsia, paraesthesiae Related secondary problems: tension headache, tiredness, insomnia, bowel changes	Avoidance or escape from anxious situations Cognitive avoidance of disturbing thoughts Distraction from tasks with performance deficit Restricted activity due to rituals or intrusive thoughts.

The Origins and Maintenance of Anxiety

Anxiety and fear are both frequently adaptive and protective. Fear crossing a road or climbing a mountain may be essential to preserve life. Anxiety may increase inventiveness and productivity, at least until a certain limit is reached.

The bodily responses of anxiety assist in preparing the muscles and circulation for the physical effort involved in running a race or playing in a match. A feeling of tension may aid concentration of attention when making decisions or taking examinations. All is well if anxiety and fear remain proportional to the needs of the situation but problems arise once symptoms become disproportionate, resulting in diminishing performance and self-confidence. In particular these may take the form of anxiety: (a) in the absence of real danger; (b) in excess of the amount of danger; or (c) lasting long after the danger has passed.

Distress also occurs when physical symptoms develop in a situation where a physical response is inappropriate. For example, arrears of a mortgage cannot be dealt with by punching the banker on the nose, and physical escape from aeroplanes for mid-flight anxiety is hardly possible.

Anxiety may be maintained by a set of factors entirely different from its original cause. The child who has received an injection or painful procedure from a doctor wearing a white coat may become anxious the next time he sees a white coat. This is an example of classical conditioning in which the pairing of two cues produces the same response when either is presented separately and parallels Pavlov's experiment with the bell and the salivating dogs (see Chapter One).

Many other factors may contribute to the maintenance of anxiety after its initial occurrence – most notably the following:

(1) Upsetting Thoughts.

(2) Avoidance and Escape.

(3) Loss of Confidence.

(4) Life Events and Vulnerability.

(1) Upsetting Thoughts

These usually occur in connection with attempts to find an explanation for the symptoms – 'Am I going mad?', 'Am I going to have a heart attack?', 'If I fail my driving test it will be the end of everything', 'I'm going to lose my job if I'm like this'. Such thinking errors fall into four classes:

(a) Overestimation of the probability of a disaster, such as a plane crash.

(b) Overestimation of the severity of a feared event, such as taking an examination.

(c) Underestimation of the subject's own coping resources, such as the ability to speak clearly when feeling anxious.

(d) Underestimation of outside rescue factors, such as help from colleagues or family.

Once such thoughts occur a feedback spiral is established. For example, your heart misses a beat, you think 'Help! I'll never manage this' and your heart starts thumping in earnest. The bodily feelings feed the thoughts which are in turn confirmed by the increase in feelings.

(2) Avoidance or Escape

To avoid anxiety-producing situations, or escape if caught in them, is perfectly reasonable in the face of real danger but may become a severe handicap if it becomes a pattern in situations where no real danger exists. The list of avoided situations gradually increases and interferes more and more with everyday life. Temporary relief is gained by escape or avoidance but on each subsequent occasion coping is more difficult and avoidance occurs earlier in the sequence. Eventually, as in the severe agoraphobic, the life style may become so restricted that the house is never left and staying at home alone is impossible.

(3) Loss of Confidence

Confidence is built upon recurrent experience of success, thus avoidance and escape sap confidence as they signify failure. One failure inevitably leads to fear of another and tasks that were once easy now seem difficult and rewarding experiences diminish – 'I was once the bloke they always came to for advice. Now they know that I am always in such a state that they don't dare ask'.

(4) Life Events and Vulnerability

Life events may feature both in the original cause and in the maintenance of anxiety. Every primary care worker will recognise that life events can produce a clinically disabling degree of anxiety in some people, as can long term stressors with unpredictable features such as caring, threat of redundancy or living with an alcoholic relative. Typical examples of such events are marriage, divorce, moving house, taking a driving test or awaiting an operation. Such anxiety may be transient but it is disabling and frequently requires help. A more serious situation occurs when two or more of these stressful events come together or when a particularly timid or socially vulnerable person is involved. Under these circumstances the severity of the resultant anxiety often seems multiplied rather than simply cumulative.

The Size of the Problem

Most authorities agree that anxiety based problems are the most common psychological conditions (Brown and Barlow 1992). They are amongst the most frequent disorders presented in primary care. It has been calculated that about 10 per cent of the population consults a doctor about tension at some time and an Oxford GP survey in 1977 (Skegg et al. 1977) found that, amongst registered patients, more than 20 per cent of women and about 10 per cent of men received at least one prescription for a psychotropic drug during a year. This figure rose to 30 per cent amongst 45-year-old women. Another survey found that 50 per cent of patients found suitable for psychological intervention in general practice suffered from anxiety based problems (Robson et al. 1984).

The Assessment of Anxiety Problems

We are aware that there is some repetition from previous chapters in this section but we feel that the importance of assessment in anxiety for both patient and therapist makes it necessary to include everything at this point in its correct order.

Summary of Anxiety Assessment

(1) Interview

- Nature of the problem.
- Resulting disabilities.
- Other problem areas.
- Present and previous ways of coping.
- What sort of help is envisaged by the patient?
- Specific information on:
    - triggers
    - situations
    - consequences
    - factors that increase or decrease the problem
    - patients interpretation of the problem
    - patients interpretation of specific symptoms or thoughts.
- Life style questions:
    - diet; including drinking (tea, coffee, alcohol, fizzy drinks)
    - exercise.
- Leisure pursuits present or abandoned.
- Ambitions, life plan or hopes.
- Platonic and sexual relationships.
- Medication prescribed or 'over the counter'.

(2) Baseline measurements.

(3) Treatment plan.

---

(1) Interview

A clear and exact statement of the *nature of the problem* and the *disability* resulting from it is obtained. Enquiries are made about *other significant problem areas* or *causative factors*, such as life events and triggers.

As much time as possible is spent seeking out:

(a) *Triggers* that precede anxiety; including physical symptoms and their attribution.

(b) *Situations* in which anxiety is likely to occur.

(c) The *worrying thoughts and images* that precede or accompany the problem.

(d) The immediate and long standing *consequences* of the problem.

(e) The factors which are associated with its *increase* or *decrease*.

(f) It is valuable to know how the *patient interprets his problem*. Classically the physical effects of panic are attributed to evidence of catastrophic events such as heart attacks and brain tumours. Under some circumstances these attributions may be less clearly defined and be labelled loss of control or simply dying. There may be no clear idea of the exact meaning of loss of control or the mechanism of dying often because they avoid thinking about the final consequences and are therefore unable to institute any coping actions or thoughts. It follows that no intervention is likely to succeed unless these interpretations are uncovered and discussed or the patient works out what is the 'bottom line' of the fear. As with all avoidance the reality generally turns out to be far less frightening than the fantasy they are trying to avoid. One patient feared death, not it turned out because of a fear of dying, but because he wanted to finish a book he was writing. Once time was set aside for this each day and progress was recommenced some of his anxiety was also alleviated.

(g) How has he tried to *cope* with the problem previously? What methods has he tried? What outside help – from professionals, friends or relatives – has he obtained and did it make any difference?

(h) Information about *what sort of help* he wants and expects and how improvement of the problem would affect him and his family is also useful.

(i) It is important to know what the patient enjoys, does well or used to do. Did he take part in sport or other exercise which he has now discontinued? Using these *assets* may be important when planning treatment.

(j) The *development* of the problem is important but historical factors may be overemphasised by the patient. He may wonder repeatedly what caused his difficulties in the first place whereas the therapist will be more concerned with what is maintaining them currently. Nonetheless some information on development may be important to confirm or modify the significance of other data.

(k) Consideration should be given to the *differential diagnosis* with particular reference to hyperthyroidism, certain cardiac conditions and hypoglycaemia.

(2) Baseline Measurements

The Diary

The most usual and valuable baseline assessment is a diary recording the situations in which anxiety occurs, its associated thoughts and feelings, a rating of severity and coping method tried (see also Chapter Four). Its exact form will depend on the individual problem and the information which is thought to be important in the particular case. Table 6.2 is an example of such a diary.

Table 6.2 Anxiety diary

Date/ Time	Situation	Feelings How bad (0%–100%)	Thoughts Belief (0%–100%)?	Coping/Outcome
5/12 6pm	Christmas rush Deliveries late	Tense 60% Anger 30%	We'll never finish 80% The boss will crucify me	Large whisky Headache
16/12 12 md	Under dryer	Trapped 70% Panic 60%	I shall lose control Everyone will look at me	Challenged thoughts Cued relaxation

It is noticeable how often the severity of a problem alters once a record is being kept. A symptom which is said to be constantly present may in fact only occur at specific and relatively infrequent times of day. It is commonly found that certain problems disappear altogether once a diary is being kept. Diary keeping may be as effective as anxiolytic drugs in some cases but no formal research exists to demonstrate this. The mechanisms involved probably include an increased sense of control and recording counteracts negative selective memory.

Questionnaires

A number of self administered inventories and questionnaires are available in the assessment of anxiety. Amongst the most useful are:

- *The State Trait Anxiety Inventory (Spielberger).* This is an American instrument with two scales of twenty questions each. The first scale measures anxiety 'at this moment' (state anxiety) and the second 'how you generally feel' (trait anxiety).

- *The Marks and Mathews (1979) Fear Questionnaire.* This is an English instrument of covering a range of anxiety related conditions divided into subsections dealing with different phobic and general anxiety features.

- *The Anxiety Inventory (Beck and Emery 1985).* This is probably the most useful instrument for everyday use. It is in a 21 question format with two scales and relating to severity and frequency with a choice of four degrees of severity.

Good anxiety management in primary care does not require the routine use of any formal questionnaires although diary keeping is almost always essential. Furthermore the excessive use of questionnaires may seem insensitive and mechanical unless sensitively handled. They are useful, however, in showing progress and change, may pick up symptoms which have been missed at interview and are essential for research measurements across settings.

Physiological Measurements

Direct measurements of pulse rate, skin conductivity and blood pressure change associated with anxiety are possible but only used extensively as a research tool. Some simple gadgets along these lines can be bought and even appear in Christmas crackers. It is extremely doubtful if they are accurate or reliable enough to have any true clinical use.

Cognitive Behavioural Tests and Experiments

These are of use in two main areas:

(a) The straightforward *behavioural approach test* is useful in phobic anxiety both as measurement and treatment for with well established avoidance the patient himself has no idea how he will react only how he fears he may react. The patient is simply asked to approach the feared situation, object or a photograph of the object and the proximity achieved measured – as the phobia improves so the approach becomes closer. The same principle is used in situational fears when the subject might be asked to go into the feared setting, for example a supermarket or to a local park if scared of dogs or ducks, and rate the fear on a previously agreed scale, for example; 0–100 (where 0 is not at all anxious and 100 is maximum anxiety).

(b) The *cognitive behavioural experiment* (Beck and Emery 1985) is used to test the validity of worrying thoughts and dysfunctional assumptions. A socially anxious person for instance might arrange to go into a restaurant and observe carefully whether everybody did stare at him as predicted.

(3) Treatment Plan

At this stage it should be possible to arrive at a *formulation* about the type of anxiety and the factors maintaining it. The formulation should result from a joint discussion between therapist and patient with eventual agreement. If agreement cannot be reached the outlook for co-operation and success is not good and perhaps the formulation needs modification or more time should be spent on explanation. At this time treatment goals should also be settled, and the patient needs to understand that the object of most cognitive behavioural programmes is to arrive at control over anxiety, not to abolish it altogether. The most successful plan is often a 'package' involving a mixture of techniques, however for the sake of convenience the main types of anxiety based problems will be described in turn, together with the treatment approaches most commonly used for each.

Types of Anxiety Based Problems

The following will be considered:

(1) General anxiety disorder.

(2) Phobias: agoraphobia, social, specific.

(3) Panic attacks.

(4) Hypochondriasis.

(5) Sleep disorders.

(6) Post traumatic stress disorder.

(7) Obsessive compulsive disorder.

(8) Withdrawal from Benzodiazepine sleeping pills and tranquillisers.

Treatment

Anxiety Management Training

This is the name given to a package of techniques for tackling anxiety. Patients may be encouraged to use some or all of these depending on the analysis and requirements of their particular disorder and may be taught on an individual basis or in groups. In fact most people benefit from incorporating all these strategies to some degree in everyday life and anxiety management training groups are often run as health promotion as well as for helping groups of patients currently suffering from anxiety.

The content consists of three groups of elements:

(1) *Explanation* of the nature of anxiety (as described above) and the *rationale* of treatment to the patient.

(2) *Control* of symptoms using relaxation, distraction, exercise, restructuring of thoughts and panic management etc.

(3) *Avoidance reduction* by graded exposure and *confidence rebuilding* by encouraging positive activities or successful coping with challenges or unpleasant circumstances.

As much of the treatment is to be done by the patient himself at home, the programme may be set out in a manual (see p. 100 and Reading List) or other written instruction which can be studied and referred to by the patient at all times. The therapist's task is to assist the clear definition of the problem(s), explain and rehearse the treatment tasks and procedures, oversee record keeping and symptom monitoring, help to produce suitable homework assignments and assist in overcoming blocks and difficulties. The written material can serve as a guide at all times. Several suitable manuals are published (see Books for Patients) but the enthusiast can also design his or her own adapted to the clinician's own style of working.

Rationale

This is the first section of the Anxiety Management Training programme and is designed to explain how thoughts and feelings interact producing anxiety through the autonomic nervous system – particularly the sympathetic division. Table 6.3 gives some idea of how this works.

Table 6.3 Autonomic nervous system

Sympathetic	Parasympathetic
Provides physical response to threat (Fight or flight)	Provides physical response to calm (Relaxation of body and mind)
Pulse rate and blood pressure raised	Pulse rate and blood pressure fall
Breathing rate increased	Breathing rate lowered
Digestion inhibited	Digestion promoted

Fear or anxiety becomes a problem when it is excessive, occurs in the wrong situation, or goes on for too long. There is quite a complex cycle of acceleration in which several different groups of factors play a part (see Figure 6.1). The patient may have a false perception of danger or some physical abnormality or be scared by the anticipation of the unpleasant symptoms starting all over again (fear of fear).

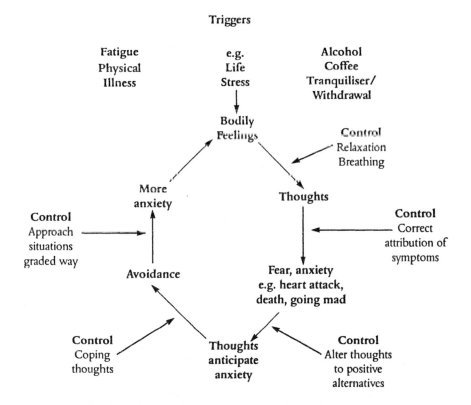

Figure 6.1. The feedback cycle of anxiety and points of possible intervention

It is explained that relief from anxiety is often sought by avoiding the situations that produce it, like crowded places, shops or meeting particular people. This may produce temporary relief, but every time something is avoided it is more difficult to face it the next time it crops up. In this way life becomes more and more unrewarding and limited.

Loss of confidence occurs because the anxiety makes it harder to do things which were once easy. Confidence is a pleasurable feeling that comes from repeated experience of success or mastery. Failure at things which were once possible leads to the abandoning of further attempts and the avoidance of similar things which might prove too difficult. Lost confidence can be regained by learning how to cope with small challenges, designed for success, before building up to progressively bigger ones.

Symptom Control

Any previous successful attempts at coping should be developed and encouraged, and additional methods incorporated within the patient's own scheme.

(1) *Deep muscle relaxation* – this is introduced as a way of

- reducing muscular tension, which is tiring and often leads to hyperventilation
- inducing a relaxed mood and sense of physical well-being
- providing an alternative distracting response which the patient can use as soon as he senses the beginning of anxiety symptoms
- as the basis for imaginal desensitisation
- to control hyperventilation.

All of these assist slowing down which counteracts the hurry usually associated with anxiety. Relaxation is taught with taped instructions along the lines that follow on page ??. Relaxation is most effective when taught 'live' but this is unlikely to be possible in primary care unless someone is enthusiastic enough to run groups. Instructions recorded in the voice of the therapist provide the next best option and this has the added advantage that the therapist must learn how to do it himself! (This is best done by pairing with an interested or stressed colleague and trying out a relaxation schedule on each other and obtaining feedback on your performance.)

The patient is advised to practise the taped sequence in full, say, twice a day. Then a shortened version of the exercises is introduced for quick relaxation. Lastly, instructions are given to recognise the cues of tension and use them to initiate the short sequence. A series of relaxing scenes may be prepared by the patient to aid mental relaxation after the physical sequence is finished. Relaxed posture and slow breathing may be stressed separately. Once learnt, the tape can be used on the train, at night, or at lunchtime at work using a Walkman and headphones to help concentration.

(2) *Exercise* – under certain circumstances exercise will provide a more appropriate first means of symptom control than relaxation. This is particularly true with those people who take hardly any exercise, who find relaxation difficult or where anger is associated with anxiety and who suffer from many of the 'fight or flight' symptoms. The use of exercise in treatment is one way of resolving the paradox that modern non-physical stress frequently produces a primitive somatic response. A businessman developing his own firm found that he was much better able to deal with the problems of the day after a brisk morning swim in the neighbouring pool. A woman with children, although always feeling tired, found a short structured jogging programme and weekly yoga class improved her sense of well-being and energy. In some areas the primary care team have been able to negotiate a package with a local sports centre and can therefore 'prescribe' a programme of swimming or circuit training to get the patients started. Aerobics is best avoided at this stage as it seems to exacerbate the anxiety symptoms.

(3) *Timetable restructuring* – the patient may at first be asked to keep an activity schedule, recording what they do hour by hour during the day (see Chapter Nine). This will highlight days or times when they do too much or too little or get into high stress situations. It is also instructive for people who are unable to sit still or spend any time on their own. The timetable is then used to plan days, weeks and months ahead in order to space what needs to be done, prioritise, and add new things like exercise or practice. Often to the patient's surprise they find that they are in fact doing more than when they were rushing at it 'hell-for-leather'.

For the more long term plans the timetable can be used to decide in advance what activities are essential in the next week or month and how they can best be arranged. This may involve leaving out some of the less essential items or making a decision that a particular evening or weekend will be kept free regardless of how many invitations have to be refused. Some skills training on how to turn down invitations or demands, how to leave work on time and how to plan to spend an evening at home may be necessary. This basic system may be extended by drawing up a programme where each area of activity has a separate column. The tasks connected with each activity are then listed in the appropriate column and a time allotted for each according to priority. If insufficient time is available the less urgent items are postponed, left out or delegated (the more stressed a person becomes the more they seem to have to take on the world by themselves. It is more time consuming initially to make the children make their own packed lunch but reduces pressure in the long run). As each item is completed it is ticked in the relevant column thereby increasing the patient's sense of control over his activities (see Table 6.4).

Table 6.4 A task programme

Priorities: 1=urgent 2=Do sometime 3=Omit or delegate

Partner	Children	Work	Builders
Wine bar with part-ner (1)	Dentist (1) Library (1) Shoes (2) Presents for party (1)	Finish report (2) Arrange meeting (1)	Phone surveyor (1) Clear room out (1)

(4) *Distraction* – is used to counteract the build up of panic or anxious thoughts and worries in three ways:

   (a)   Concentrating on the surroundings, for example, conversations, items of clothing of others present or concentrating on a pre-arranged object like a spot on a watch dial. The latter can also be used as a cue for relaxation.

   (b)   Mental activity such as; reciting a poem, singing, doing calculations, remembering a list or classification or rehearsing positive or coping self statements. These activities are more powerful if they can be done aloud, if circumstances permit.

   (c)   Physical activities such as; jogging, doing exercises, having a bath or just keeping busy.

(5) *Control of upsetting thoughts and images* – these occur in the presence of tension and anxiety, making matters worse as described in Figure 6.1. They have the following characteristics:

   (a)   They are *automatic* – they occur fleetingly without effort.

   (b)   They are *distorted* – they do not fit the facts.

(c) They are *unhelpful* – making change difficult.

(d) They are *plausible* – they go unquestioned.

(e) They are *involuntary* – very difficult to switch off.

A routine can be followed to identify these thoughts. A recent occasion when the anxiety symptoms were troublesome is identified and recalled. The situation is described in terms of time, place, activity and companions. The onset of anxious feelings is remembered and these feelings are rated out of 100. The associated thoughts are then recalled in terms of words, images and meaning. Once the thoughts have been identified their role in the provocation or increase in anxiety can he examined, followed by an attempt to challenge them in terms of unreasonableness, unreality and exaggeration. Alternative ways of thinking about the problem can then be explored. A few examples will illustrate the sorts of ways in which these techniques can be used. For instance the thought 'Everyone will stare at me' can be tested in reality by experimenting in the situation and seeing if the staring actually occurs. The thought 'Palpitations mean I am having a heart attack' might be replaced with 'The palpitations are due to anxiety and I can control that'. The image of collapsing in the street and being surrounded by a hostile crowd might be countered by the question 'If someone collapsed near you in the street, would you feel hostile towards them?'

In practical therapy the three most useful lines of questioning are:

(a) Is your thought or image true and accurate?

(b) Would there be another, less anxiety provoking, way of looking at it?

(c) What would be the worst thing that could happen and if the worst did happen what would be so awful about it and what could you do to cope or minimise the risk?

Obviously particular types of problem may require one line of questioning rather than the others. Once the patient is trained in identifying and challenging anxiety provoking thoughts there is a period of intensive practise using the charts (see Table 6.5).

Table 6.5 Thought challenging chart

Date/Time	Situation	Feelings (How severe 0%–100%)	Anxious Thoughts/Image (How real 0%–100%?)
7/11 5pm	Unhappy child with fever	Anxiety 95% Fear 85%	Meningitis 80% Dying 75%

Avoidance and Loss of Confidence

A description is obtained of any situations or thinking patterns which are being avoided. These are then arranged in a hierarchical list, starting with the least difficult situations and progressing to the most difficult ones. A graded approach is adopted in which the easiest situations or tasks are tackled first and repeated until they can be managed without undue anxiety or difficulty. As confidence in this task is built up the next most difficult task is attempted until a satisfactory point or the top of the hierarchy is reached. Practice must be regular and frequent, and if a block occurs because one step is too hard it must be broken down into smaller components so that success is achieved. This is not always easy and may require some creative thinking by the patient and therapist. By its nature practice has to take place in the patients own time with only encouragement, planning and some role playing or rehearsal in the session.

Written information exists at various levels to help patients with general anxiety disorder ranging from a complete self-help package *Stresspac* (White 1995) through detailed booklets to be used in conjunction with a therapist (Butler) to single advice and information sheets. The patient instruction leaflet that we use is based on the work of Butler and summarises the programme (see Appendix 1 to this Chapter).

Types of Anxiety Based Disorders

General Anxiety Disorder

This means anxiety that arises when there is no obvious external object or situation responsible. Cognitive factors in the shape of negative thinking patterns and catastrophic images are paramount in producing and maintaining this type of anxiety. It is the most common type of anxiety seen in primary care and its treatment encompasses many of the techniques that are useful in the treatment of the other varieties.

It has already been pointed out that anxiety is both necessary and universal. Fearlessness is only found in mythical Greek and Teutonic heroes and almost all of these came to sticky ends. It is only when distress exceeds the danger that a clinical problem arises. Although, by definition, in generalised anxiety there is no specific fear, there may be a number of stress factors present which need to be considered. These can arise from marital or child-rearing difficulties, money problems, work relationships, exams, moving house, existential worries and many other situations which may require a practical problem-solving approach to go hand in hand with management of the anxiety symptoms.

Phobias

Phobias are anxieties occurring in response to a particular situation. They may be very specific, for example, fear of spiders, rats, thunder or flying, or more general and related to social situations or anxiety about illness. The latter are obviously of particular importance to the primary health care worker as are phobias of blood, injections and medical procedures.

Agoraphobia

This is the most common and diffuse member of the phobic family. Originally it is derived from the Greek for fear of the market place. This meaning has acquired new force with the advent of the modern supermarket. It is now extended to cover a wide range of patterns of fear related to the central theme of being in public, away from home and in some sense trapped,

Table 6.6 Percentage of agoraphobic people reporting certain situations that provoke anxiety

Situation	%
Joining a line in a store	96
A definite appointment	91
Feeling trapped in a hairdresser etc.	89
Increasing distance from home	87
Particular places in the neighbourhood	66
Thinking about my problem	82
Domestic arguments and stress	87

Source: Burns and Thorpe 1977

with escape socially or physically difficult. Common examples found in many case histories are as in Table 6.6.

The fear produced in these situations has a number of physical features. Some of these are produced by direct stimulation of the sympathetic nervous system and adrenal medulla; such as high pulse rate, sweaty hands and rapid breathing. Some are mediated by hyperventilation; such as tingling fingers, dizziness and carpo-pedal spasm. Experience of such unexplained sensations increases fear and apprehension which in turn leads to an increase of the symptoms. Fear of the distressing symptoms occurring in the future is also important. Such 'fear of fear' may lead to increasing avoidance of a wider and wider range of activities, eventually producing the classic long-standing agoraphobic who has not gone out alone for many years. This in turn may lead to a number of secondary problems. For example, one of us dealt with a problem of truancy which was eventually tracked down to an agoraphobic mother who was only able to leave the house in the company of her school-age daughter. Shopping and visiting were thus only possible if the girl remained at home.

The fearful thoughts described by agoraphobics often involve death, becoming insane, losing control, making a fool of oneself or collapsing. Various factors are described as improving the problem. Chief amongst these is the presence of a reliable, 'safe' person such as the child described above but more often a spouse or close friend.

The full range of possibilities described under General Anxiety may be involved in the treatment of Agoraphobia but the main drive is towards:

(1) Explanation of the nature of the condition.

(2) A programme of exposure to the feared situation(s) which may be either;

    (a)   rapid (flooding or implosion); or

    (b)   gradual (desensitisation in vivo or in imagination).

Rapid exposure is a straightforward and effective way of treating phobic anxiety. After a suitable explanation of the rationale of exposure in reducing fear, the patient is accompanied by the therapist into the feared environment, for example, a shopping centre or a train. With the support and encouragement of the therapist she remains in this environment until her symptoms begin to subside. After the early accompanied sessions she is encouraged to spend time by herself in the feared situation thus demonstrating that, with time, anxiety subsides even in the absence of the therapist.

Although this is an effective method of treatment, it will often require the services of a trained professional capable of helping the patient through the very high levels of anxiety frequently generated for several hours at a time during the early stages of treatment. For obvious reasons this may be difficult to arrange in primary care.

Graded exposure is the most suitable approach for a home-based programme initiated in the community (Mathews *et al.* 1977). This is based on the principle that fear decreases with familiarity and even daunting tasks can be tackled if broken down into small steps. There are many common place examples of this approach. The rider is advised to get straight back on his horse after a fall; the new swimmer takes a few strokes, then swims a width and finally a length of the pool.

It may be instructive to go out once with the patient but then a relative or friend can be enrolled as a co-therapist. The rationale of exposure treatment is explained to both the patient and anyone else who is helping with the programme. The patient, with help, then draws up a list of all the situations that he finds in any way problematic and these are then arranged as a hierarchy in order of difficulty (see Table 6.7).

Table 6.7 Agoraphobia hierarchy (unmixed)

Neutral Situation: At home in front of TV

(1) Preparing to post a letter.

(2) Going to the letter box (50m) with partner.

(3) Going to small corner shop with partner.

(4) Letter box without partner.

(5) Supermarket with partner on Monday (quiet day).

(6) Supermarket alone on Monday.

(7) At supermarket check-out with partner, three people waiting.

(8) At supermarket check-out with partner on busy night with queue.

(9) At supermarket on a quiet day alone.

(10) Taking the bus to out-of-town supermarket.

The hierarchy is then used to draw up a comparable list of clearly defined goals starting from the least worrying and rising to the most threatening. These items are then tackled in order, by means of regular daily practice with the help of a partner if possible. Anxiety is measured by means of a fear diary in which the patient records the degree of disturbance each item causes on a rating scale from 0 = absent to 100 = the greatest anxiety ever experienced.

Each item may have to be repeated many times before symptoms decrease sufficiently to move on to the next item. Eventually in this way the top of the hierarchy is reached.

If an item proves too difficult the programme may be modified either by a return to re-practise the previous item or, the step between the two lines is sub-divided so that smaller intermediate grades can be tackled. It will be evident that, on the hierarchy example given, there are a number of potential intermediate steps should these be required. As soon as reasonable progress has been made the patient is encouraged to practise freely, experiencing a range of situations of comparable difficulty to those already mastered. In this way the whole repertory of behaviour is increased and the gains made are thus consolidated. Daily practice of both new and mastered items is important in order to avoid regression and discouragement. This is a very suitable approach for the primary care workers whose main task is to plan the extensive between–session tasks, help with setbacks and encourage the patient to change their behaviour in such a way that they will want to go out more.

Social Phobias

The social phobic is afraid of social or performance situations in which he fears his behaviour will cause him humiliation or embarrassment (DSM IV Ref). Some of the features of agoraphobia may be present and a clear distinction may not always be possible. By and large the social phobic's problems revolve round fears that he will behave in an unacceptable way leading to rejection or loss of 'face'. Thoughts such as 'I'm stupid and sound boring', 'People are looking at me' or 'I shall make a fool of myself and never be able to hold my head up again' are common. These thoughts may first occur at a difficult social situation which causes previously hidden assumptions about social adequacy to be activated (Clark 1995). Once a threat to self esteem is perceived it will be fuelled by a number of maintaining factors:

(1) Attention shift to internal monitoring (sensations, images, felt sense). This information is then used to infer the thoughts and opinions of others.

(2) Safety behaviours intended to prevent negative evaluation in fact:

   (a) prevent disconfirmation (if you don't expose yourself to the feared situation you can't tell if your fears are justified)

   (b) increase the internal self-focus

   (c) cause the feared symptoms such as, sweating, trembling and concentration loss

      (d)   make the sufferer appear withdrawn promoting the social response he fears.

(3) Avoidance of social situations entirely prevents disconfirmation.

(4) Mental rehearsals and 'post-mortems' focus on internally constructed feelings, fantasies and images and promote selective retrieval of past failures.

(5) Excessively high and rigid standards of social performance; 'I must always be brilliant', 'If I appear anxious people will despise me'.

Treatment should begin with a *formulation* based on a review of several recent episodes, the recognition of associated negative automatic thoughts and safety behaviours and the identification of the contents of self-awareness.

    A *social activities diary* is used to keep track of events and examine them in terms of the *formulation*.

    The *intervention* will address the following:

(1) Planning to drop predicting the outcome of future events and the use of safety behaviours.

(2) Challenging rigid assumptions and introducing more flexible alternatives.

(3) Building confidence by scoring and crediting positive images and self statements.

(4) Experiments to test the environment. Is the predicted response in fact accurate with regard to trembling, disfluency, sweating etc.? Do safety behaviours in fact protect? If not drop them.

(5) Recognise that 'post-mortems' deal with feelings and shift to processing external events only.

(6) Review the advantages and disadvantages of 'post-mortems' and if they serve no useful purpose ban them.

(7) Use video and audio feedback to demonstrate reality. (*Source:* Clark 1995)

People often come for help when they have 'failed again' or have to face some situation that they feel they cannot manage or have failed at in the past. Presentations at work, a wedding speech or seminars for students can give serious problems. Help may need to be multifocal including; planning of material to be presented, recording and challenging of cognitions, live rehearsal in session, imaginal desensitisation and role play for dealing with variety of outcomes.

Specific Phobias

Fear of blood, wounds, injections and dental treatment are amongst the single object phobias which have particular medical relevance. Blood and injury phobias are the only ones accompanied by a drop in blood pressure and fainting is a realistic fear and a possible reaction. An effective treatment for blood and injury phobia has been shown to be possible in one session (Hellstrom, Fellenius and Ost 1996). This consists of a brief behavioural analysis followed by a regime which consists of:

(1) Inducing tension of voluntary muscles in for example, the arm which serves to increase blood pressure.

(2) Discrimination training to recognise the first signs of a drop in BP when confronted with a blood or injury stimulus which triggers the use of the tension inducing sequence.

One session therapy has been shown to be as effective as five sessions. The session should be conducted as follows:

- patient is instructed to tense muscles in arms legs and face and keep tensing until a warm feeling is felt in the face

- return to normal *not relax*

- repeat after 20–30 secs

- repeat with slides or videos presented of blood and injury scenes.

One session is also shown to be as good as five at follow up.

Single animal, object or situation fears are extremely common and indeed it is probable, at least in childhood, that all of us are affected to some degree. Many of these are not a problem, as avoidance causes no disability, or such a minor problem as not to warrant behavioural treatment beyond brief explanatory counselling. It seems more sensible to treat a postman who experiences anxiety once a year when he gets on the plane for his annual holiday with a small dose of diazepam rather than a cognitive behavioural programme. If, however, the flying phobic is an oil company worker who must take the helicopter to an off-shore rig twice a week, then desensitisation is fully worthwhile. In this latter case desensitisation in imagination may have to be used as it is difficult to manipulate real-life exposure to graded flying situations. In fact there are courses available run by Avia Tours at weekends from airports in the UK (see Useful Contacts). As well as exposure the identification and re-formulation of catastrophic thoughts and images is undertaken. It is important to incorporate as much real-life practice as is feasible and tapes and slides (some of which are available commercially – see note at end of chapter) can be used to fill some of the gaps.

Other single phobias are managed by exposure using such materials as are available and the design of these programmes can be a fascinating exercise in resourcefulness with interesting visits to zoos, parks, pubs and public lavatories. The more frequent and the longer the exposure trials, the better and quicker are the results. Finally it should be emphasised that much of these programmes can be undertaken as homework assignments with very limited person-to-person contact, thus improving the patient's own sense of control over his problem and increasing the programme's suitability for primary care use. More time than the standard consultation may be needed at assessment but after that the therapist has only to monitor progress and help surmount difficulties and set-backs.

Management of Panic Attacks

By their very nature panic attacks occur suddenly and often unexpectedly and the GP will often be the first on the scene. His explanation and emergency management of the attack, particularly if it is the first of its kind, may have a lasting and important effect on the subsequent course of the problem. If he grunts and gives intramuscular diazepam the patient cannot be blamed for thinking that he has an inexplicable and probably serious condition which will only respond to potent medication. Whatever the hour of the night it is essential to get an exact description of the symptoms, details of any recent stressful circumstances and the patient's own ideas about the cause of his problems. Fears of suffocation, heart attacks and strokes often figure largely in the thoughts and imagery of the patient and any management is likely to prove ineffective unless such fears are discovered and discussed. An adequate physical examination is also necessary, as much as an anxiolytic as to exclude any physical cause for the problem. The attack commonly consists of an intense feeling of fright or impending doom which is associated with a wide range of physical sensations mostly mediated by the autonomic nervous system. These physical feelings can be misinterpreted so that the patient may fear he is going to die in an unspecified way, go mad or make a fool of himself. The physical symptoms most frequently found are, dizziness, giddiness, palpitations, numbness, paraesthesia of the hands, feet and round the mouth, nausea, breathlessness or a sensation of a band round the chest. The essential difference between panic disorder and other anxiety related problems is that the patient is preoccupied with what is happening right now rather than future threats.

In panic attacks the patients invariably misinterpret their sensations and regard them as being much more serious than they are. The aim of treatment is to help the patient re-attribute their sensations to innocuous causes. The efficacy of cognitive behavioural treatment is now well established (Arntz and van den Hour 1996).

Many panic sensations closely resemble the effects of hyperventilation. There is now considerable evidence (Clark *et al.* 1985) that in many, though not all cases, hyperventilation does play a key role in panic attacks. A careful description of the type and frequency of the attacks will often confirm that this is likely to be the case. In the recurrent problem this information is supplemented by a Panic Attack Diary which records the frequency and type of attack.

Treatment of panic attacks should be directed; (a) towards explaining the nature of the panic reaction, its similarity to the effects of hyperventilation and seeing that the symptoms are correctly attributed; and (b) to teaching controlled respiration as a method of managing attacks.

The management takes place in four phases:

(1) Interview and baseline diary record. The assessment should include observation of physical signs such as sighing, yawning, gulping or burping which may indicate hyperventilation. This can also be looked for by asking the patient to place one hand on his chest and one on his abdomen and breathe as usual to see which hand moves with his breath. If the chest hand alone moves the patient is breathing incorrectly and may already be experiencing unpleasant symptoms.

(2) Experimental voluntary hyperventilation (The Challenge Test). The patient is asked to overbreathe for about two minutes. He is then asked to stand up and concentrate on and describe his physical symptoms. (A symptom rating scale is available in Clark and Hemsley 1982.) It is important that during the introspection period the patient is asked to stand up as some symptoms such as 'jelly legs' may occur only on standing. The symptoms may then be terminated by re-breathing into a paper bag. The patient is then asked to rate the similarity of his symptoms during the experiment to those that he experiences during an attack, where 100 = identical and 0 = no similarity, so that the extent to which overbreathing is involved can be gauged.

(3) An explanation is then given, with an information sheet, of the mechanism of physical reactions in panic and the possible relationship to hyperventilation. The patient can learn to distinguish when he is hyperventilating and this in itself, by explaining why he feels so bad, helps him keep calm and exert some control over the panic.

(4) Training in slow, smooth abdominal breathing which is incompatible with hyperventilation is then given. Initial training can be done with a

tape on which 'in-out' – pause' breathing instructions are recorded at the rate of eight and twelve breaths per minute (7.5 and 5 seconds per cycle respectively). This is incompatible with hyperventilation. Practice is then continued without the tape. Finally the patient hyperventilates and terminates it by switching to controlled breathing. For others who have a more chronic tendency to hyperventilate, relaxation may be necessary to calm down generally, then to say 'relax' very slowly on all the out breaths allowing a long pause before automatically needing to take another small in-breath. When he feels confident that he can start to control the panic sensations by using one of these techniques he is encouraged to go into a situation that he has previously avoided, and practise his newly acquired control techniques. The programme is frequently effective even in those cases where there is no demonstrable hyperventilation, probably as a result of; (i) acquired perceived control; and (ii) reattribution of catastrophic thoughts and images (see Appendix 2 to this Chapter for patient information sheet).

Hypochondriacal Fears

Excessive health anxiety is extremely common and is a particular problem in primary care with its emphasis on continuity of patient management. A distinction should be made between fear of a disease (disease phobia) and the false belief of having a disease (disease conviction). The former has been shown to be more closely associated with anxiety and the latter with somatic symptoms (Kellner Hernandez and Pathak 1992). Many such cases are managed at an entirely superficial symptomatic level which is unsatisfactory, both for the clinician who is often employing investigations, referrals and treatments which he knows to be useless, and for the patient who realises that his problems persist, or even increase, inspite of medical advice. The GP is in a unique position to deal with this problem to his own relief as well as the patient's. Specialists will often inadvertently reinforce the problem by expressing apparent surprise and concern that they find nothing wrong *within their speciality* thereby implying to the Hypochondriacal patient that there must certainly be something seriously wrong in another field.

The *formulation* of the problem involves early illness-related learning (family experience and modelling of illness behaviour) followed by a critical incident which activates negative automatic thoughts and imagery. These then form a feedback cycle involving behavioural, affective, cognitive and physiological elements (see Figure 6.2).

In practice the significant factors in the presentation are:

Previous experience

Experience and perception of
(i) Illness in self, family; medical mismanagement
(ii) Interpretations of symptoms and appropriate reactions
'My father died from a brain tumour.'
'Whenever I had any symptoms I was taken to the doctor in case it was serious.'

↓

Formation of dysfunctional assumptions

*'Bodily symptoms are always an indication of something wrong;
I should always be able to find an explanation for my symptoms.'*

↓

Critical incident

Incident or symptom which suggests illness
*'One of my friends died of cancer a few months ago.
I have had more headaches recently.'*

Activation of assumptions

↓

Negative automatic thoughts/imagery

'I could have a brain tumour:
I didn't tell the doctor that I have lost some weight.
It may be too late.
This is going to get worse.
I will need brain surgery.'

↕

HEALTH ANXIETY, HYPOCHONDRIASIS

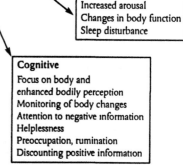

Behavioural
Avoidance and self-imposed restrictions
Repeated self inspection
Repeated manipulation of affected area
Consultation, reassurance seeking
Scanning for information
Preventative measures

Physiological
Increased arousal
Changes in body function
Sleep disturbance

Cognitive
Focus on body and
enhanced bodily perception
Monitoring of body changes
Attention to negative information
Helplessness
Preoccupation, rumination
Discounting positive information

Affective
Anxiety
Depression
Anger

Figure 6.2. Cognitive behavioural model of the development of hypochondriacal problems
(Reproduced by kind permission of Dr Paul Salkovskis and the Oxford University Press)

(1) Increased *physiological arousal* (e.g. palpitations or sweating) causing;

(2) Increased *scanning and awareness of bodily sensations* with selective attention to illness-confirmatory observations (e.g. repeated swallowing> sore throat > ideas of throat cancer).

(3) *Avoidance behaviours* in particular reassurance-seeking which inspite of its manifest lack of effectiveness is pursued using a wide range of contacts (such as professional, family and friends) in an even wider range of settings (for example, social, professional, literature and the media).

The *cognitive behavioural management* for hypochondriacal fears focuses on:

(1) The setting of mutually agreed goals related to health anxiety rather than reassurance about symptoms. This is often difficult but the primary care worker is both better and worse off in this respect than the mental health professional. He has advantages in that he is consulted early in the sequence of reassurance seeking and his function in health care is well understood by the patient. Unlike the mental health professional he does not have to justify his role but on the other hand he is the gate-keeper for investigations and referral and may be approached by the patient solely as a means of access to these services.

Two guidelines are useful when considering whether further investigation/referral should be undertaken. The first is to decide if the investigations are justified in the judgement of the clinician unfettered by the importuning patient. If there is no such justification then they should not be undertaken, as to do so is wasteful and detrimental to proper care. The second condition arises from the first. Since in medicine it is difficult to be absolutely certain about anything, the clinician must use some professional courage in resisting demands for further reassurance. He may point out that the referral/investigation/reassurance cycle has proved ineffective so far so however long is spent on it it is unlikely to be effective in the future. Unfortunately medical training and public perception may make this more difficult; clinicians are pilloried for missing an insignificant physical defect in a patient but readily forgiven for a major mishandling of human misery ('Organic factors must always be excluded first' is still medical school teaching).

(2) However strong his conviction, most of the time the patient will admit that he may be wrong and will agree to the programme of non reassurance and referral (if only for a limited time) much to the reassurance of the clinician. Once the patient has agreed to explore

health anxiety as a possible cause of his symptoms, the emphasis shifts to gathering and testing evidence for and against the belief he is 'ill'. It is important to work with the patient and avoid confrontation. Evidence for and against the patients interpretation of the symptoms is carefully evaluated. For example reassurance may be withheld and the resultant effect observed. The effect of selective attention may be demonstrated and manipulated. The relationship between catastrophic images and the resultant physiological arousal can be shown experimentally (Warwick and Salkovskis 1990).

Sleep Disorders in Adults

Disordered sleep is so often a feature of anxiety-based conditions that it seems logical to deal with it at this point, although it may equally reasonably be classified as a habit problem. Sleeping difficulties of children present a number of different features and are considered in Chapter Twelve.

Assessment

Medically, insomnia has frequently been regarded in the past as a single disorder with a single treatment – hypnotic. In recent years it has been realised that there are many different elements to insomnia and many associated problems, and that hypnotics often create more problems than they solve. It is not commonly realised that most sleeping pills are benzodiazipines and hence ineffective after short periods and addictive over time.

An important step in assessment is to discover whether the lack of sleep is a relatively isolated problem, possibly learnt by the gradual adoption of faulty habits, or whether it is a symptom of an under-lying disorder such as anxiety, which may have to be treated first and to some extent separately. Once associated difficulties have been adequately considered an assessment is made of the sleep pattern itself. This should reveal:

(1) The time of going to bed, the time of going to sleep and how the latent period between the two is occupied.

(2) The number, time and length of middle-night waking periods and how these are occupied.

(3) The time of final waking in the morning.

It is also important to find out the patient's idea of what constitutes a 'good night's sleep' and what ill-effects he expects if he is deprived of it. All of this information can be obtained at interview and may be confirmed by a baseline record chart recording these details from night to night over a week or a fortnight. This method of recording may present some practical difficulties.

It is, for example, sometimes a problem to record the exact moment you fall asleep, but worthwhile records are usually obtained and the information they contain often surprises the sufferer. A patient who believes quite genuinely that he doesn't sleep a wink is then astonished when his record shows relatively minor periods of night waking. This sort of information may in itself promote change by relieving anxiety attached to the problem and increasing the patient's sense of control over it.

Management

This is tailored to the type of problem revealed by the assessment, but a number of techniques are frequently used and have been shown to be effective (Schramm *et al.* 1995). These can be incorporated in a short patient information sheet (q.v.). The elements of this sheet are:

(1) Information – that sleep requirements often diminish (sometimes dramatically) with age and that four hours per night may be quite sufficient for the older person.

(2) Eliciting and challenging sleep related negative automatic thoughts. For example that lack of sleep in itself, unless enforced, causes ill effects.

(3) Adjustment of sleeping goals – going to bed later and being prepared to get up early and start other activities.

(4) Stimulus control – ensuring that bed is only a place for sleeping (and, if appropriate, sex which of course itself aids relaxation and sleep) and not for eating, watching TV or coping with tomorrow's problems.

(5) Preparing for periods of insomnia by making sure that there is a warm, comfortable place with perhaps a kettle, teapot and paperback book to get up to during the night.

One patient found that watching a horror video promoted sleep and although this would appear to be somewhat unusual, it does emphasise the point that individual variations have to be considered and that the programme cannot be slavishly applied to everyone. It is common that reading in bed will promote somnolence in some people but wakefulness in others. Cassette tapes of novels, poetry and music are also popular and the world service radio in the middle of the night. The leaflet we use for patients is reproduced in Appendix 4.

Post-Traumatic Stress Disorder

A number of public disasters such as tragedies involving train crashes, ships sinking and fires in public places have focused attention on helping survivors recover from their ordeal. There is also increased emphasis on the psychological effects of more individual traumas such as rape (Rothbaum and Foa 1993), road traffic accidents (Mayou, Bryant and Guthrie 1993, Blanchard *et al.* 1996) burglary and hospital admission or childbirth. In fact any occurrence which for some reason has a major impact on the person. Major trauma shatters the certainties of existence leaving the sufferer unsafe, perplexed, questioning, demoralised and guilty. The primary health care team will often form the point of first, possibly only, help in such cases and some idea of the nature and course of post traumatic stress will help to guide the primary care worker.

The main features of pathological post-traumatic stress are:

(1) Re-experiencing the trauma in intrusive thoughts, images or dreams.

(2) Numbing and dulling of emotions associated with lack of interest in rewarding activities. There is avoidance of situations or activities perceived to be associated with the trauma.

(3) Increased arousal manifested in irritability, insomnia and anger with markedly enhanced startle response to any situation or stimulus perceived to be associated with the trauma.

Many of the symptoms of PTSD are similar to those of depression and both conditions often co-exist but it is important to correctly distinguish the two.

The *formulation* in PTSD addresses aims to give the patient back apparent control over his shattered internal and external environment. *Crisis intervention* after major disasters has been undertaken in debriefing groups (Hodgkinson and Stewart 1991). The format of the groups allows survivors to explore together the *facts* of the disaster and their survival, the *feelings* engendered and the *significance* to themselves as people and to their future lives. This is followed by the mobilisation of *resources* from within individuals, from within the group and from outside agencies. In this way a sense of meaning and control may be regained. It is unlikely that many primary care workers will have the task of dealing with major, multi-injury disasters but the framework of exploration of facts, feelings and significance followed by the mobilisation of resources will be appropriate to use in consultations with individuals who have suffered recent injury.

Crisis intervention may be sufficient to restore normality but some will not have had access to this or it will not have proved adequate. In these people other management will be required along the following lines:

(1) Treatment of co-existent depression (if present) either with antidepressants or cognitive therapy.

(2) Review in fine detail memories, images and flashbacks associated with the traumatic experience in an attempt to organise its meaning to the individual. Then encourage them to vary and shift the set maladaptive pattern of reporting and flashbacks which only serve to reinforce the trauma not to lessen it. For example: imagining a change of facial expression, different clothes, people in other situations. Sometimes photographs or newspaper articles can be used to provide new viewpoints.

(3) Challenging negative automatic thoughts and dysfunctional beliefs following normal cognitive therapy techniques. In particular issues connected with anger, detachment and guilt will be addressed.

(4) Desensitisation to arousal reactions, particularly those concerned with disaster-related images and thoughts, by graded exposure in imagination or imaginal flooding.

(5) Graded exposure to avoided situations and graded expansion of activities to cope with withdrawal or numbing of emotional response.

Obsessive Ruminations and Compulsive Rituals

Elements of obsessionality and the occasional compulsive ritual are common in daily life – most people can remember avoiding the cracks in the paving stones when out walking as small children. Ruminations and obsessions can however become extremely disabling. Recurring ideas of a distressing kind can prevent logical thought and most of the day can be taken up with rituals involving washing and checking, or a mother may be alone at home hiding knives for fear of harming her baby.

Relatives and friends, whilst complaining of the disabling nature of the rituals, often co-operate in making them possible. The parents of a patient obsessed with ideas of contamination were prepared to see the furniture removed wholesale from their sitting room whilst the patient sat in splendid isolation on a metal-framed deck chair placed on a carpet of old newspapers. One can only speculate that a more spirited defence of their domestic rights by the parents in the early stages might have materially altered this unfortunate young man's intractable clinical course.

The *formulation* in obsessive compulsive disorder looks at three main elements:

(1) Obsessional thoughts associated with anxiety.

(2) Compulsive rituals (thoughts or actions) which neutralise the thoughts producing temporary relief but preventing extinction.

(3) Avoiding situations which might provoke the thoughts.

Clinical depression frequently co-exists with obsessive compulsive disorder and should be recognised and treated before more specific therapy is started.

Obsessions and compulsions are not commonly seen in primary care but if serious, *management* will require more resources than are usually available and home visits are a crucial component in assessment. Early referral to a unit specialising in this work is often indicated. Excellent results are obtainable using *exposure* and *response prevention* programmes (Marks 1985). The ritual situations are sought out by the patient in the company of a therapist who assists him in resisting the urge and at the same time models appropriate behaviour. Milder cases can be treated in primary care particularly with the help of medication from the Selective Serotonin Re-uptake Inhibitor (SSRI) group of antidepressants simply by instructing the patient to resist his ritualising by degrees (Abel 1993). Depending on the baseline frequency of hand washing he may decide that he will reduce it from 5 to 3 times after a visit to the toilet or after his normal checking routine he is not going to allow himself to return home to check the doors or gas taps. The rationale of all response prevention approaches is that intrusive thoughts produce anxiety which is then relieved temporarily by the ritual. If avoidance both overt and covert is confronted and the urge to ritualise is resisted the anxiety eventually diminishes (cf. flooding treatment for phobias described earlier).

Where obsessional thoughts dominate without overt ritualising two strategies may be used:

(1) *Habituation Training* may be carried out in a number of ways:

    (a)   deliberate instruction to form and hold the thought;

    (b)   writing down the thought repeatedly like the 100 lines beloved of old-fashioned school teachers and reading them at preset times during the day rather than when they occur spontaneously.

    (c)   Listening through a Walkman to a 'loop' tape recorded by the sufferer again at times under his control and low emotion.

Measurement is taken of the duration and intensity of the thoughts within the session and the frequency, intensity and duration of thoughts between sessions. With satisfactory progress the thoughts become less intense and less troublesome.

(2) *Thought Stopping* – the patient interrupts the circular thought pattern by shouting 'stop' and substituting a pleasant scene or thought. This is done first with the therapist help, then out loud by the patient and finally by the patient silently to himself. The technique can be strengthened by the use of an elastic band, strategically placed round the patients wrist which is 'pinged' painfully as the thought stopping occurs.

The hypochondriacal patient who consults frequently in general practice may be a particular type of obsessive-compulsive. His compulsion is to seek and obtain reassurance but this of course produces only temporary relief and he is soon back.

Benzodiazepine Withdrawal – Tranquillisers and Sleeping Pills

Associated with anxiety and sleep difficulties, one major problem which presents itself regularly is that of dependence on tranquillisers and sleeping pills. Adverse publicity has made many people aware of the dangers of regular consumption of these drugs. Often, however, awareness has come too late when dependency has already developed, sometimes after relatively short-term use started at a time of acute stress.

Self-help groups in the community such as Tranx, where they exist, are excellent in providing group support. In other cases withdrawal may be attempted by gradual dose reduction week-by-week over a predetermined number of weeks. The mode of action of Benzodiazepines means that even relatively low dosage may cause habituation and the lowest doses may be the hardest to eliminate during a gradual reduction programme. It is usual to change short-acting benzodiazepines to equivalent dosage of the longer half-life varieties before beginning to cut down. Beta blockers and antidepressants may be used to aid symptom control during withdrawal.

The type and duration of withdrawal symptoms vary enormously from patient to patient but they can undoubtedly be extremely persistent and severe over several months (Lister and File 1984). Treatment is aimed at reducing anxiety. This may stem both from the original problem or personality trait and from fear of the extent and intensity of the withdrawal symptoms. The latter often mimic other anxiety symptoms quite closely and may be minimised by a range of the techniques described previously under anxiety management. In some cases, however, patients may also need help just to 'live with' the symptoms for a time and find ways to adjust their lives to make them easier during the period of withdrawal. Commonly, advice will also be required to help with insomnia, panic attacks, perceptual disturbances and a number of other particular problems which may occur at this time.

Cognitive methods may be helpful in enabling the patient to re-attribute symptoms to withdrawal rather than personal inadequacy, impending breakdown or death. and to come to terms with what they see as a 'wasted' period of their life. Symptoms are monitored for frequency and intensity and as far as possible positive coping strategies are advised which can be applied to each symptom as soon as it occurs.

Several other points are important. It has been suggested that alcohol, even in small amounts, may exacerbate symptoms and that sudden falls in blood sugar may prove a problem at this time so that the importance of regular eating should be stressed. A careful balance needs to be struck between the suggesting of symptoms and failing generally to prepare the patient so that he may again resort to medication when caught unawares by an unexpected event such as perceptual disturbance.

First Aid in Anxiety

'First aid' advice for the anxious patient is a frequent requirement in general practice. Often the patient's attempt at coping with anxiety symptoms consists of trying to pretend that they do not exist, pushing them out of their mind and increasing the often already frantic pace of their daily life. Such a course works for a while but is doomed to disaster as, of course, the symptoms do exist, they cannot be pushed away for ever and hurry is often already part of the problem. The failure of these home-made strategies may well increase the anxiety by inducing a sense of helplessness.

At the first interview simple advice can be given to accept symptoms at face value, try consciously to slow down, make an effort to look at natural surroundings and plan the day ahead with a timetable. Monitoring of anxious episodes allows the anxiety to be acknowledged as a problem and reduces the stress of trying unsuccessfully to fight it. This may give immediate relief and be all that is necessary in the mild, transient case. As anxiety increases, once a certain point is reached efficiency decreases. The sufferer may counter this effect by even more effort and his alarm at his lack of success may initiate an anxiety cycle. A simple simile such as that of mental wheelspin may serve to explain this process and enable the sufferer to gain sufficient confidence to cope with this problem from his own resources after a few minutes' discussion.

Acknowledgement

Much of the material in this chapter has been influenced by or derived from the work of The University of Oxford Psychological Treatment Research Unit, the Warneford Hospital, whose help has been invaluable. We are particularly grateful to Dr Gillian Butler, Professor David Clark and Dr Paul Salkovskis who not only allowed many of their ideas to be adapted and used but who made many helpful comments on the original draft and to Professor Michael Gelder for his permission to make use of the material.

References

Abel, J. (1993) 'Exposure with response prevention and serotonergic antidepressants the treatment of obsessive-compulsive disorder: A review and implications for interdisciplinary treatment.' *Behaviour Research and Therapy 31*, 3, 463–478.

Arntz, A. and van den Hour, M. (1996) 'Psychological treatments of panic disorder without agoraphobia.' *Behaviour Research and Therapy 34*, 113–121.

Beck, A.T. and Emery, G. (1985) *Anxiety Disorders and Phobias.* New York: Basic Books.

Blanchard, E.B., Hickling, E.J., Taylor, A.E., Loos, W.R., Fornouris, C.A. and Jacard, J. (1996) 'Who develops PTSD from motor vehicle accidents?' *Behaviour Research and Therapy 34*, 1–10.

Brown, T.A. and Barlow, D.H. (1992) 'Co-morbidity among anxiety disorders: implications for treatment and DSM IV.' *Journal of Consulting and Clinical Psychology 60*, 835–844.

Clark, D.M. (1995) Personal communication.

Clark, D.M. and Hemsley, D.R. (1982) 'Effects of hyperventilation: individual variability and its relation to personality.' *Journal of Behaviour Therapy and Experimental Psychiatry 13*, 41–7.

Clark, D.M., Salkovskis, P.M. and Chalkley, A.J. (1985) 'Respiratory control a treatment for panic attacks.' *Journal of Behavior Therapy and Experimental Psychiatry 16*, 23–30.

Hellstrom, K., Fellenius, J. and Ost, L.-G. (1996) 'One versus five sessions of applied tension in the treatment of blood phobia.' *Behaviour Research and Therapy 34*, 101–112.

Hodgkinson, P.E. and Stewart, M. (1991) *Coping with Catastrophe.* London: Routledge.

Jacobson, E. (1938) *Progressive Relaxation.* Chicago, Illinois: University of Chicago Press.

Kellnerm, R., Hernandez, J. and Pathak, D. (1992) 'Hypochondriacal fears and beliefs, anxiety and somatisation.' *British Journal of Psychiatry 160*, 525–532.

Lister, R.G. and File, S.E. (1984) 'The nature of lorazepam-induced amnesia.' *Psychopharmaeology 83*, 183–7.

Marks, I.M. (1985) 'Behavioural treatments of phobic and obsessive compulsive disorders: A critical appraisal.' In R. Hersen *et al.* (eds) *Progress in Behavior Therapy.* New York: Academic Press.

Marks, I. and Matthews, A.M. (1979) 'A brief standard self-rating scale for phobic patients.' *Behaviour Research and Therapy 17*, 263–267.

Mathews, A.M., Teasdale, J., Munby, J., Johnston, D. and Shaw, P. (1977) 'A home-based treatment programme for agoraphobia.' *Behavior Therapy 8*, 915–24.

Mayou, R., Bryant, B. and Guthrie, R. (1993) 'Psychiatric consequences of road traffic accidents.' *British Medical Journal 307*, 647–651.

Robson, M.H., France, R. and Bland, M. (1984) 'Clinical psychologist in primary care: controlled clinical and economic evaluation.' *British Medical Journal 288*, 1805–8.

Rothbaum, B.O. and Foa, E.B. (1993) 'Sub-types of post-traumatic stress disorder and duration of symptoms.' In J.R.T. Davidson and E.B. Foa (eds) *Post-traumatic Stress Disorder: DSM IV and Beyond*. Washington DC: American Psychiatric Press.

Schramm, E., Hohagen, F., Backhaus, J., Lis, S. and Berger, M. (1995) *Behavioural and Cognitive Psychotherapies 23*, 109–27.

Shapiro, F. (1989) 'Efficacy of eye movement desensitisation in the treatment of traumatic memories.' *Journal of Traumatic Stress 2*, 199–223.

Skegg, D.C.G., Doll, R. and Perry, J. (1977) 'Use of medicines in general practice.' *British Medical Journal 1*, 1561–3.

Speilberger, C.D., Gorsuch, R.L. and Lushmere, R.E. (1970) *STAI Manual 1970*. Palo Alto, CA: Consulting Psychologists Press Inc.

Warwick, H. and Salkoviskis. P. (1990) 'Hypochondriasis.' *Behaviour Research and Therapy 28*, 2, 105–119.

Materials

The Beck Anxiety Inventory published by The Psychological Corporation.

Recommended for Further Reading

Barlow, D.H. (1988) *Anxiety and its Disorders*. New York: Guilford Press.

Beck, A.T. and Emery, G. (1985) *Anxiety Disorders and Phobias*. New York: Basic Books.

Kennerley, H. (1990) *Managing Anxiety*. Oxford: Oxford University Press.

Mathews, A.M., Gelder, M.H. and Johnston, D.W. (1981) *Agoraphobia – Nature and Treatment*. London and New York: Tavistock Publications.

Rachman, S.J. and de Silva, P. (1996) *Panic Disorder – the Facts*. Oxford: Oxford University Press.

White, J. (1995) 'Stresspac: A controlled trial of a self-help package for the anxiety disorders.' *Behavioral and Cognitive Psychotherapy 23*, 89–107.

Books for Patients

Butler, G. and Fennell, M. *Managing Anxiety; Controlling Anxiety; Managing Social Anxiety; How to Relax*. All from Booklets Secretary, Warneford Hospital, Headington, Oxford. Price £2.50 – £3.00 each.

Coleman, V. *Life Without Tranquillisers*. Judy Piatkins (Publishers) Ltd.

Herbert, C. (1995) *Understanding Your Reactions to Trauma*. Available from: Booklets Secretary, Warneford Hospital, Headington, Oxford. Price £5.

Marks, I.M. (1978) *Living with Fear*. New York: McGraw Hill.

Melville, J. (1984) *The Tranquilliser Trap and How to Get Out of it*. London: Fontana.

Mills, J.W. (1982) *Coping with Stress*. New York: John Wiley.

O'Rourke, M. (1996) *Home Improvements: Self Help for Aggressive and Abusive Behaviours*. Published by the author Farnham Road Hospital, Guildford GU2 5LX.

Tallis, F. (1996) *How to Stop Worrying*. London: Sheldon.

Yaffe, M. (1988) *Taking the Fear Out of Flying*. Newton Abbot: David and Charles.

Leaflet

Getting a Good Nights Sleep. A Guide to Handling Sleep Problems. Produced by Lorex Sythelabo Ltd. in connection with the Medical Advisory Service – a good leaflet. Adapted from Colin Elspie and Colin Shapiro.

Programmes for Patients

Fear of Flying. Tape Programme from Webucational, PO Box 81, Wimborne, Dorset BH21 3UT.

Taking the Strain. A five tape and leaflet package adaptable for either professional or patient use. Produced by: Cestrian Psychological Services, 19 Clare Avenue, Hoole, Chester CH2 3HT Tel: 01244 400448.

White, J. (1995) Stresspac. Psychological Corporation.

Useful Contacts

The Sleep Matters Self-Help Group Helpline Tel: 0181 994 9874 (Mon-Fri 5pm to 10pm).

Fear of Flying Courses Information from British Airways Customer Relations at Heathrow Airport or direct from Avia Tours 01252 793250 or 061 832 7972. The courses are run at Manchester or Heathrow Airports at weekends.

Appendix 1: SELF HELP FOR ANXIETY

Anxiety is necessary to help warn of danger and cope with hazardous jobs like driving in fog or working with dangerous tools. It can also help increase productivity and produce original ideas. Problems with excessive anxiety are, however, very common and about one person in ten consults a doctor about them at some time. Tablets such as tranquillisers are one answer and they do help for a while but gradually they lose effect as you go on taking them. They may also give rise to side effects as you try to stop them.

What is anxiety?
It affects both body and mind producing worrying feelings of fear and apprehension together with physical feelings of tension, trembling, churning stomach, nausea, diarrhoea and palpitations. These physical feelings may easily be put down to other worrying causes such as cancer or heart disease – thus increasing fear.

When is anxiety a real problem?
When it interferes with life in the absence of real danger or goes on for too long after the danger is past.

Why does this happen?
All of us come under stress at some time or another. Some of us feel the effects more than others but even those who become anxious rather easily can learn to cope with it.

What are the consequences of persistent anxiety?
(1) *Upsetting thoughts* such as that you may have a serious physical illness or be in real danger increase:
   - Bodily Feelings
   - Anxiety
   - Fear of anxiety

(2) *Avoiding situations or places that make you anxious.* It is normal to avoid real danger but anxiety may lead you to avoid things like shops, crowded places and trains which are not really dangerous. At first avoidance makes you feel better but:
   (a) Relief is only temporary – you may worry what will happen next time.

(b)   Every time you avoid something it is harder the next time you try and face it.

(c)   Gradually you want to avoid more and more things.

(3) *Loss of confidence.* Confidence is built up by doing things successfully. If you find that you can no longer do things that you used to do successfully, confidence is lost and can only be built up again gradually by tackling the easiest tasks first.

> *Remember*   (a) Anxiety does produce physical symptoms like rapid heart rate but it does not produce physical harm like a heart attack.
>
> (b) It makes you tired by using energy uselessly but does not cause nervous breakdowns.

Controlling symptoms

Many people already know some ways of making their symptoms better and some things which make them worse. Write these down and see if you can use this information to help in other circumstances.

Relaxation can help in relieving uncomfortable muscular tension, tiredness and worry. It also helps to slow down the speeding up and mental wheelspin which occur with anxiety.

Tape recorded instructions show you first how to relax your whole body, then how you can do it quickly in a number of different situations and finally how to use it to cope with the onset of feelings of anxiety and tension. The exercises teach you where your particular centres of tension are and what it feels like to be totally relaxed.

Regular practice is essential and should be at a settled time of day which is reserved for it. When you have completed the relaxation exercises try to imagine yourself in a situation where you have felt perfectly calm and contented. Recreate the sights and sounds of that situation in your mind. A list of relaxing situations such as days in the country or on holiday is useful for this purpose.

Start to use relaxation in circumstances when you are beginning to feel anxious – good exercises for this purpose are relaxing the forehead and neck, dropping the shoulders and practising slow shallow breathing. A key word like 'calm' or 'relax' can be used to start the sequence. Physical exercise like jogging, swimming, cycling or playing a ball game may also help to relieve the symptoms.

Rapid anxious breathing can make you tremble, feel dizzy, produce a thumping heart with tingling sensations in your hands and feet. This can be very worrying and give you the idea that you may be having a serious illness like a stroke or heart attack. These symptoms are controlled by slow, shallow breathing at 8–12 per minute.

Rushing and posture – plan your timetable in advancing order to avoid rushing. You will probably find that you get just as much done. When you have finished or are having a planned break, sit with a comfortable relaxed posture – not hunched up.

Distraction – tense worrying thoughts tend to produce a vicious circle. Try to turn your attention off these thoughts and fill your mind with something else – for example:

(1) Concentrating on what is going on around you – shop goods, people, cars or countryside according to where you are. There are many possible variations.

(2) Mental activity such as remembering a list or a poem or doing arithmetic.

(3) Physical activity such as walking, gardening or ironing.

Controlling upsetting thoughts – half formed upsetting thoughts or images can make you feel anxious or keep anxiety going. The thought that the sharp pain in your chest may be due to a heart attack makes it much more sinister and threatening. It is important at first to study your thinking and find out exactly what your upsetting thoughts are. This is quite difficult as they are automatic and come and go very quickly so that initially you may not be aware of them and need to practise hard in order to identify them.

Try to write them down exactly as they occur when you feel tense. They may be quite simple like 'Here we go again' or 'This is the way it started last time'. Once you know what you are thinking you can examine the thoughts carefully and identify those that are exaggerated or unrealistic. 'I didn't get the job so nobody will employ me', I feel tense about talking at the meeting which means I will make a hash of it' or 'I punished William unfairly so I am a lousy mother'. There are more positive and reasonable alternatives to all these thoughts. Try to write these down and then look at some of your own thoughts and see if you can find more reasonable alternatives. This is quite difficult at first but becomes easier with practice and a bit of help.

Dealing with avoidance and loss of confidence

Avoidance easily builds up with anxiety and makes things harder. It is countered by gradually getting back into the habit of doing things which build up confidence. The steps are as follows:

(1) Make a list of all the things that you avoid or make you anxious.

(2) Arrange these in order of difficulty.

(3) Select the easiest item on the list to start practise.

(4) Repeat this item until it can be done without difficulty.

(5) Move onto the next item and so on until you can do the whole list.

> *Remember* To be helpful practice must be regular, frequent and prolonged.

Appendix 2: COPING WITH A PANIC ATTACK

During a panic attack you are extremely likely to breathe very fast and/or deeply. This will have the effect of reducing the amount of carbon dioxide you will have in your lungs which will create a lot of unpleasant body sensations which are likely to make you afraid. A vicious circle of fear leading to overbreathing which leads to unpleasant body sensations (faintness, dizziness, tingling, headaches, racing heart, flushes, nausea, chest pain, shakiness, etc.) which cause more fear which leads again to overbreathing and so on, gets established.

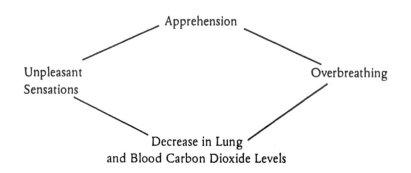

To stop this very nasty process you have to raise the amount of carbon dioxide in your lungs. You can do this in two ways:

(1) If you have a paper bag handy hold it tightly over your nose and mouth so that no air can get to your lungs from outside the bag and breathe the air in the bag for several minutes until you calm down.

(2) If a bag is not handy or it would be embarrassing to use one (say in a supermarket) then you should change your breathing so that you breathe in less air in a given period of time. You can probably do this most easily by slowing down your breathing in small steps. Attempt to breathe in smoothly and slowly and to let your breath out just as slowly. As you slow your breathing down you are bound to increase the depth of each breath somewhat. However, try to avoid a very big increase in depth because that would undo the good you have done by slowing down. The ideal you are aiming for is smooth, slow, regular and fairly shallow breathing. If you have managed to slow down for a few seconds

but feel out of breath[1] and a strong urge to take a quick gulp, *don't.*
Resist it by swallowing a couple of times, that should get rid of the
urge; if it doesn't then go ahead, take a gulp *but* once you've let the air
in *hold it* for about five seconds and then let it out *slowly.* If you can hold
a gulp for a few seconds you prevent it from lowering your carbon
dioxide levels. To sum up, breathe in and out as slowly and evenly as you
can and avoid any big increase in depth as you do so.

To help yourself slow down you could:

(1) Remember how you breathed with the tape and try to do that.

(2) Count to yourself while breathing. To start off with you might say 'one
thousand' to yourself while breathing in and 'two thousand' while
breathing out so your breathing would be:

in	*out*	*in*	*out*
one thousand	two thousand	one thousand	two thousand

and soon you might be able to say more to yourself while breathing in and out
and so take longer doing it. For example:

in	*out*
one thousand two thousand	one thousand two thousand
in	*out*
one thousand two thousand	one thousand two thousand

(This instruction leaflet is reproduced by kind permission of P. M. Salkovskis and D.
M. Clark.)

---

1   The feeling of being out of breath that people sometimes get when anxious is paradoxically
often caused by breathing too much. Taking in *less air* for a little while will often make it go
away. We don't know why some people become breathless after over breathing but it is a
well established fact that they do.

Appendix 3: DEEP MUSCLE RELAXATION

The technique described here is adapted from the Jacobson method (Jacobson 1938). It is the one most commonly used by behaviour therapists and depends on the alternative tensing and relaxing of various muscle groups with emphasis on learning to discriminate between the two. With practice, progressively deeper relaxation of any or all muscle groups can be produced at will.

The technique is most effective when taught by an instructor in person either to individuals or groups, followed by practice using a tape recording made at the live session. Under many circumstances, however, this will prove too time – consuming and commercial, and often previously prepared tapes or written instructions have to be used. (See 'Books for Patients' at the end of this chapter.)

The subject may use a couch, bed or even the floor but is probably best seated in a comfortable reclining chair. Uninterrupted quiet is essential. Later they may wish to practise in a hard chair or even standing up so that they can apply it in a variety of situations. Most instructors develop their own routine and there are small variations in order and wording. The following is given as an example:

> Anxiety and stress are often associated with physically tense muscles although you do not always realise that your muscles are tense. The series of exercises that we are going to do will help you to distinguish between tension and relaxation in the muscles and teach you how to relax the tension away at will. We will work through the various groups, first tensing them then relaxing them at the key word 'Relax'. We will start with the right hand and arm. Make a tight fist and, bending the elbow, coil the forearm up to the shoulder. Get the muscles of the forearm and upper arm as tight as you can and notice the feeling of tension in them. When they are as tight as possible begin to uncoil the arm from the shoulder allowing the forearm to rest beside you with the fist open, fingers and palms downwards and, to the key word 'Relax', allow the last little bit of tension to run out of the fingertips. (Pause 15 seconds.) I now want you to make a fist again and coil the forearm and arm up to the shoulder trying to get all the muscles a little firmer and a little more tense than last time. When you have got everything as tight as you possibly can, let the arm uncoil again noticing how different the relaxed muscles feel from the tension of a moment before. Try to relax the arms, (pause 5 seconds) forearms, (pause 5 seconds) and fingers a little more than the last time. Try to find that last little bit of tension and release it.

A similar double sequence of tension and relaxation is then used with the following muscle groups in turn:

Left Arm. This is really just a repeat of the right arm. It is included for the sake of symmetry and to provide further practice of the general principles with another easy muscle group.

Shoulders and Back of Neck. The tension phase is achieved by pulling the neck back into extension and pulling the shoulders up so that they press firmly into the neck on either side. Relaxation allows the neck to come forward and the shoulders to fall, releasing the tension. This latter part of the sequence can be taught as a single manoeuvre to be used at the cue of anxious sensations in public as it is invisible to other people present. The instruction 'When you begin to feel tense just concentrate on letting your shoulders drop' is often found to be helpful. Neck tension is a specific problem in a number of painful conditions and here also the technique is of use.

Forehead and Eyes. This is the most important group for the control of tension headaches. The eyebrows are pulled down into a deep frown and the eyes screwed tightly shut. The forehead is then allowed to smooth out and the eyes relax and open. Attention is drawn to the tingling 'leathery' feeling of the frontalis areas as the muscle relaxes.

Jaw and Tongue. The big masseter muscles at the side of the jaw are clamped tightly and the tongue firmly pressed against the roof of the mouth. Relaxation consists of unclenching the jaw and letting it fall slightly open whilst at the same time the tongue falls loosely down from the roof of the mouth.

Muscles at the Front of the Neck. The strap muscles are tensed to bring the chin down pressing tightly into the sternal notch. As the muscles relax the chin comes forward and up.

Chest and Breathing. This is of great importance in the control of hyperventilation and the emergency management of panic attacks. A deep breath is taken which is then forced out against a fixed diaphragm and closed throat producing a feeling of pressure in the ribs and intercostal muscles. The patient is asked to note how the muscles feel and then gradually let the breath go allowing the chest muscles to relax and a pattern of slow, shallow, rhythmic, even breathing to take over (see Coping With a Panic Attack, pp.104–105). These four descriptive words can be used as key words that the patient remembers when using the sequence in future. It should be added that some instructions ask the subject to take deep breaths but, except at the beginning of the sequence, this has no value and may make the physical consequence of hyperventilation worse by increasing respiratory alkalosis.

Back and Buttocks. The tension phase consists of pulling together the shoulders and the buttocks and arching the back. The simile of a bridge between two pillars is useful to give the patient the idea. After relaxation the whole body rests completely heavy on the chair or couch 'like a lump of lead' whilst the muscles of the shoulders and back are checked to release the last bit of tension.

Stomach. The stomach muscles are pulled tight producing a great feeling of tautness round the umbilicus 'as if somebody heavy was about to step on your stomach'. As the muscles are relaxed the sensation of slow, shallow, rhythmic, even breathing takes over again but this time concentration is on how the stomach muscles move in response to this.

Thighs, Legs and Feet. Unless there are special reasons such as local cramps, these are generally taken together. In tension the knees are pushed hard down in extension and the ankles and toes pushed out in full plantar flexion 'like trying to reach a point just out of reach beyond the toes'. The sensation of tightness in the thighs, calves and toes is noted. With relaxation the joints ease slightly into flexion and the knees fall slightly apart. Once more attention is drawn to the difference in the physical feeling of the two phases.

After the completion of the sequence of muscle groups, the patient is asked to check each in turn to make sure it is completely relaxed. This is followed by a pause of about one minute to enable the full feeling of complete relaxation to be appreciated and savoured. In order to allow normal activities to be resumed without a sudden jar a backward count from five is usually incorporated to end the programme. The complete sequence takes just over 30 minutes and can be recorded on one side of a C90 cassette tape.

The phrases 'let it go a little bit further' and 'let the last little bit of tension flow out of the muscles' are usually used frequently during the sequence as they can be recalled more easily later when the patient is practising by himself. In the same way it is important to incorporate a key word such as 'relax' or 'calm' which can be remembered as a cue.

The complete programme is taught initially but subsequently this is modified, when applied in practice, by omitting the tension phase and selecting parts which are most practical and useful in real life situations. For example, whereas the whole programme could not be used in a check-out queue, the breathing exercises, some isometric exercises and the relaxation phase of the head and neck exercises are perfectly feasible. Often some form of relaxing imagery, a pleasant scene or idea, is included in the beginning or end of the programme. This is useful but the image should be selected according to the patient's own individual requirements. People often choose a beach, garden or secure place at home. Whatever the image it can be induced and strengthened by considering the sounds, smells, colours and so on, that accompany the image.

Appendix 4: HELP WITH SLEEPING PROBLEMS

Many people come to their doctor complaining of being unable to sleep. They assume that they may become ill if they do not get enough sleep. In fact this is unlikely to happen as the body will take all the sleep it needs unless this is forcibly prevented. The amount of sleep people require varies enormously and often gets less with age. A person who had ten hours a night at twenty may require five or less at sixty. Some people fear that they will not be able to perform as well if they do not get a certain amount of sleep. This fear is also usually groundless and performance can be as good after a restless night as a good one.

It is possible to compare the amount of sleep you have had with your performance and the way you feel the following day by keeping a record as below:

Date	Hours of sleep	Activities (next day)	Competence 0–10	Alertness 0–10

From this you can draw your own conclusions as to whether your present pattern is harmful.

If you decide to try and increase the amount of sleep that you are getting, it is important to make sure that you are prepared for sleeping and that being in bed is linked in your mind only with sleeping not with other preoccupations. Usually excitement or hectic activity will prevent sleep, while calm and relaxation help in getting off, but this also varies a lot from person to person – for example, reading keeps some awake and sends others to sleep. It is important therefore to study and get to know your own pattern. The following suggestions may be helpful:

If You Have Difficulty in Getting to Sleep:

(1) Go to bed only when sleepy and do not try to get more sleep by going to bed early.

(2) Do not read, watch TV or eat in bed unless you are sure, from past experience, that these activities help you to get to sleep.

(3) When in bed try to get all your muscles as relaxed as you can. Taped or written instructions may help this.

(4) Try not to think about getting to sleep or worry about the day's activities. If you are unable to control worry then keep a note pad and pencil by the bed and write them down for a 'worry time' during the day then try instead to think about pleasant events or places.

(5) If you cannot find some pleasant thoughts at that moment listen to any relaxing sound from outside the house for instance birds, people or distant traffic.

(6) If you are unable to get to sleep after 10 minutes, get up immediately and do something different such as reading or going into a different room. Return to bed only when sleepy.

(7) Set your alarm and get up at the same time each morning regardless of how much sleep you received during the night.

(8) Do not take a nap during the day.

(9) If there is a time you are prone to fall asleep during the day or evening then set an alarm to limit the time and do not expect to sleep so well at night.

If You Wake During the Night

(1) Once you are fully awake do not lie in bed worrying about daily problems and not sleeping – get up.

(2) Go to a different room, make a drink if you feel like it, and sit comfortably in a chair reading a book or a magazine. (It is often worthwhile preparing a chair with a reading lamp, rug if necessary or heater and a suitable paperback the night before.)

(3) Only return to bed when you feel sleepy. When in bed relax and think of pleasant events or places.

(4) If sleep does not come in ten minutes, return to the chair and repeat the cycle.

> *Remember* Worrying about not sleeping is much more tiring than just being awake.

Chapter Seven

Relationship and Sexual Problems

This chapter covers the more intimate and social sides of interpersonal skills. Problems related to work will be dealt with later, although there will be some overlap. Social difficulties are examined in terms of the wider environment of relationships and this section should be read in conjunction with that on social phobia in Chapter Six. Many patients find that the breakdown of relationships results in uncontrolled anger outbursts and there will be some consideration of how these may be managed. Particular aspects of partnership and sexual problems will then be considered.

Relationship Difficulties

Social Interactions

Everyday behaviour between people in society requires a wide range of skills (Argyle 1967). In the ordinary way these are acquired by gradual learning involving trial and error within family, school or leisure activities. Equally if there are any problems most of these areas of life may be affected, leading to a reduction in social reinforcement and thus loss of confidence. Failure to use effective social skills may be because there has never been an opportunity to learn them. Equally it may be due to some other factor, commonly social anxiety or co-existing depression which stems from distorted thinking patterns and rigid inflexible life rules (see Social Phobia Chapter Six). In other words there may be a *skills deficit* or a *performance deficit*.

The cognitive behavioural interview has to estimate the type and proportion of these deficits in any individual problems. Detailed information is obtained about the current situations being avoided or causing problems, the presence of negative automatic thoughts, rigid personal rules and factors such as illness or isolation which may account for that lack. There are a huge number of cultural, social and personal variables which must be taken into account. There are also considerable intercultural differences. Assertive behaviour in one country may seem aggressive or submissive in another.

Performance Deficits

A wide variety of co-existing problems may hinder social performance. Depression, obsessionality and most forms of anxiety are obvious examples. Wider problems like physical and mental handicap and illness will play a part. The most frequent difficulty is, however, anxiety about the social situation itself which is based on the fear of making a fool of oneself in front of other people (negative social evaluation). This has been discussed earlier in Chapter Six. In the social skills context, a useful component of treatment is to help the patient divide the feared tasks into manageable components which are then tackled in a graded approach. For example, a patient is afraid to ask a friend for coffee as she thinks she may not be able to end the visit if she becomes too panicky. It may be helpful first to invite the visitor when there is a quick natural end to the time available such as having to fetch a child from playgroup in half an hour's time.

When setting goals for homework practice it is important to make tasks as easy as possible in order to ensure success. Patients may need reassuring that this is not 'cheating'. For example, someone who becomes anxious when eating with other people in public might first try going into the canteen and buying a sandwich and a carton of drink so that he can walk out at any time. Once he becomes more confident he can order a full meal, first perhaps by himself and then with friends.

Skills Deficits

The appropriate behaviours in various situations may never have been learnt, perhaps because of illness or a particularly isolated upbringing. Training can be provided in both an individual and a group setting. Group settings have the advantage that they provide a ready-made social situation for role-play and modelling. Such groups can be usefully set up within primary care by counsellors, nurses or health visitors as resources permit. It is necessary for leaders to acquire a knowledge of the content of social skills training and to see where it fits into the management of a variety of problems. The outline given below is insufficient to enable someone to lead a group and those interested in doing so are advised to read further (Falloon *et al.* 1974; Trower *et al.* 1978) and attend practical training sessions or workshops.

Outline of Social Relationships Group

Before accepting a patient as a group member an assessment interview should be carried out on an individual basis in order to estimate his or her needs and suitability for membership. It is the responsibility of leaders to remember individual needs once the group gets going and to fit these as far as possible into the working framework. A typical group programme might include:

(1) *Early sessions.* The rationale is explained by demonstrating that *assertive* behaviour includes:

    (a) the ability to express one's own wishes and to strive to achieve them (more use of 'I')

    (b) respect for one's own rights and at the same time the rights of others

    (c) by this means getting positive responses from others and avoiding being punished and ignored (positive and negative reinforcement).

Aggressive and servile behaviours on the other hand invite punishment or extinction. These points are clarified by modelling and role-play in the session and home work practise and recording between sessions. Work on *dressing, grooming, presentation* and *posture* is also included as appropriate.

    The influence of age, sex, status, the type of occasion (for example, diplomatic ball vs teenage disco), number of people present, and nature of the transaction (for example, complaint about shoddy goods or asking for a date) and the way that they influence appropriateness are discussed. The same format of modelling, role-play and homework is then applied.

(2) *Non-verbal communication* including the influence of personal space (i.e. the comfortable distance to engage in any activity with another person), facial expression, smiling, eye contact and gestures.

(3) *Vocal characteristics* ('How to say it') involving tone of voice, volume, emphasis, clarity, pace, fluency and pitch and the information these give us about the state of the communicator (for example, anxiety or diffidence) and the importance of the communication.

(4) *Initiating, continuing and terminating conversations* including suitable opening and closure phrases and also the importance of listening, relaxing, turn-taking and allowing silences.

(5) *Accepting, refusing and asking* in such a manner as to get the desired response, such as explaining that you can't go out that evening but you would still like to see the person again, etc.

(6) *Losing arguments and accepting other people's points of view* without being aggressive or losing dignity.

(7) *Intimate situations*, including how to give and accept compliments graciously; the importance of touching and closeness, tone of voice and remembering things (such as birthdays) that are important to the other person; how to give and accept presents and services.

(8) *Complaints* both in the home and in the world outside involve the same rules. These include being clear, not allowing the conversation to generalise onto other irrelevant issues, not getting angry and making it possible for an agreed solution to evolve.

The *format of the group session* may be as follows:

(1) Introductions if necessary and general report of the week including any positive events.

(2) Report on homework.

(3) General theoretical points raised from homework and in preparation for the exercises.

(4) Modelling and role-play exercises.

(6) Discussion of the emotions and thoughts provoked by the exercises.

(7) Setting of homework.

After four to six sessions less time is spent on general exercises and more may be devoted to role-playing individual members' problems. At this time blocks to treatment may be uncovered in the form of individual negative self-statements and obstructive assumptions which were not apparent at the initial interview. These can then be discussed and re-framed into more helpful, flexible alternatives.

Without elaborate group work some of these points can be discussed or role-played in the consultation. One patient was greeted by his almost estranged wife with the unexpected suggestion that they went out for a drink together. He replied 'What's come over you all of a sudden?' and a row ensued. At a brief consultation he was able to find positive alternative responses. The use of these, to his delight, later greatly improved the relationship.

Anger Management

Communication breaks down into anger in three main circumstances. First, when a cherished goal is obstructed, for example, the promised return telephone call never comes. Second, when important underlying life rules are broken, for example, 'I should always be treated considerately and with respect' (Beck 1976). Third, when anger serves to protect the individual from criticism or threat as, for example, when the response to correction by a superior at work is an outburst of rage against the critic ('The man on a short fuse').

The *assessment* of the problem includes the usual functional analysis aided by diary keeping. Particular attention is paid to the distorted thinking preceding the outburst and its consequential effects. It may be helpful for the patient to draw up a 'profit and loss account' demonstrating the advantages and disadvantages of the angry response. A resulting *formulation* should show the internal as well as external factors provoking anger, the consequences on the patient and others and the possible advantages of change.

Strategies for management include:

- Relaxation and exercise.
- Increasing variety and amount of pleasurable activities.
- Problem solving training.
- Distancing from anger triggers both in time ('wait before responding'), space ('calmly leave the room') and thought ('think about the pros and cons first').
- Breathing control (see Panic in Chapter Six).
- Recognising and challenging distorted thinking.
- Introducing positive self-statements.
- Recognising and modifying obstructive personal rules.
- Setbacks should be recognised as opportunities for re-assessing and learning more, rather than just as 'failures'.

Partner Therapy

The high rate of failed relationships is a sad fact of modern life. Certainly increased prosperity, leisure and expectation of life may place strains on relationships in developed Western society which have to some extent replaced the more obvious stresses of disease and poverty. Many relationships start with high affection, commitment and expectations only to see these desirable features drain away to the distress of both partners. Strangely both partners may find that they can feel valued and communicate with others perfectly satisfactorily at work or leisure but feel neglected and misunderstood by the person closest to them. The theory of cognitive therapy predicts that the basic technical skills are lacking in such relationships inevitably leading to disillusionment, miscommunication and misunderstanding (Beck 1988).

Table 7.1 The twelve deadly expectations

(1) 'Our love (i.e. romance and excitement) will continue unabated over time.'

(2) 'My partner should be able to anticipate my thoughts, feelings and needs.'

(3) 'My partner would never hurt me or retaliate in anger.'

(4) 'If you truly loved me you would always try to please me (i.e. meet my every need and desire).'

(5) 'Love means never being angry or upset with your partner.'

(6) 'Love means always wanting to be together.'

(7) 'Our personal interests, goals and values will always remain the same.'

(8) 'My partner will always be open, direct and honest with me.'

(9) 'Because we are in love, my partner will always respect, understand and accept me no matter what I do.'

(10) 'It would be terrible if my partner ever embarrassed, belittled or criticised me.'

(11) 'Our level of sex, affection and commitment must never decline.'

(12) 'We must always agree with each other on important matters.'

Brief therapy with couples has been shown to be highly effective (Halford and Osgarby 1996) and can be a useful intervention in primary care. One partner in a distressed relationship may make an appointment with his, or more often her GP, and present superficial, ostensibly more acceptable 'medical' symptoms. Sensitivity, time and some gentle probing may be needed on the part of the GP to uncover the real problem. Once the true cause of the distress is discovered and discussed, it is best to see the other partner alone in a second consultation in order to maintain the balance and attempt to assess 'secret factors' such as undeclared sexual affairs. It may be a necessary part of therapy to encourage honesty between partners and it is, of course, important to discover if either partner is so involved elsewhere that they have no intention of continuing with the marriage. Other typical 'secrets' may include jealousy, dislike of stepchildren, venereal disease, incest and other 'skeletons in the cupboard'.

Once these initial interviews are complete a decision can be taken with both partners about further treatment. It can be explained to the couple that a relationship such as a marriage may develop problems in itself which are almost independent of the individual people involved. Most of us can recall marriages where both partners are charming agreeable people with everybody, except their husband or wife. In such cases it is the relationship that needs the attention and there is no such thing as a sick or guilty party. Actions and words will receive a major part of the attention during the early stages of therapy with additional factors such as distorted thinking and assumptions gradually assuming more importance later. This model suitably modified to address the features of the individual problem is discussed and modified with the partners.

If the couple accept the *formulation*, two further questions are helpful. First, are both prepared to commit themselves to trying to make the relationship work? Second, are both prepared to change in order to achieve this? It may seem rather unfair to ask questions at this early stage but it is helpful to get some sort of commitment in each other's presence.

After the decision to continue has been taken, the assessment should include a detailed description in behavioural terms of the incidents which lead to conflict, the thoughts, feelings and misapprehensions attached to them and the partners' expectations of each other. It should also stress the (often forgotten) positive factors in each other and the relationship. Time should be spent on deciding on goals of treatment that are clear and acceptable to both. Once detailed information is obtained about precipitating factors, it may become clear that only one or two aspects of life such as sex or money difficulties are leading to problems. It is useful to find out about what a couple used to do together and trace the development of the problem which is now engulfing both of them.

Table 7.2 The three hidden agendas

(1) My partner doesn't care about me (Positiveness).

(2) My partner is not interested in me (Responsiveness).

(3) My partner doesn't treat me as an equal (Status).

Often at least one partner is ambivalent about asking for help and a low-key early session may be helpful in making both sides aware of the difficulties. Any changes suggested at the assessment stage should be designed to be non-threatening and to give positive results, to encourage confidence on both sides. Time is spent uncovering the unrealistic expectations and hidden agendas (q.v.).

Both partners can be asked to keep independent weekly records of behaviour which they feel has led to unhappiness and rows. They may also note positive behaviours and give a daily satisfaction rating. A checklist of commonly occurring problem areas in marriage may be of help in making sure that nothing has been left out. This might include:

- Sex
- Communication
- Alcohol, smoking and food
- Religion
- Free time and holidays
- Money
- Housing
- Friends
- Children
- Relatives

Intervention Strategies

These are a selection of commonly helpful techniques all or some of which can be applied as appropriate:

Disengagement. Partners are asked to aim to treat each other as friendly flatmates. They may greet each other on arrival and departure, enquire about each other's day, give an idea of when they might expect each other home and whether they might eat together.

Love Days or Evenings. Each partner in turn makes an effort to try and please the other unconditionally. This is useful before dealing with areas of conflict.

Going Out. Planning a night out together – just a walk, drink or local cinema rather than an expensive treat where too much is invested or expected – can be used. Other companionship exercises include planning a perfect weekend or holiday and seeing what each other would like to do. Some of these activities, once discovered, can then perhaps be incorporated in the normal week's timetable.

Using 'I'. This makes needs and wants clear without resorting to hints, double meanings or unfair questions, i.e. those with only one permitted answer, such as 'Do you mind if we don't go out on Friday – I've got to work late at the office.'

Timetabling. The idea of this is to change the couple's routine at certain times when there is a high probability of conflict. Suggestions should be the result of a discussion of ideas put forward by the couple. The therapist only has to make sure that the ideas are realistic and are expressed in terms that can be clearly translated into precise actions. Some examples might be:

(1) 'Change Sunday lunch' to the evening so that all members of the family can go out in the morning.

(2) Decide to get up 15 minutes earlier in the morning and alter some of the responsibilities. In this way frayed tempers are avoided and duties shared more evenly, possibly getting the children to help.

(3) Have separate bank accounts so each partner can feel in control of their finances, clarifying who pays what.

Role-playing. It can be illuminating for couples to role-play their reception of one another when they meet in the evening. Areas of modification usually become apparent. This technique can also be used to teach or improve basic skills such as asking a favour, making a protest or appreciating something the other has done.

Reverse role-playing, if used with care, can make a partner see how it feels to be in the other's shoes and increase their awareness of which aspects of behaviour to change.

Contracting. Behavioural contracts are like commercial ones in that they express clearly, usually in writing, the duties and rewards of both parties. They can aid clarity, recall and compliance in changing behaviour but, more important, if used properly they are seen to be fair and equitable. The first step is for a grid to be drawn up as follows:

	Increase Sought	**Decrease Sought**
Her behaviour (according to him)	Serving fish Coming out for drink	Nagging about plumbing Going to bed at 9pm
His Behaviour (according to her)	Help with Kevin's bath Talk together at homecoming	Socks on the floor Late without 'phoning

Figure 7.1 Contract grid

Once the grid is complete the actual contract can be agreed. These are of two types:

(1) A *quid pro quo* contract. This is a straightforward exchange of behaviour. In the example given above serving fish twice weekly might be exchanged for 15 minutes' help at Kevin's bath time. The behaviours are equal and interdependent.

(2) A *parallel* contract. Each behaviour is treated independently and has its own reward, and sometimes punishment for breach. For example, husband phones before being late. Reward: a chat on arrival. Punishment: supper removed at 7 p.m. on ensuing nights.

Problem-solving Techniques. These are often clearly lacking in troubled marriages. There are three stages:

(1) *Defining the problem* – this should be clear, specific, unemotional and brief.

(2) *Generating solutions* – only one problem is taken at a time but no solution is too ridiculous or way-out to be mentioned.

Table 7.3 Problem solving

Step 1 Define the problem *precisely*.

Step 2 List every possible solution *however far fetched or stupid it may seem.*
  (1)..
  (2)..
  (3)..
  (4)..

Step 3 Consider carefully and discuss if possible the pros and cons of each solution.

Solution	Advantages	Disadvantages
....	....	....
....	....	....
....	....	....
....	....	....
....	....	....
....	....	....
....	....	....
....	....	....
....	....	....

Step 4 Choose the best solution or combination of solutions.

Step 5 Plan how to carry out the solution stepwise.
  Step 1..
  Step 2..
  Step 3..

(3) *Selecting a solution* – again it is important to be clear and specific. Who is going to do what, when, where and how often? Some provision for follow-up and monitoring change can also be made.

A useful technique which provides a framework for problem solving is *executive sessions*. The rules are as follows:

(1) Either partner who has a problem may approach the other and ask for a session.

(2) The second partner fixes a time and place for the session, which must not be unreasonably delayed – a suitable example would be 'in the kitchen at 7 p.m. after the children are in bed'.

(3) At the session the first, convening, partner has ten minutes to put the problem, during which time the responding second partner must listen but not speak.

(4) The second ten minutes gives the responding partner the right to reply, during which time the convenor must listen but may not speak.

(5) The final ten minutes is spent generating solutions along problem–solving lines, which are then tested. If success is not achieved either partner may call another session.

The highly structured nature of this system allows reasoned communication between partners who normally cannot speak without fighting.

New Behaviours. These may be suggested to increase or decrease interdependence such as joining clubs or evening classes either together or apart.

Cognitive Factors. Thinking errors and dysfunctional schemata and assumptions play an extremely important part in marital problems (Beck 1988, Bagarozzi and Winter Giddings 1983). They come to light in the initial assessment and as blocks to progress later in treatment.

Prevention. Much of the drive of marital and couples therapy has been towards repairing damage. It makes a lot of sense, however, to attempt to teach the relevant survival skills early in the relationship so that the couple have the technical knowledge to avoid damage altogether (Beck 1988).

Markham and his co-workers (Markham *et al.* 1994) have devised and evaluated a programme (Prevention and Relationship Enhancement Programme, PREP) which can be used both by couples preparing to set out on their relationship together and those who have already developed problems. The research evaluations have shown an enduring beneficial effect in the relationship outcomes over several years follow-up (Markham and Halweg

1993). This group conceptualise the main problems in relationships as occurring in four categories:

(1) *Escalation.* When trivial issues at the start of an argument grow during the exchange until major verbal and sometimes physical wounding occurs.

(2) *Invalidation.* Where one partner refuses to recognise the importance of the other's concerns and sets him or her down.

(3) *Withdrawal and Avoidance.* One partner, usually the woman, feels that she cannot get a concern properly discussed and the other continually withdraws from the issue either by physically leaving or by terminating the conversation in other ways. The pursuer then chases more vigorously and the evader withdraws ever more rapidly.

(4) *Negative Interpretations.* One party implies a hidden harmful reason for the others behaviour which does not in reality exist and acts accordingly.

The PREP programme goes on to address ways of exploring these problems and learning more adaptive ways of handling them. The programme has had considerable success in the US and in Germany as part of premarriage programmes. In the UK where the course of relationships is less traditionally defined there is a potential problem in recruitment. The PREP team hold workshops in Denver for leaders who direct group work and consultants who work on a one-to-one basis with couples. Both leaders and consultants can be drawn from non-professional volunteers who are prepared to take the training.

Partner problems have been discussed in the context of heterosexual couples but the principles involved apply equally to any other type of relationship including same sex partners, parent and child, workmates or flatmates where conflict may occur.

Sexual Problems

Sexual problems are presented fairly frequently in day to day general practice, but can easily be ignored to the detriment of patients and their relationships. Occasionally a patient will visit specifically to complain of a sexual difficulty or more often it will be seen as an accompaniment to physical or psychological illness or as a side effect of medication. Unfortunately it is often overlooked by patient and doctor while concentrating on what seems to be the more 'important' issue. If a family planning service is offered and health visitors are also alert to sexual problems arising after childbirth, or from the stress of looking after young families, then numbers may increase significantly. Since effective psychological help is available it is a pity if reluctance on the part of professionals to discuss sexual issues prevents people obtaining help which may greatly enhance their quality of life.

When sexual difficulties are acknowledged early, brief explanations, advice and reassurance may be enough to sort problems out. In other cases, more formal psychosexual therapy may be needed. This can be provided by the primary care worker, by referral either to a specialist sexual dysfunction clinic or to services in the voluntary sector, such as Relate counselling. Success rates are reasonably high if prognostic factors are taken into account when deciding whether or not to offer therapy (Hawton 1995), and this type of treatment is rewarding for both patients and therapists. It is well suited to primary care where the time and place of appointments may be convenient for both partners. This setting is also well situated to provide the regular but often short appointments usually required in the most straightforward cases. The most common simple problems develop as a result of stress, illness, surgery or after childbirth and a well timed brief intervention in primary care can prevent the development of more intractable difficulties.

Such cases still require a thorough assessment of the complaint although a short treatment programme will often be enough. Treatment should concentrate on information and permission giving and usually some form of sensate focus or goal setting to restart contact between the partners. Often couples say they are waiting until they both 'feel like it'. Unfortunately this can result in an indefinite cessation of sexual activity but sensate focus or well judged Timetabling can either restore sexual activity quite quickly or reveal more serious underlying reasons. Acknowledgement of the problem in attending the surgery may in itself often relieve anxiety and improve communication between the couple. One example of this was a woman of sixty who attended the surgery because she had lost interest in sex for some months. Her husband had been threatened with redundancy six months before and as a result of this stress the couple did not have sex for three months. When the employment problem was resolved the wife was unable to regain her interest. Brief discussion about possible causes of the problem, a lot of reassurance and specific instructions to ban intercourse and do some sensate focus, resulted in a return to their former activity level in three weeks.

The sex therapy programme (Appendix 1) from Masters and Johnson (Masters and Johnson 1970) is essentially behavioural. Graded tasks desensitise anxiety to sexual behaviours and allow new behaviours to be learned. Considerable success can be achieved with this alone, but as with many other behavioural techniques, a cognitive component has been added to provide a more comprehensive approach when the former is insufficient.

Bancroft (1996) proposes that cognitive behavioural therapy addresses four broad areas:

(1) Improving communication and understanding between the couple.

(2) Learning new methods of conflict resolution and expression of negative feelings.

(3) Cognitive restructuring of sexual concepts and meanings.

(4) Modification of the sexual behaviour and response *per se*.

Beyond the cognitive behavioural, there is still a gap in knowledge surrounding the physiological mechanisms that mediate between the behaviour and cognitions. Further understanding may lead the way to new therapies and benefits (Bancroft 1996).

Equally sexual problems resulting from physical illness, handicap and old age should not be overlooked. The treatments described below can be used and imaginatively adapted to help a couple obtain sexual pleasure and satisfaction within their physical limitations (Greengross 1976).

Sexual problems in *men* may be classified as:

(1)   Erectile problems.

(2)   Premature ejaculation.

(3)   Non-ejaculation.

and in *women*:

(1)   Loss of interest or libido.

(2)   Orgasmic dysfunction.

(3)   Vaginismus.

In *men* and *women* they may be classified as:

(1)   Problems with frequency of intercourse.

(2)   Lack of education and information.

(3)   Difficulties related to illness, ageing, surgery or physical disability.

The commonest causes are:

(1)   Anxiety-based, following a traumatic conditioning experience or due to stress.

(2)   Anger or resentment in the relationship leading to inability to share pleasure with the partner.

(3) Related to moral or religious commitments.

(4) Related to physical illness or disability.

(5) Related to alcohol, drugs, circulatory problems, ageing or endocrine disorders such as diabetes.

(6) Arising from the stresses of infertility treatment.

(7) Fear of pregnancy or infection.

An outline of the main categories of the problem and approaches to treatment follows, but before embarking on more complex problems and for further information, the reader is recommended to consult one of the specialist texts (Hawton 1985, Bancroft 1989, Zilbergeld 1980). If treatment is misinformed or misdirected, couples may become disheartened and a later second round of therapy is difficult to initiate.

Assessment

A sexual history should be obtained from each partner, together or preferably one at a time. Joint interviews help mutual understanding of the problems. Seeing couples separately, however, allows a partner to disclose secret facts and worries. If these are relevant they should be discussed in the joint sessions. Some secrets from the past such as previous infections, experiences or relationships may have no influence on the presenting problem and disclosure of these should be carefully judged. If there is current deceit in the relationship which one partner is unwilling to discuss, then it may be necessary to discontinue ideas of treatment for the time being.

It is important to obtain the following information:

(1) A precise description of the problem and the circumstances leading up to the initial and current difficulties.

(2) Thoughts, feelings and images related to sexual experiences and traumas. These may not be accessible on initial interview but can emerge later in therapy from diaries used for monitoring cognitions at different stages in the programme.

(3) Stress or mental illness in one or both partners.

(4) The state of the current relationship.

(5) Any current medication or physical illness.

(6) Details of past and current methods of contraception, information on knowledge and application of safe sex in both gay and heterosexual couples.

(7) Cultural or religious values. The sexual difficulties need to be understood in the context of cultural or religious mores and adjustments made in the content and presentation of therapy as well as access to it.

(8) Diaries (see Chapter Four) are useful after the first session to assess thoughts and feelings associated with past and current sexual experiences and the general relationship. Negative body image, low self-esteem and childhood experiences may all be revealed. Standard questionnaires, such as GRIMS and GRISS (Collier 1989) are useful, but a tailor-made diary designed at each session is generally more acceptable to the patient and more useful in gaining information.

As in all functional analyses, precise detail is important even if it is difficult to obtain immediately. When considering erectile difficulties for example, it is important to find out whether there is an erection which is lost, no erection at all, or whether premature ejaculation is the cause. It should be noted if the patient has early morning erections, whether the difficulty is the same with masturbation or other circumstances. This will provide the information to determine the exact nature of the problem. An illustration of the importance of accurate assessment is the case of a man who suffered from non-ejaculation after 18 months in hospital under heavy medication. It was discovered that until recently he had used 'withdrawal' as his normal method of contraception, that the problem predated his illness and it was the withdrawal method, not the drugs or illness that was responsible for the non-ejaculation.

Treatment

(1) *Assessment and Functional Analysis.* This in itself is sometimes therapeutic in clarifying problems for the couple concerned. It can also provide an opportunity to remove blame from one partner in particular, for both partners to take some responsibility for the problem and overcome avoidance in discussing the issue.

(2) *Education or Information.* Questions in the assessment can serve to highlight gaps of sexual information. This then allows physiological details to be explained, old wives tales and myths (Baker and De Silva 1988) to be explored and a rationale for treatment to be given. Books for home reading are very useful at this stage (see Books for Patients at the end of this chapter).

(3) *Permission Giving.* Discussion or reading for homework assignments can be an opportunity to introduce sexual behaviours which the couple had not previously considered or had thought to be improper. A

patient may be reassured that there is nothing wrong with masturbation, oral sex, or having sex in the afternoon. If attitudes stem from a patient's religious or moral upbringing or convictions and these are in conflict with current wishes, then a session with a sympathetic and liberal religious leader may be helpful in interpreting what is and is not acceptable. Obviously care should be taken not to offend, shock or suggest unwanted behaviours or encourage anyone to break strongly held convictions or taboos. Other attitudes can be counterproductive, for instance in desensitisation where in early stages a behaviour may need to be initiated without necessarily being desired in advance. It is difficult but sometimes necessary to discuss the possibility of trying a task while still feeling fairly neutral about it, as with other more phobic behaviours. Feedback is crucial as another stage or approach should be considered if no enjoyment is forthcoming.

(4) *The Modified Masters and Johnson Approach* (Masters and Johnson 1970) see Appendix 1.

This programme for sexual difficulties, like many other treatment approaches in this book, is based on the model of desensitisation in vivo, and hence stages are presented to the patient in a hierarchical manner (see below and Chapters Five and Six). However, the hierarchy must be constructed individually for each patient or couple as an assumed standard format may be quite inappropriate. Many patients think a 'treatment' does not work for them and naturally become disenchanted and at worst, feel that they have failed when in fact the therapist has adopted too rigid an approach. When blocks occur in therapy, a return to the assessment analysis, subsequent cognitive and behavioural information, and some re-formulation may lead to a different hypothesis and therapeutic approach.

(5) *Masturbation Programme* (Heiman, LoPiccolo 1976) see Appendix 2.

(6) *Pharmacotherapy and Sexual Aids.* Pharmacotherapy and sexual aids are used increasingly in the treatment of sexual dysfunction. However a CBT assessment to gauge the contribution of psychological factors will help in deciding which approach to use and when. Cognitive therapy and behavioural approaches may both be indicated in helping the patient or partner come to terms with the use of external aids. A quadriplegic can be helped with cognitive therapy to develop 'cerebral' rather than physiological orgasm. Modelling or anxiety management techniques may be helpful for a patient or partner to

give am intracavernosal penile injection (see the Caverject video –
details at the end of this chapter).

Pharmacological Treatments

Erectile Failure. There are currently two forms of intrapenile injection. These
are used as diagnostic and increasingly as therapeutic agents in psychogenic
impotence. The first one used was Papaverine and now Caverject or Prostaglandin E seems to be the treatment of choice. They produce a satisfactory
response without the danger or inconvenience of priapism. Trials are under-
way for an external vasodilator cream and for oral medication Sildenafil, but
at present these are not available. Apart from Yohimbine which is moderately
effective, penile injection is the only pharmacological treatment generally
available.

Premature Ejaculation. Oral medication for the treatment of premature
ejaculation has advanced dramatically since the advent of SRRIs and the use
of Clomipramine. These appear to provide a very effective response when
results for psychological and behavioural strategies are less convincing.
However, the response is based on a side effect of a drug which, for other
patients, who may be taking the medication for depression, causes partial or
complete loss of libido and sometimes erectile problems (treatable as above).
While continuing on the medication, these problems are not amenable to
psychological intervention other than providing an explanation and reassurance that the drug effect is reversible. The improvement effects for premature
ejaculation are not always sustainable after withdrawal from the drug and it
may soon be shown that, as with many other psychological problems, a
combined drug and psychological treatment may be most successful (see
Appendix 3).

   With both these conditions, the assessment will help point the way in
choosing a treatment approach (Althof 1995). The following factors should
be considered:

(1) When the symptom developed. Drug therapy may be less desirable
    where symptoms are of recent onset.

(2) The extent of sexual experience and confidence. Anxiety reduction and
    education may be more appropriate in those patients with infrequent
    sexual encounters or lack of experience.

(3) The quality of the couple's relationship may contraindicate therapy
    where this seems to be a major contributor to the problem. On the
    other hand, a course of pharmacotherapy for the presenting patient
    can improve the motivation of the partner to continue with a

psychological treatment programme, knowing that there may be hope for some improvement where past failure had demoralised them.

(4) The ability to tolerate side effects.

Physical Treatments and Sexual Aids (From Bhugra and Crowe 1995)

(1) *Vacuum pumps.* These are usually supervised in specialised clinics but are feasible for use in primary care (details are given at the end of this chapter).

(2) *Surgical procedures.* The use of these is largely confined to correction of congenital and acquired abnormalities. The relatively simple Fenton's operation to enlarge a physically tight vagina is feasible for the experienced surgeon working in primary care. The rest lie outside our scope but occasionally advice may be sought by a worried patient or relative (Masters and Johnson 1970).

Bibliotherapy

Patient self-help books are useful but their effects are greatly enhanced by therapist contact. Books and videos are particularly recommended in primary care to maximise the efficacy of brief contact and help the less experienced therapist (Trudel 1991).

Premature Ejaculation

When Stage Four of the sensate focus is reached (or earlier if ejaculation occurs during Stages One, Two or Three, see Appendix 1), the woman should be asked to stimulate her partner until he reaches the point of orgasm. When he indicates to her that he has reached this point, she immediately stops until the urge has decreased when stimulation can be restarted. When this cycle has been repeated three of four times they may continue to orgasm. At Stage Four the same stop–start technique is used with the penis inside the woman eventually proceeding to ejaculation (Semans 1956).

An alternative technique, now less used, is for the woman to squeeze the penis just below the glans to abolish her partner's urge to ejaculate. After the urge subsides stimulation is restarted. This technique can create anxiety in both parties about damage to the penis and the other seems equally effective.

Men who have a regular masturbation habit or who have no current partner can also learn to control premature ejaculation by using the stop–start techniques when masturbating. At the same time it may be useful to learn to increase the awareness of the point at which ejaculation becomes inevitable.

It is possible for uncontrolled rapid masturbation to reinforce premature ejaculation when intercourse is resumed with a partner.

Drug therapy alone or in combination with the above techniques should also be considered either as the treatment of choice or if the man is making no progress with cognitive behavioural methods.

Erectile Problems

Temporary impotence is a common, although extremely worrying, condition frequently associated with periods of increased stress or depression. Exploration and explanation of the problem may be all that is necessary. The attitude of the patient's partner is important, as it is very helpful if they are understanding and relaxed. Some, however, see their partner's erectile failure as a result of their own loss of attractiveness or even of his excessive sexual activities elsewhere. These attitudes should be explored and corrected. If further therapy is needed, for most men the ban on intercourse and first two stages of sensate focus provide a lot of confidence. Genital touching is introduced in Stage Three. The partner should stroke and fondle the man's penis and then stop so that the exciting sensations are lost and the contrast of feelings recognised without anxiety. They then stimulate him again so that the sensations return. This teasing technique should be continued for some time whether he gains an erection or not. When his confidence has increased they may try to stimulate him to orgasm without penetration.

The next stage is to attempt the teasing technique with the penis inside the vagina using the female superior position. First there is no movement and later a gradually increasing amount of thrusting is allowed.

Failure of an erection at any point in this programme can be dealt with by going back a couple of stages. This should restore confidence or may shed more light on any particular difficulty which has not been dealt with. More general problems may be revealed at this stage and a few sessions spent on cognitive or anxiety management techniques can be integrated into the programme. Occupational stresses are frequently a precursor of sexual problems and have become more common in recent years.

Vaginismus

This can be treated successfully but sometimes more time and resources may be needed if there are complicated or deep-seated psychological problems resulting from sexual abuse or other trauma.

It is important to discover the woman's thoughts and feelings about genitalia (of both partners) and sexual intercourse. The problem is often revealed at vaginal examination and it may be possible after discussion of anxieties to pursue the examination sympathetically and embark on a therapy programme. After the assessment consultation, the woman is asked to find a relaxed opportunity to examine and touch her genital areas. Considerable avoidance may be encountered and it may be necessary to help and encourage her to do this first in the surgery. Pelvic floor exercises (Kegel, 1952) will help her to obtain some feeling of control over the vaginal muscles and will also be useful later. As the vagina is approached, there is often extreme tension in the feet, legs and thighs and practising general differential relaxation exercises (see Chapter Six) will help to alleviate this.

The next stage is to ask the woman to insert her finger a short way into the vagina, gradually progressing to complete insertion followed by the insertion of two fingers. A lubricant may help. If difficulty is encountered at this stage, an examination by a female therapist may facilitate progress and the patient can then try to insert her own finger under supervision. Graded dilators may be preferable at this stage as they sometimes permit a more relaxed position to be adopted allowing introspection on any anxieties or negative feelings caused by having something in the vagina. Use of dilators may be continued for a time before an attempt is made to insert a finger. The use of tampons is sometimes considered to be a major goal and achievement and helps to consolidate progress.

Practice is then transferred to pleasuring sessions with first the woman and then her partner placing a finger near, then just inside the vagina. The woman should feel relatively relaxed and comfortable with the finger or dilator in her vagina before any attempt is made towards movement or penetration with her partner's penis. Penetration with a finger or penis should always be under the woman's guidance and control so that at no stage does she feel frightened or forced. Methods of contraception should be discussed again now as ideas that may only have been hypothetical at the assessment stage with vaginismus patients now become a reality.

In cases of vaginismus, perhaps more than in other sexual difficulties, blocks may occur in treatment. Negative attitudes may be revealed and resolved but if this is impossible referral may be the best course of action. For example, a woman of 28 had never had intercourse, although she was able to enjoy mutual masturbation with her boyfriend. Using graded dilators considerable progress was made, until halted by her being unable to face her feelings, related to an incestuous relationship in her childhood. Brief psychotherapy helped her resolve some of these feelings and she was able to return to sex therapy and achieve intercourse some weeks later. Another patient was so tense that, after relaxation failed, graded dilation was eventually achieved under intravenous diazepam which has led to successful consummation of the marriage.

References

Althof, S. (1995) 'Pharmacological treatment for rapid ejaculation: preliminary strategies, concerns and questions. *Sexual and Marital Therapy V10*, 3, 247–252.

Argyle, M. (1967) *The Psychology of Interpersonal Behaviour*. Harmondsworth: Penguin.

Bagarozzi, D.A. and Winler Giddings, C. (1983) 'Behavioural marital therapy: empirical status, current practices, trends and future directions.' *Clinical Social Work Journal 11*, 26–9.

Baker, C. and De Silva, P. (1988) 'The relationship between sexual dysfunction and belief in Zilbergeld's myths: an empirical investigation.' *Sexual and Marital Therapy 3*, 2.

Bancroft, J. (1996) 'Sexual problems.' In D. Clarke and C. Fairburn (eds) *Science and Practice of Cognitive Behaviour Therapy*. Oxford: Oxford University Press.

Beck, A.T. (1976) *Cognitive Therapy and the Emotional Disorders*. New York: New American Library.

Beck, A.T. (1988) *Love is Never Enough*. London: Penguin.

Bhugra, D. and Crowe, M. (1995) 'Physical treatments of erectile disorders.' *International Review of Psychiatry 7*, 217–223.

Collier, J. (1989) 'The sue of the GRIMS and GRISS in the assessment and outcome of sexual problems.' *Journal of Sex and Marital Therapy 4*, 1, 11.

Falloon, I., Lindley, P. and McDonald, R. (1974) *Social Training: A Manual*. London: Psychological Treatment Section, Maudsley Hospital.

Greengross, W. (1976) *Entitled to Love: The Sexual and Emotional Needs of the Handicapped*. London: Maltby Press.

Halford, W.K. and Osgarby, S. (1996) 'Brief behavioural couples therapy: A preliminary evaluation.' *Behavioural and Cognitive Psychotherapy 24*, 263–273.

Hawton, K. (1995) 'Treatments of sexual dysfunction's by sex therapy and other approaches.' *British Journal of Psychiatry 15*, 307–314.

Hawton, K. (1985) *Sex Therapy – A Practical Guide*. Oxford: Oxford University Press.

Heiman J. and Lo Piccolo, J. (1976) *Becoming Orgasmic: A Sexual Growth Programme for Women*. New Jersey: Prentice-Hall.

Kegel, A.H. (1952) 'Sexual functions of the pubococcygeus muscle.' *Western Journal of Surgery, Observation and Gynaecology 60*, pp.521–4.

Markham, H. and Hahlweg, K. (1993) 'The prediction and prevention of marital distress: an international perspective.' *Clinical Psychology Review 13*, 29–43.

Markham, H., Stanley, S. and Blumberg, S.L. (1994) *Fighting for Your Marriage*. San Francisco: Jossey Bass.

Masters, W.H. and Johnson, V.E. (1970) *Human Sexual Inadequacy*. London: Churchill.

Semans, J.M. (1956) 'Premature ejaculation – a new approach.' *Southern Medical Journal 49*, 35–7.

Trower, P., Bryant, B. and Argyle, M. (1978) *Social Skills and Mental Health*. London: Methuen.

Trudel, G. (1991) 'The use of bibliotherapy in the treatment of sexual dysfunctions.' *British Journal of Sexual Medicine Spring 1991*, pp.18–20.

Recommended for Further Reading

Argyle, M. (ed) (1981) *Social Skills and Health.* London: Methuen.

Beck, A.T. (1988) *Love is Never Enough.* London: Penguin.

Bancroft, J. (1996) 'Sexual problems.' In D. Clarke and C. Fairburn (eds) *Science and Practice of Cognitive Behaviour Therapy.* Oxford: Oxford University Press.

Bancroft, J. (1989) *Human Sexuality and its Problems.* London: Churchill Livingston.

D'Ardenne, P. (1996) 'Sexual health for men in culturally diverse communities – some psychological considerations.' *Sexual and Marital Therapy 11,* 3, 289–296.

Greengross, W. (1976) *Entitled to Love. The Sexual and Emotional Needs of the Handicapped.* London: Malaby Press.

Hawton, K. (1985) *Sex Therapy – A Practical Guide.* Oxford: Oxford University Press.

Jehu, D. (1979) *Sexual Dysfunction A Behavioural Approach to Causation, Assessment, and Treatment.* Chichester: John Wiley.

Markham, H., Stanley, S. and Blumberg, S.L. (1994) *Fighting for Your Marriage.* San Francisco: Jossey Bass.

Priestley, P., McGuire, J., Flegg, D., Hemsley, V. and Welham, D. (1978) *Social Skills and Personal Problem Solving.* London: Tavistock.

Zilbergeld, B. (1980) *Men and Sex.* London: Fontana.

Books for Patients

Alberti, R.E. and Emmons, M.L. (1983) *Your Perfect Right.* San Luis: Impact.

Delvin, D. (1974) *The Book of Love.* London: New English Library.

Dickson, A. (1982) *A Woman in Your Own Right – Assertiveness and You.* London: Quality Books.

Kaplan, H. (1981) *The Illustrated Manual of Sex Therapy.* St Albans: Mayflower Book, Granada Publishing Ltd.

Zilbergeld, B. (1980) *Men and Sex.* London: Fontana.

Equipment

The PREP Training Package from PREP Educational Products Incorporated, Denver, Colorado.

Clairol Massage Vibrator Ann Summers Branches or mail order.

Graded Vaginal Dilators' Suppliers (Stanley Vaginal Trainers):

John Bell and Croyden, Wigmore Street, London WI.

Downs Surgical, Parkway Close, Parkway Industrial Estate, Sheffield S9 4WS.

Gregoire A. (Compiler) (1991) Product Review. *Sexual and Marital Therapy 6,* 2, 217–220.

Impotence Systems

Pos-T-Vac Vacuum Therapy System from Eurosurgical Ltd., Merrow Business Centre, Guildford, Surrey GU4 7WA. Tel: 01483 456007 Fax: 01483 456008

ErecAid System, from Cory Bros., 4 Dollis Park London N3 1HG. Tel: 0181 349 1081/5

Senselle and KYJelly – retail pharmacies

Using Caverject (Training Video) Provided free by Upjohn who also provide leaflets and a demonstration kit from local representatives or Pharmacia and Upjohn Ltd., Davy Avenue, Knowlhill, Milton Keynes, MK5 8PH

Appendix 1: THE MODIFIED MASTERS AND JOHNSON APPROACH TO THERAPY
(Masters and Johnson 1970)

After assessing and defining the problem, patients are given a brief explanation and rationale of treatment. Sexual intercourse or mutual masturbation is banned in the early stages in order to prevent performance anxiety (masturbation alone is still permissible unless contributing in some way to the problem).

Stage One

At this stage the aim is to increase pleasurable non-sexual contact between the couple. They are instructed to caress each other over all parts of the body except the genital areas and the breasts (sensate focus). This should be done in turn with one partner touching and giving pleasure. The other is allowed to do nothing except concentrate on the thoughts and feelings aroused and give some feedback on how, where and in what way they enjoy being touched. Each partner should take it in turns to initiate these sessions. At least half an hour three times per week should be put aside for practice. Where one partner has felt under pressure to have intercourse frequently, it may be easier to give that partner the responsibility to start or get them to make a commitment to practise, say, twice a week at set times. The same pre-set technique may be used separately from Masters and Johnson programmes to regulate intercourse under those circumstances where the demands of one partner for sex have over-whelmed the other, resulting in the latter avoiding all kinds of physical contact.

Initially couples may find that these instructions are too false or embarrassing but the use of a lubricant or body massage oil may help to get them started. Couples with sex problems may have built up elaborate avoidance behaviours and claim to have no time for the homework. Whether this is the cause or an effect of the problem should be clarified and the timetable re-structured in order to make time for sessions. This may have other unexpected benefits in improving their lifestyle and reducing stress more generally.

Some couples genuinely find these exercises too threatening. They may need to spend time trying to initiate some more ritualised physical contact such as kissing 'Hello' and 'Goodbye', holding hands when out walking and doing some touching when clothed. Such extreme cases are not common and may suggest the possibility of phobic reaction calling for desensitisation before further therapy.

Stage Two

Once the initial difficulties are overcome, another week of sensate focus exercises without any attempt at intercourse or genital touching is helpful. The aim now is to increase the pleasure of being touched by being more directive to the partner. Each in turn describes the sensations felt in different areas and may guide their partner's hand to indicate the direction and pressure of touch. They should be reminded that sensations will probably not be the same every day so that continuing feedback is important. The importance of the intercourse ban and the hazards of cheating should be stressed. Even if they have intercourse satisfactorily at this time they may increase anxiety about future failure. If it goes badly they may undo the progress made so far and tension and frustration will return. If, however, the problem has only been a short-term one, it may have resolved completely at this stage allowing intercourse to be resumed. This calls for clinical judgement.

Stage Three

When both partners feel ready and can enjoy Stages One and Two with no anxiety, they can begin to include the genital areas in the session. They should continue as before with light touching all over the body but gradually increase the time devoted to the genitals and breasts as well. It should be stressed that the aim is not sexual arousal but to explore different ways of giving pleasure. Lotion or oil can still be used to prevent soreness and increase sensitivity. Guidance and feedback from the partner should be encouraged. When the man is being given pleasure by the woman, the aim is not to achieve an erection but one may occur. If he has a partial erection, she should carry on caressing, but if a full erection is obtained she should stop the touching, allow it to diminish and then continue as before. The idea is to enjoy genital pleasuring with no goals of arousal or fears about sexual performance.

Stage Four

This is reached when the woman can be relaxed and aroused and the man can obtain a full erection. The penis can now be inserted into the vagina. The woman should be in control of this in the female superior position astride the man on her knees at about the level of his chest. She can then place the penis in her vagina and move slowly back until it is fully inserted. They should both remain motionless and enjoy the sensation of the penis inside the woman. They should not go on to intercourse or worry about how long the erection lasts. If the erection diminishes they can change positions, return to pleasuring and repeat the cycle if a full erection returns. This exercise increases confidence by allowing time to concentrate on feelings and communication without being worried about performance. If lubrication is needed, KY jelly or Senselle, both available from chemists should be recommended.

After several sessions have been spent doing this exercise, it can be prolonged and include some movement. The man should attempt to thrust gently – just enough to maintain the erection – alternating with the woman moving gently for as long as they both find it pleasurable. This may be followed by more rapid movements proceeding to climax. As in earlier stages they may stop, withdraw for a while and lie quietly before resuming the exercise. They should not aim to reach a climax every time but to continue to enjoy sexual feelings without the pressure to perform.

The rate of moving from one stage to another depends on mutual agreement of the partners. Even if they remain at a particular stage for some time a commitment to regular practise and review is very important.

Some couples find it therapeutic to practise their homework at a different time or in a different situation or room from that associated in the past with distressing experiences. As an example, a female patient with loss of libido found it hard to initiate the sensate focus stage of therapy in bed. This created negative thoughts related to her husband's former demands and also fear that any contact or cuddle was bound to lead to intercourse. She felt much safer on the sofa which had not previously been associated with sexual activity.

Cognitive Aspects

Couples should be asked to keep a diary of their homework and record in it any emotions and thoughts evoked by the exercises. The assumption of the 'spectator' role is a particularly common block to progress that may be discovered in this way. One or other partner feels that they cannot lose themselves in the pleasurable sensations but rather that they remain as an onlooker seeing everything which takes place from outside. Other negative thoughts unearthed in this way may help to identify attitudes or past experiences of sex and relationships which are hindering progress. Some of the techniques of marital or cognitive therapy may be used to relieve these problems. For example, a patient felt angry and resentful during sensate focus. Closer examination of her thoughts showed that her anger was due to her partner being so relaxed, when she was aware of all the jobs which needed doing in the flat and of her unfinished thesis lying on the desk. Some re-dividing of the chores and adjustment of her work timetable made her think of the relationship as more equitable. She was then able to relax and enjoy sexual activity.

Another patient felt that sex was stupid. She felt angry that physical contact only occurred during sex and adopted a 'spectator' role. Increasing day-to-day non-sexual physical contact helped her to begin to enjoy sex. Another discovered that her 'switching off' was always related to seeing her partner's erect penis which brought images of an incident on holiday where she was flashed at and which was still causing nightmares and flashbacks (see PTSD in Chapter Six).

Appendix 2: TECHNIQUES FOR SPECIFIC PROBLEMS: MASTURBATORY PROGRAMME FOR ANORGASMIC WOMEN
(From Heimam and Lo Piccolo 1976)

This is another multi-stage programme and some stages are used for self exploration for negative body image and low self-esteem and can be implemented before or alongside the Masters and Johnson Programme.

Stage One

Self-exploration is a useful exercise for those women who suffer from anorgasmia, vaginismus or whose sex life is affected by a negative body image and low self-esteem especially for those who have been sexually abused. Time needs to be set aside so that a relaxed and private situation can be found. The woman should then just examine and explore her naked body, being aware of and if necessary recording the thoughts and feelings produced by different areas. A mirror can be used to examine the genital areas and a book with diagrams of the female genitalia can be used to identify the specific parts. Patients should be reassured that everyone differs slightly in case minor variation make them worry that they are anatomically abnormal.

Stage Two

The patient touches herself on the breasts and genital areas but without attempting arousal. This graded approach helps any phobic fears or points of avoidance to be identified.

Stage Three

The woman is asked to continue visual exploration and try to identify any sensitive areas by touch.

Stage Four

The sensitive areas are now stimulated to try and increase pleasurable feelings. A lubricant such as baby cream may be used to increase sensation or avoid soreness.

Stage Five

The length of the session should be increased to allow time to try and vary the intensity of stimulation, with occasional pauses. Encouragement is given to concentrate on erotic fantasies to increase arousal and reach orgasm.

Stage Six

If orgasm has not been achieved by this stage a vibrator may be used. These can be obtained from mail order or specialist shops. The patient may also be encouraged to role play orgasm with movement, moaning and crying aloud. This helps to release inhibitions about voluntary movements and overcome fears of losing self-control. If the idea of using a vibrator is unacceptable, it may be helpful to stress that it only needs to be used temporarily to obtain orgasm although it can be used in loveplay later if so wished.

Stage Seven

The partner should now be involved and orgasm attempted in his presence. This helps to overcome feelings of inhibition and shows him how to stimulate his partner to produce orgasm.

Stage Eight

The partner may try and stimulate the woman to orgasm using the vibrator as necessary. She gently guides his endeavours.

Stage Nine

The couple may have intercourse, using the vibrator and manual stimulation of the woman. Once she gains more confidence in her ability to achieve orgasm if preferred the vibrator may be dispensed with on occasions.

Chapter Eight
Disorders of Habit and Appetite

Under this heading will be considered two main groups – motor habits such as tics and spasms; and disorders of appetite including eating disorders, problems with alcohol, drug misuse, smoking and gambling. Sleeping problems have been discussed with anxiety disorders, and enuresis and encopresis will be discussed later under problems of childhood, although all of these may also be legitimately regarded as habit disorders. These are a wide and somewhat disparate group of problems which cannot be easily fitted into one model of development or plan for modification. Unfortunately in several of these areas problems are becoming much more common. When the predecessor to this book was prepared (France and Robson 1986) drug misuse was still only occasionally encountered by most primary health care teams and eating disorders in young women were much less common or at least much less apparent.

These problems may all be regarded as learned habits, possibly with initial rewards but long term costs. These costs range in severity from mild social embarrassment in the case of some muscle spasms to an early painful death from lung cancer in the case of the smoker. Another way of saying the same thing is that reinforcement for repeating the habit is much more immediate than the reinforcement for controlling it. We have seen in Chapter Five that reinforcement is much more effective when it is provided immediately. It is often the task of the therapist to try and devise strategies for overcoming this imbalance.

Another feature common to these conditions is the crucial importance of an accurate assessment of the problem – when and in what environment it is likely or unlikely to occur, with what consequences and with what associated thoughts and emotions. This analysis leads to accurate and appropriate baseline measurements which in turn may lead the sufferer to understand aspects of the problem which seemed previously purely automatic. The original rather simplistic stimulus–response model for these disorders was theoretically appealing but clinical results were often disappointing.

There have been three developments of great significance in understanding and treating these disorders in recent years.

First, Prochaska and Di Clemente (1992) proposed a five stage cyclical model which can be applied to several of the disorders in this category. The model suggests that the following stages occur;

(1) *The Pre-Contemplator Stage*; change is not yet on the agenda and the full need for it not yet appreciated. The clinician may give information about the facts and risks.

(2) *The Contemplator Stage*; when patients consider the problems associated with their behaviour and the problems and possibilities of change. They are still ambivalent and not yet ready to act but are receptive to information and reflection.

(3) *Preparation*; much of the ambivalence is for the moment resolved. The patient wants to change but is not certain how to go about it.

(4) *Action*; work has begun on change and the real difficulties are being met.

(5) *Maintenance*; for the moment change has been achieved but this cannot be considered fixed or permanent.

An essential part of the model is that the stages do not occur in a fixed progression and regression to the stage before is also possible. It follows from this model that the health worker must assess carefully which stage the patient has reached and give help and understanding appropriate to that stage.

To help achieve this Miller and Rollnick (1991) (see also Rollnick and Miller 1995) introduced *motivational interviewing* which facilitates the patient developing his own motivation by exploring areas of ambivalence rather than having solutions imposed by the therapist. In this therapeutic partnership the patient can decide when change is desirable as a result of his own examination and eventual resolution of the pros and cons.

Motor Habit Problems

There are as many types of motor habit problems as there are sufferers. Even the apparently commonly occurring ones such as eye blinking, nail biting and hair pulling will have individual features in each case, which emphasises the importance of assessment.

Functional Analysis. This should particularly emphasise any factors that make the problem more or less probable, such as nail-biting in the office or an increase in muscle spasm on Sundays when the children are at home to lunch. The problem may mainly affect the sufferer or be an irritation to others such as the teacher or different members of the household. An awareness that habits are often inadvertently reinforced by attention from others is important and should be explored. The removal of the problem may have extremely negative effects for the sufferer if it results in him being ignored or feeling insignificant.

Baseline Measurements. These are planned using the information gained from the functional analysis particularly with regard to expected frequency and severity of the habit. It is obviously impossible to count every occurrence of a muscle twitch which is frequent and repetitive. In these cases some form of time sampling or interval recording would have to be used. If these techniques are adopted it is useful to take samples at different times of the day and at weekends when circumstances are likely to be different. Baseline records are probably most useful when taken by the sufferer as the process of self-monitoring may promote change in itself. Clearly, however, there are situations, for example, with unconscious habits or handicapped children, where an independent observer must be used. The brief of the observer must always be clear and well defined as described in the section on data collection (see Chapter Four).

Principles of Intervention. The information produced by the interview and the baseline measurements should enable an hypothesis to be formed. A decision is then taken, if possible with the full co-operation of the patient, about the type of intervention most likely to prove effective.

Here there are a number of different possibilities. The habit may be seen to be largely secondary to another problem such as general or situational anxiety. Treatment of this may be all that is required. A local government worker had to pass urine whenever she was attending a committee meeting. She responded well to a very short programme consisting of an explanation of the likely anxiety based mechanism of the problem and distraction by counting the number of times the chairman said 'of course'.

As mentioned earlier self-monitoring will often alleviate a habit by promoting an understanding of the muscular mechanism involved and producing a sense of perceived control of the problem. A tally counter of the sort which is used to record the attendance at jumble sales is extremely useful. It is possible to obtain these from sports shops.

It may be possible to alter the stimulus situations in which the problem occurs, for example, by eliminating long hours of boredom and inactivity, or to make it more difficult to perform the response, for example, by encouraging the wearing of gloves by a hair-puller or spot picker. These factors will both be discussed in more detail when smoking is considered. With certain habit disorders, differential reinforcement of an alternative incompatible activity is also to be considered. This may be particularly useful with children or as part of a self-control programme. Nail-biters can sometimes be helped by learning to make a fist or squeeze the thumb between the index and middle fingers in response to a desire to bite. The parent ignores biting but notices and praises when the chosen alternative takes place.

Patients presenting tight or recurrently sore throats in the absence of obvious infection are fairly frequent in general practice. Acting on the hypothesis that this problem results from increased pharyngeal constrictor tone, treatment by relaxation training of the adjacent neck muscles, sometimes with the help of simple electro–myographic biofeedback, has produced considerable relief in a number of cases.

The most specific and long-established behavioural method of treating habit spasms is by massed practise in which the patient deliberately learns to perform the tic or twitch for varying periods voluntarily or at set times depending on the frequency or type of tic. At its simplest, massed practise programmes are very easy to plan and initiate in primary care since long therapist contact is unnecessary. Practise may be done first in the surgery, then in front of a mirror which reduces avoidance. Video feedback may also be useful. There are probably a number of different elements contributing to the effectiveness of massed practise. First, the subject learns in detail the component movements of the tic and thus brings it to some extent under voluntary control; second, repeated practice tends to extinguish the habit; and third, relief from fatigue and boredom provides negative reinforcement on stopping. A number of other theoretical models have also been suggested to explain the manifest effectiveness of this rather improbable procedure. Once the muscle groups involved in the movements have been clearly identified by the patient it is often possible to involve the same or opposing muscles in an incompatible behaviour. This can be used to supplement or replace the massed practise if this proves to be insufficient in itself to eliminate the habit.

Appetite Disorders

Eating Problems

From the primary care perspective it is important here to include obesity, which presents a major and largely unsolved dilemma to the primary care team as well as the twin scourges of anorexia nervosa and the ever increasing problem of bulimia. This often has to be tackled in primary care both because of the absence of sufficient specialist resources and also because low-contact manual based treatments have been shown to be effective (Treasure *et al.* 1996). In addition bulimia is often part of a multi-problem presentation which may be seen as a physical health problem initially.

Obesity

Many general practitioners feel uneasy when confronted with this problem. On the one hand it is a major health hazard directly causing a number of diseases and contributing to others which challenge the family doctor's preventive role. On the other hand it is realised that converting it into a *medical* disorder involving a passive patient and a doctor 'who has got to do something about it' distorts the nature of the problem and will usually be counter–productive in terms of successful management. Aside from these issues the problem is a vast one and it is debatable if one-to-one treatment, even if desirable, can be offered with the resources available.

In this context group treatments have numerous advantages. They can be organised by any member of the team who has the enthusiasm, particularly health visitors and practice or district nurses. This, in itself, to some extent weakens the dependent medical model which is further weakened by self-help support between group members who are all trying to cope with the same problem. It is possible to deal with more clients at one time and to go into aspects of the problem, such as relapse prevention strategies (Perri *et al.* 1994) in far greater depth than would be possible on an individual basis.

There are some snags. The group programme has to be fairly general and cannot be tailored to meet exactly the requirements indicated by the assessment of each individual's problem. It is quite possible, however, to incorporate some individual assessment and time during sessions for members' particular difficulties. The programme given in Appendix 1 is not intended to be in any way definitive but merely to give an example of one programme which has been used in a NHS health centre in the UK. Commercial slimming organisations such as Weight Watchers are also popular and to some extent useful. They do, however, have a number of disadvantages. They are expensive, often contribute to the abstinence violation effect (Marlatt and George 1984) by suggesting, for example, that eating one doughnut equals total failure, and fail to provide any cognitive input.

A caveat has to be added at this point as it is now believed that weight may be more genetically determined than was once though and each of us may have a relatively fixed 'set point' that allows only small fluctuations to be achieved with ease (Keesey 1980). This theory may account for the extremely poor outcome of most weight reduction programmes.

Anorexia Nervosa and Bulimia Nervosa

These problems are clearly interrelated and may co-exist. Both, but particularly the less common anorexia, are serious and they carry the highest mortality rate in mental health. They will therefore often require appropriate in-patient and specialist treatment. The general practitioner and other members of the primary care team do have an important role in early detection of the vulnerable patient. They may be able to prevent the problem assuming major proportions by taking early action to point out the dangers both to the potential patient herself and to her parents. Unfortunately the units specialising in the treatment of these problems are, in the UK, currently overwhelmed by the potential number of patients. Consequently early management or even all management may have to be given in rather inappropriate general hospital settings. Here the emphasis is often directed solely to obtaining sufficient weight gain to make discharge physically safe. This 'Strasbourg goose' approach may be necessary to preserve life but offers little in the way of help after discharge or help with the emotional and environmental–mental factors that have been maintaining the condition. Although this is predominantly a female problem, particularly rife amongst gymnasts and dancers as well as academic young women, it is being seen increasingly in young men and boys.

The cognitive behavioural approach (Fairburn 1995) has been shown to produce good results in about 50 per cent of patients and together with some related psychological elements such as motivational interviewing (Miller and Rollnick 1991) is now the treatment of choice with the most promising long term outcome (Cooper and Steere 1995).

Assessment

Interview assessment should concentrate especially on the following points:

(1) The patient's exact description and perception of her problem.

(2) Her attitude to her shape and weight. In particular:

(a)   Its importance in her life.

(b)   Reaction to weight changes.

(c)   The reaction of others.

(d)   Her own preferred weight.

(3) What is the patient's and her family's attitude to food?

(a)   Is it abundant and important in their lives?

(b)   Was great store always set on finishing all food prepared and having second helpings?

(c)   Attitude to dieting.

(d)   Sense of control over eating?

(3) Has the patient ever been overweight and if so what were the attitudes of parents, peer-group and self to that?

(4) How many of these factors operate in her present life?

(5) Are there excessive or unreasonable academic expectations from the patient herself, her parents or others?

(6) Is the eating problem a form of avoidance of distasteful aspects of life or is it being rewarded by excessive attention? Is it being used to control or punish parents?

(7) Are there related problems, for example loneliness, anxiety, depression or boredom on the one hand, and certain physical situations like the presence of particular feared foods or returning to the family home on the other.

(8) Relationships inside and outside the family, including with partners and at school or work.

(9) Physical well being including:

(a)   Presence or absence of periods.

(b)   Physical examination including appearance, present weight, state of teeth and parotids.

(c)   Serum electrolytes – potassium in particular will tend to fall in vomiting patients.

Intervention

Even during the assessment the motivational interviewing approach (Miller and Rollnick 1991) should be a guide to exploring the patient's ambivalence about her condition. As the first interview proceeds and in subsequent interviews it becomes all important to help the patient resolve her doubts.

The main drive is to guide the patient in exploring her own ambivalence about continuing or attempting to change her anorexia. The central elements of this should be:

(1) Rationale; explaining and exploring shape and weight and the connected loss of self-esteem. It is important to provide a manual, for example, *Getting Better Bit(e) by Bit(e)* by Schmidt and Treasure (1993), or one of the alternatives mentioned under Recommended Further Reading. Not only are these manuals excellent in guiding the occasional therapist but they have been shown to be effective as a therapy in themselves. In order to make some of the important points about bulimia both to the patient and her parents, the short facts sheet may be useful (see Appendix 2).

(2) Instituting a diary recording eating, vomiting, laxative use and weight which will provide a record of change.

(3) Helping the patient to examine her life with or without bulimia. This can be done in the form of letter to 'Bulimia' or to a friend in the future describing life with or without the condition (Schmidt and Treasure 1993). All these measures are directed towards helping the patient to resolve her ambivalence. Miller and Rollnick (1991) state that 'direct persuasion, aggressive confrontation and argumentation are the *conceptual opposite* of motivational interviewing and are explicitly proscribed in this approach'.

(4) Sometimes it may be worth encouraging both anorexics and bulimics to make lists of feared foods such as those likely to lead to bingeing, starving or self-induced vomiting, and of situations, for example being alone, which they find to be particularly difficult. The dichotomy between inherently 'good' and 'bad' foods may be explored as part of the overall picture.

(5) Measures to label correctly and to counteract associated factors such as anxiety, indecision, depression and social isolation. An attempt should be made to explore and fill the gap left by abandoning the 'professional anorexic or bulimic career'. Many of these patients' lives revolve round their problem and there may be a real danger that they will become 'nothing people' if their problem disappears.

(6) A weight target should be set and instructions given to eat three meals per day with provision for appropriate snacks. An anorexic is more likely to be able to cooperate with a programme designed to lead to gradual weight gain which in turn allows her to come to terms with

her changing shape. Frequently it is this resistance to 'becoming fat' that leads to the breakdown of home-based programmes. It is essential that the patient is allowed to discuss her fears about this without confrontation and preferably away from her parents. Bulimics who are within their recommended weight limits should aim to maintain this or possibly lose small amounts. It is sometimes helpful to ask the patient to make out a daily target diet in advance. Each item is ticked off in turn providing some sort of self-reward for each day successfully completed.

Many attempts at modification of these problems at home founder because the patients have learned a pattern of deception and denial over the years which they find it difficult to abandon. This tends to emphasise the importance of the non-confrontational approach. Sometimes, however, the problems seem insurmountable and it is important to remember that these conditions are potentially lethal and that even expert units experience a considerable failure rate. If the situation is deteriorating to the point of danger with the BMI falling progressively further below 17, admission is essential. It is possible, however, that the primary care worker may be able to modify patient or family attitudes early in the condition in such a way as to prevent an intractable full-blown problem developing.

Smoking

It is unlikely that anyone reading this book will need convincing that smoking is extremely harmful and yet, alas, it is still extremely widespread. The evidence of successive reports by The Royal College of Physicians of London and the Surgeon General's department in the USA need not be reviewed here. There has been a net reduction of smoking in the USA and UK in recent years although it is uncertain which factors have brought this about. In the UK it may be that a general trend towards physical fitness and the cultivation of healthier living habits has been more effective than the pathetically small budget of the Health Education Council and the dedicated efforts of organisations like ASH (Action on Smoking and Health) in the face of massive tobacco advertising and the damaging models presented by parents, teachers and nurses. Doctors cannot be exempt from responsibility as, although they have stopping smoking in greater numbers than other professionals, the damage done by the smoking doctor as a model far outweighs that caused by most other groups. Such gains as have been made by older men and women stopping have to an extent been offset by young women and girls who have taken up the habit in greater numbers. Most smokers start in their teens perhaps to assert themselves as independent and follow their group. It is possible that one of the unlooked for effects of feminine equality is a greater readiness to smoke. The harmful effects of smoking seem irrelevant and remote at this age to both sexes. Later in life many smokers want to stop but find it difficult to do so. Many of these would-be non-smokers seek help from doctors, clinics or anti-smoking preparations.

On the surface it would appear that smoking prevention might be a particular fruitful field for the behaviour modifier. The cues are often clear-cut, the behaviour easily studied and measured and the potential reinforcers for quitting considerable in terms of money and health. If the therapist is also the patient's family doctor or a primary care colleague who is in a powerful position to comment on matters of personal health so much the better. A survey of the multitude of techniques that have been used to achieve quitting, however, shows almost uniformly disappointing results (Chapman 1985). The best results have often been achieved by simple advice in a medical setting following an episode of illness like a myocardial infarct or in association with some chronic condition where smoking is likely to prove particularly harmful (Raw and Heller 1984, Jarvis and Russell 1983). This seems to give some support to the theory that doctors are particularly well placed to influence the problem.

Apart from the giving of simple advice there is no clear view of the best approach. Recently great hopes have been raised by nicotine replacement therapy, usually with chewing gum (Nicorette) or patches (Nicotinell). Although results were good under experimental conditions with about 40 per cent abstinent at one year follow-up, it seems that random prescription in the surgery is unlikely to do as well. This is probably because maximum effect is achieved only when the gum is part of an overall treatment plan.

Some doubt has been cast on the value of non-smoking clinics (Chapman 1985) but it has been confirmed again recently that the most promising results may be obtained using a group treatment package (Jason et al. 1995). Nicotine replacement preparations, Nicotinell and Nicorette are an important adjunct (Russell et al. 1980) particularly in those who smoke over twenty a day. The group scheme that follows was used by a general practitioner led group from a health centre and achieved 30 per cent abstinence at one year follow-up without the use of nicotine substitution.

The simple recording of smoking behaviour is now widely done in primary care as part of the health promotion initiatives. This has been shown to be important as although numbers quitting after these recordings are small in terms of percentage their nation wide figures are impressive and outweigh more specialised interventions in total effect. Percentages increase after brief advice from the GP and associated with nicotine replacement produces a further improvement (Russell *et al.* 1993). More intensive group treatment courses can improve the quitting rate up to 30 per cent but only, of course, at a much greater expenditure in terms of professional resources.

The provision of a non-smoking group, however, indicates a commitment to smoking cessation on the part of a Primary Health Care Team and may have unmeasured wider effects amongst practice patients. Formerly such groups were run solely along stimulus control lines (see France and Robson 1986) but it is probably equally if not more effective to have a loose structure which can include the following elements which are based on the work of Prochaska and Di Clemente (1992) and Rollnick and Miller (1995):

(1) Information and rationale.

(2) Advantages and disadvantages of quitting (*Motivational Interviewing Approach*) (Miller and Rollnick 1991).

(3) Self-monitoring with group work on difficulties and possible solutions. For those wishing to adopt a structured approach a summary of the group programme formerly used at our clinic is reprinted in Appendix 3. Further research into specific behavioural methods may produce positive results, particularly if it involves the motivational interviewing approach (Miller and Rollnick 1991, Rollnick and Miller 1995). It is striking, however, that to date all the elegant behavioural approaches have failed to produce results better than those achieved by an attention–placebo condition.

Alcohol Misuse

The alcoholic or potentially alcoholic patient presents a particularly difficult problem in primary care. The general practitioner has an opportunity of identifying a potential problem and offering advice early if he enquires routinely about alcohol use amongst his patients. He is often accused of neglecting this opportunity by the mass media and special interest organisations. He may realise, however, that merely identifying the problem is of little use if the patient continues to deny it himself and refuses to accept help, or the resources available to provide help are inappropriate or inadequate.

Notoriously many drinkers are unwilling to accept that they have a problem until it is well advanced. This attitude is compounded by the traditional illness model of the problem adopted by the profession and organisations like Alcoholics Anonymous, useful as they often are. The model emphasises that alcoholism is a disease which, once acquired, is lifelong. The sufferer is always one drink from the gutter ('one drink, one drunk'). The only treatment is directed towards a goal of total abstinence with the threat of loss of control always looming large. This goal, it is said, can only be achieved initially by means of lengthy in-patient therapy disruptive to career, family and self-esteem alike. Small wonder that many who privately suspect that they are developing a mild drinking problem prefer to deny it until they can do so no longer.

The above model may be useful for the severely dependent alcoholic who has had daily withdrawal symptoms for at least six months, who engages in withdrawal drinking and whose drinking repertoire has become narrowed to a stereotyped pattern. It is, however, counter-productive in the much larger group of drinkers, including those commonly seen in primary care, who are only mildly to moderately dependent or binge drinkers. This group are characterised at the most by mild or moderate withdrawal symptoms a few times a week for less than six months and only the beginning of narrowing of the repertoire. They do not exhibit a 'priming effect' if one drink is taken. To encourage them to believe that disaster will follow a single drink is not only untrue but damaging as it encourages the belief that all is lost if any lapse from abstinence occurs. This belief may help the initial cessation of the problem but it actually hinders the rather more important objective of maintaining long-term change. Success may be measured in various ways which makes outcome research difficult (Sobell, Sobell and Douglas 1995). It may increase the Abstinence Violation Effect (AVE) (Marlatt and George 1984) which occurs when someone committed to abstinence finds himself unable to cope with a particularly high risk situation. He crosses the 'forbidden line', perceives himself as having failed totally in his endeavour and gives up. In reality all that has happened is one lapse which affects the person's ability to continue his programme only in his own perception.

Controlled drinking programmes have the great advantage that the AVE is much less likely to be a problem. Even where abstinence is the goal as much time as possible should be spent on relapse prevention (RP) strategies. It will be apparent that RP and AVE are important not only in the management of drinking problems but also in other forms of drug abuse including smoking.

Assessment

This will depend upon the type of problem presented. Is the problem acknowledged and understood by the patient? Is the patient there to find out whether a problem he himself suspects in fact exists? Does the doctor suspect a problem which the patient has not accepted?

In the last two situations the Drinkwatchers (Ruzeck 1984) unit system is the most helpful rule of thumb:

$$1 \text{ unit alcohol} = \text{half pint of beer}$$
$$1 \text{ glass of wine}$$
$$1 \text{ glass of sherry}$$
$$1 \text{ single whisky.}$$

Too much   = more than **21 units** per week for men

= more than **14 units** per week for women.

These levels are on the conservative side and recent opinion suggests that they may be raised a little. If, however, they are being consistently exceeded then there is a potential or actual problem. This information alone will be very helpful to many patients.

Further assessment, once it has been decided that there is a problem, will consist of a standard behavioural analysis as described in Chapter Three to determine the environmental factors influencing the patient and the problem. Of particular value are the following factors:

- A narrowing of the repertoire of drinking behaviour.
- Importance of drink in everyday life.
- Increased tolerance to alcohol.
- Repeated withdrawal symptoms.
- Repeated relief or avoidance of withdrawal symptoms by further drinking.
- Subjective awareness of compulsion to drink.
- Reinstatement of the previous elements after abstinence.

Further assessment can be by means of the Severity of Alcohol Dependence Questionnaire (SADQ) (Stockwell *et al.* 1979) which is divided into five sections dealing respectively with (i) physical symptoms; (ii) affective symptoms; (iii) craving and relief drinking; (iv) daily consumption and; (v) recurrence of symptoms after abstinence. As well as giving detailed factorial information, the questionnaire serves to distinguish mild to moderate dependence in those with scores up to 35 from severe dependence at scores of 36 and above. For the clinical reasons explained at the beginning of this section this distinction may be extremely important.

Goal Choice

Using the *motivational interviewing* (Miller and Rollnick 1991) approach the patient may list his reasons for and against cutting down on his drinking. If and when he decides to reduce his drinking the same technique will help to decide whether to go for a goal of controlled drinking or abstinence. With the information now available the therapist should be able to assist the patient in deciding whether he chooses a goal of controlled drinking or whether abstinence is more desirable and appropriate. If the former, the type of controlled drinking must be clearly defined.

Intervention

Some, particularly the severely dependent patient, will need to be referred to specialised agencies at this time. If successful with these, he may require more help at the primary care level later, particularly with relapse prevention.

With the others many different intervention elements may be needed. Chick (1995) summarises the minimal intervention with the acronym FRAMES:

Feedback about personal risk or impairment.
Responsibility – emphasis on personal responsibility for change.
Advice to cut down, or if indicated, abstain.
Menu of options for changing drinking pattern.
Empathic interviewing.
Self-efficacy: an interviewing style which emphasises this.

(Rollnick, Kinnersley and Stott 1995)

Self-monitoring for stimulus recognition and control is important so that the high risk situations may be identified and alternative ways of coping rehearsed. Elements of social skills training will help the patient learn to refuse alcoholic drinks without embarrassment. The type of non-alcoholic drinks available may be discussed so that an appropriate choice may be made in advance of need. It is important to consider and reframe the Abstinence Violation Effect mentioned earlier and adjustments in life style should be considered.

There are a list of useful self control tips at the end of this chapter which can be used to hand-out to patients (see Appendix 4).

Alcoholics Anonymous have a long and honoured place in the management of this problem and branches exist in all areas and can be contacted through the telephone book. For the reasons discussed above they may not always be the most suitable agency. In Britain Drinkwatchers (Accept Services) publish a lot of information about controlling drinking and run groups where the sensible drinking approach is advocated. Unfortunately they are not available in all areas. Patients in primary care often need help after in-patient treatment or to wean off Alcoholics Anonymous attendance to a new form of social life. Similar considerations apply to gamblers.

BBC Further Education programmes (such as *That's the Limit*) are accompanied by useful books which take a broad approach to the problem.

The Scottish Health Education Group publish an excellent pocket-sized behaviourally based kit for GPs to give patients whom they suspect are drinking too much. It is entitled DRAMS (Drinking Reasonably And Moderately with Self-control). The kit consists of a medical record card for the doctor and a booklet for the patient. The latter contains information on the medical and non-medical effects of alcohol, information about how to cut down and specimen diary sheets.

An excellent overall review of the detection and management of alcohol problems in primary care has been produced by Chick (1995).

Street and Other Drugs

The number of other substances that can be misused is endless and the problem is becoming more important year by year. In many cases the substance is either dangerous, illegal or uncontrollable or all three so that controlled use is not a preferred option. Apart from that, however, most of the factors operating with alcohol problems, particularly the Relapse Prevention model and the importance of the Abstinence Violation Effect apply as well to other substances. Recognition of the problem and early straightforward advice about ways of stopping may be very effective but in many cases the user will require ongoing support. Many GPs and other primary care workers may feel a reluctance to get involved with drug users, usually for one of two principle reasons:

(1) Drug users are seen as morally defective and responsible for their own avoidable problems.

(2) Drug users are often manipulative and unreliable and consume a disproportionate amount of resources.

The first argument is untrue and unjust and shows a profound ignorance of the problems and needs of an increasingly large group of patients. The second, whilst more understandable, is equally fallacious. Many groups of sick people consume a disproportionate amount of resources and the manipulation and unreliability of drug users is part of their core problem. The only responsible attitude is that drug users are patients and should be given the same services as other patients. The treatment of problems leading to drug and alcohol misuse should if possible be addressed simultaneously using cognitive methods to disentangle the various strands.

In many cases the primary health care team will be supporting users who are not (yet) prepared to attempt to leave their habit. Even in this case there is a great deal to be done.

Assessment

This will include:

(1) The quantity and type of drugs used.

(2) Attitude to continuing/quitting.

(3) Contact with other services, such as prescribing clinic, needle exchange etc.

(4) Contact with the social side of the drug culture.

To talk to drug users a knowledge of their language is necessary. The following vocabulary sheets are by no means exhaustive but should be a start:

- ○ A vocabulary of terms common in the drug culture (see Appendix 5).
- ○ A contract sheet for controlling prescribing management from primary care (see Appendix 6).

Both are given at the end of this chapter. The contract may be adapted for other management problems.

Intervention

This becomes much easier if three principles are observed:

(1) Damage limitation, rather than quitting, may be the goal.

(2) Written contracts for prescribing Methadone and other drugs subject to misuse (see Appendix 6) should be used and observed to the letter.

(3) Included in the contract is a clause that only one doctor prescribes and they appoint a named deputy when they are absent.

Management may be divided into three stages:

(1) *Support* – the user needs to feel that his or her medical advisers understand their problem in a non-judgmental way and will provide the normal medical services whether or not the problem is drug related.

(2) *Maintenance* – consists of providing information and services to the drug user to prevent, as far as possible, unnecessary harm occurring as a result of the habit. Any gaps in drug knowledge identified in the assessment should be filled, the whereabouts of specialist and support services should be made known together with clinical advice for any problems which may occur. Many areas now have a specialised drugs

service which the primary care worker or the user can contact for advice. GPs are permitted to prescribe Methadone without a Home Office Licence and this may avoid excessive travelling for the user. If the GP elects to prescribe it it is important to have a written contract with the user (see Appendix 6) which covers issues including:

(a) Time, amount and frequency of prescriptions.

(b) Relationship with a single named doctor (or pre-arranged deputy if he or she is absent).

(c) Undertaking to keep appointments.

(d) Agreement to discussion with other (named) members of the Drugs service or Primary Health Care Teams.

(e) Prescriptions will not be replaced.

(f) Dosage alterations will be the responsibility of the Specialist Drugs Team.

(g) Non-compliance will result in review of the decision to prescribe.

(3) *Assistance in Usage Reduction* – this may be undertaken with the agreement of both parties once a relationship has been established. As with the other problems in this group the *motivational interviewing* approach of encouraging the patient to work out the advantages and opposing disadvantages of continuing the drug habit may be used. They may also be encouraged to consider how their lives appear to others at present as well as projecting how this could change in the future. Once motivation is established practical issues such as work, leisure and how to establish relationships outside the drug culture may have to be addressed.

Gambling

This has become a high profile problem in recent years because of a great increase in availability of outlets. Fruit machines are widespread in various forms and scratch cards provide instant access. In the recent years the National lottery in the UK, which provides both the pseudo-glamorous twice weekly draws and instant access scratch cards, has not only been given tremendous publicity but has also been promoted as supporting good causes which has tended to make it more socially acceptable. There has been much recent literature on the cognitive behavioural management of the problem (Lesieur and Rosenthal 1991, Griffiths 1995). Many of the issues and techniques mentioned earlier in this chapter will also apply to gambling.

Assessment

This looks at the exact environment both external and cognitive in which the gambling takes place and assesses the nature and importance of the individual rewards both in the obvious sense but also, more importantly, in the thinking and social life of the gambler. It also looks at the costs, financial, domestic, social and occupational. Compulsive gambling like drug misuse may lead to crime, particularly fraud, to feed the habit and this aspect should be assessed. The *motivational interviewing* approach (Rollnick *et al.* 1993, Rollnick and Miller 1995), may be very helpful as with other problems in this field. A diary record is then instituted.

Management

This may consist of cognitive, social and behavioural aspects (Blaszczynski and Silove 1995). The role of gambling in the clients thinking and emotions can be recorded and challenged in the usual manner. Problems with the social, domestic and work environment are addressed. Response prevention and response chain lengthening may be helpful (see this chapter p.172). *Gamblers Anonymous* (see address at end of this chapter) provide support and a useful series of self-help publications.

References

Blaszczynski, A. and Silove, D. (1995) 'Cognitive and behavioural therapies for pathological gambling.' *Journal of Gambling Studies 11*, 195–220.

Chapman, S. (1985) 'Stop smoking clinics: a case for their abandonment.' *Lancet 1*, 918–920.

Chick, J. (1995) 'Alcoholism: detection and management in general practice.' *Primary Care Psychiatry 1*, 153–161.

Cooper, P.J. and Steere, J. (1995) 'A comparison of two psychological treatments for bulimia nervosa: implications for models of maintenance.' *Behaviour Research and Therapy 33*, 8, 875–885.

Fairburn, C.G. (1995) *Overcoming Binge Eating.* New York: Guilford.

France, R. and Robson, M.H. (1986 and 1991) *Behaviour Therapy in Primary Care.* London: Chapman and Hall.

Griffiths, M. (1995) *Adolescent Gambling.* London: Routledge.

Jarvis, M. and Russell, M.A.H. (1983) 'Smoking withdrawal in patients with smoking related diseases.' *British Medical Journal 286*, 876.

Jason, L.A., McMahon, S.D., Salina, D., Hedeker, D., Stockton, M., Dunson, K. and Kemball, P. (1995) 'Assessing a smoking cessation intervention involving groups, incentives and self-help manuals.' *Behavior Therapy 26*, 393–408.

Keesey, R.E. (1980) 'A set point analysis of the regulation of body weight.' In A.J. Stunkard (ed) *Obesity*. Philadelphia: W.B. Saunders.

Lesieur, H.R. and Rosenthal, R.J. (1991) 'Pathological gambling: a review of the literature.' *Journal of Gambling Studies 7*, 5–39.

Mahoney, M.J. and Mahoney, K. (1976) *Permanent Weight Control – A Total Solution to the Dieter's Dilemna*. New York: Norton.

Marlatt, G. A. and George, W.H. (1984) 'Relapse prevention: Introduction and overview of the model.' *British Journal of Addiction 79*, 261–73.

Miller, W.R. and Rollnick, S. (eds) (1991) Motivational interviewing: Preparing people to change addictive behaviour. (passim) New York: Guilford Press.

Perri, G., Shapiro, R.M., Ludwig, W.W., Twentyman, C.T. and McAdoo, W.G. (1984) 'Maintenance strategies for the treatment of obesity: an evaluation of relapse prevention training and post-treatment contact by mail and telephone.' *Journal of Consulting and Clinical Psychology 52*, 404–13.

Prochaska, J. and DiClemente, C. (1992) 'Stages of change in the modification of problem behaviours.' In M. Hersen, R. Eisler and P. Miller (eds) *Progress in Behavior Modification 28*. Sycamore Ill: Sycamore Publishing.

Raw, M. and Heller, J. (1984) *Helping People to Stop Smoking*. London: Health Education Council.

Rollnick, S., Kinnersley, P. and Stott, N. (1993) 'Methods of helping people with behaviour change.' *British Medical Journal 307*, 188–190.

Rollnick, S. and Miller, W.R. (1995) 'What is motivational interviewing?' *Behaviour and Cognitive Therapy 23*, 325–334.

Russell, M.A.H., Raw, M. and Jarvis, M.J. (1980) 'Clinical use of nicotine chewing gum.' *British Medical Journal 28*, 1599–1562.

Ruzek, J. *Drinkwatchers Handbook*. London: Accept Publications.

Schmidt, U. and Treasure, J. (1993) *Getting Better Bit(e) by Bit(e)*. Hove: Lawrence Erlbaum.

Sobell, M.B., Sobell, L.C. and Douglas, D.R. (1995) 'Portraying alcohol treatment outcomes.' *Behavior Therapy 26*, 643–669.

Stuart, R.B. and Davis, B. (1972) *Slim Chance in a Fat World*. Illinois: Research Press.

Treasure, J., Schmidt, U., Troop, N., Tiller, J., Todd, G. and Turnbull, S. (1996) 'Sequential treatment for bulimia nervosa using a self-care manual.' *British Journal of Psychiatry 168*, 94–98.

Wood, G.T. (1996) 'Treatment of bulimia nervosa: when CBT fails.' *Behaviour Research and Therapy 34*, 3, 197–212.

Recommended for Further Reading

Association for the Advancement of Behavior Therapy Special Series Edition (1995): 'Body dissatisfaction, binge eating and dieting as interlocking issues in eating disorders research.' *Behavior Therapy 26*, 1, 1–119.

Edwards G. (1987) *The Treatment of Drinking Problems: A Guide for the Helping Professions*, (2nd Ed). Oxford: Blackwell.

Fairburn C.G. (1995) *Overcoming Binge Eating*. New York: Guilford.

Griffiths, M. (1995) *Adolescent Gambling*. London: Routledge.

Heather, N. and Robertson, I. (1983) *Controlled Drinking*. London: Methuen.

Raw, M. and Heller, J. (1984) *Helping People to Stop Smoking.* London: Health Education Council.

Schmidt, U. and Treasure, J. *Getting Better Bit(e) by Bit(e).* Hove: Lawrence Erlbaum.

Books for Patients

Chick, J.A. and Chick, J. (1992) *Drinking Problems.* London: Optima Books Positive Health Guides.

Cooper, P. (1993) *Bulimia Nervosa: A Guide to Recovery.* London: Robinson.

Custer, R. and Milt, H. (1985) *When Luck Runs Out: Help for Compulsive Gamblers and their Families.* Bicester: Facts on File Ltd (Tel: 01869 253300).

East, R., Towers, B. and Moreton, W. (1982) *No Smoke: A Self-help Handbook for People Who Want to Give up Smoking.* Published by the authors at Kingston Polytechnic, Kingston, Surrey.

Moody, G. *The Wheel of Misfortune.* London: Gamblers Anonymous.

Orbach, S. (1978) *Fat is a Feminist Issue* and (1982) *Fat is a Feminist Issue 2.* London: Hamlyn.

Oswald, I. and Adam, K. (1983) *Get a Better Nights Sleep. Positive Health Guide.* London: Martin Dunitz.

Preston, A. (1993) *The Methadone Handbook.* Published by the author in association with Community Drugs and Alcohol Advisory service, Dorchester, West Dorset NHS Trust.

Preston, A. and Malinowski, A. (1994) *The Detox Handbook – A Users Guide to Getting Off Opiates.* London: ISDD, Waterbridge House, 32–36 Loman Road, SE1 0EE (Tel: 0171 928 1211).

Schmidt, U. and Treasure, J. (1993) *Getting Better Bit(e) by Bit(e).* Hove: Lawrence Erlbaum.

The Mayflower Project *The Safer Injecting Guide.* Frimley: Acorn Drug and Alcohol Services (Tel: 01276 62566).

Useful Addresses

Accept Services (UK), Accept Clinic, 200 Seagrave Road, London SW6 IRQ. Advice on controlled drinking.

Anorexia and Bulimia Care (Southern) Mrs Maureen Morris, Arisaig, Back Lane, Monks Eleigh, Suffolk IP7 7BA, Tel: 01449 740145. Mrs Doreen Williams (Northern Branch), 15 Fernhurst Gate, Aughton, Ormskirk, Lancs L39 5ED, Tel: 01695 422479.

ASH (Action on Smoking and Health) 5–11 Mortimer Street, London WIN 7RH. Supply of non-smoking leaflets.

Gamblers Anonymous, PO Box 88, London SW10 0EU, Tel: 0171 384 3040.

Scottish Health Education Group, Woodburn House, Canaan Lane, Edinburgh.

Equipment

Tally Wrist Counters obtainable from sports shops.

Nicotine Chewing Gum 'Nicorette' manufactured by AH Leo, Sweden. Supplied in the UK by Lundbeck Ltd., Lundbeck House, Hastings Street, Luton, Bedfordshire.

Appendix 1: SUMMARY OF A GROUP WEIGHT LOSS PROGRAMME

Framework Requirements

(1) *Introduction.* This consists of an initial talk to the potential group to enable them to decide if they wish to take part. It is explained that weight reduction is achieved by; (a) planned reduction of eating in a sensible and manageable way; (b) increase of exercise – to increase energy usage; and (c) control of various environmental factors influencing the other two. The disadvantages of crash diets, cranky diets, drugs and other pitfalls are discussed briefly. It is pointed out that the long term objective is a permanent method of controlling weight, tailored to the tastes and needs of the individual and their current life style.

(2) *Pre-Programme.* Those who wish to take part then enter a two-week self-measurement period during which they try to maintain their previous habits in order to; (a) provide a baseline of weight and diet; and (b) get clients used to the tools and procedures that they will be using throughout the programme.

(3) *The Main Programme.* This consists of three sections:

    (a) An initial intensive supervision period with weekly meetings. This adjusts the diet to obtain a weight loss of 1–2 Ibs per week and in so far as possible adapts the programme to suit individual lifestyle requirements.

    (b) A longer supervision programme with monthly meetings to enable the target weight to be achieved at the proper rate.

    (c) A final meeting for assessment of the content of the programme, evaluation of its benefits and long term planning for the members.

Material Required

One pack per client containing:

(1) Specimen baseline self-observation form.

    (a) Daily Food Intake

    (b) Daily Exercise Expenditure.

(2) Calorie or unit value booklets or charts which can be of any type as long as they are accurate and fairly comprehensive.

(3) Planning charts for the main programme.

    (a)   Food in calories or units.

    (b)   Exercise in calories used.

(4) Advice sheets for helping to control environmental factors.

    (a)   To suppress uncontrolled eating (Sheets 1 and 2).

    (b)   To strengthen appropriate eating (Sheet 3).

Each member should provide themselves with a book or a loose-leaf folder which they can use to reproduce these materials as necessary.

(5) A chart giving various forms of exercise in terms of calories expended.

Pre Programme

Week 1

Weigh and agree final or intermediate target weight. (For the substantially overweight a final target weight may be dispiriting so an intermediate target may be desirable.) Look at issues of body image and self-esteem including the wearing of tight clothes. The subject of avoidance and the significance of weight change is put into perspective in discussion. Provide and introduce calorie or unit diet sheets. Provide and explain the baseline self-observation form which will be used to record all food and exercise during the baseline period. Although it is stressed that no attempt should be made to alter normal eating and exercise habits during this period of recording, it is best if weighing is only carried out at the sessions in early stages in order to avoid frenetic frequent weighings and between-weighing-machine variation. An additional advantage is that most primary care computer programmes are now able to calculate rapidly Body Mass Index which is individuals weight in kilograms divided by the square of their height in kilos. For guidance a BMI of over 25 indicates slight overweight, over 30 obesity and over 35 serious obesity. Later the client must use their own bathroom scales.

Week 2

Attitudes to weight, exercise and dieting are discussed within the group and the opportunity used to talk about pitfalls and misconceptions including 'glandular trouble', crash diets, cranky diets and the place of anorectic drugs. The likely weight gain from stopping smoking may be discussed at this point. The long term objective of a permanent improved method of eating is outlined. The previous week's self-observation forms are checked and any difficulties discussed.

The value of increasing exercise is discussed and members are asked, as homework, to consider consistent and measurable ways in which this could be done, such as cycling to the station (10 mins) instead of taking the car. It is important that, if possible, additional exercise is taken in a form that the client enjoys and is therefore likely to continue.

Main Programme

Week 3

This is an extremely full session during which the dietary and exercise modifications designed to produce controlled weight loss are introduced. The initial eating reduction is somewhat arbitrary but usually a daily programme set at around 75 per cent of baseline calorie intake will be about right. Fine adjustment can be undertaken later. It is important that the programme contains all the client's favourite foods albeit in reduced quantities. Deliberate abstinence from much-loved foodstuffs leads to an unnatural dichotomy between 'good but unattractive' and 'bad but delicious' foods which makes the latter loom large in the client's mind and tempts him or her to lapse. This may contribute to the abstinence violation effect of one lapse resulting in a feeling of total failure. This will be considered in more detail when drug and alcohol problems are discussed.

If possible an increased exercise programme should be planned and introduced at the same time.

At the end of the sessions the first advice sheet (To Help to Make Your Diet Work, Part 1) is distributed to be read before the next week.

Week 4

After weighing, the adjustments necessary to obtain the target 1–2 lbs weight loss, are made to the programme and any difficulties are discussed. The help of one group member to another is particularly useful in overcoming snags as such suggestions are more powerful than those of the leader. The achievements of the individual increased exercise programmes are then considered and an attempt made to obtain an increased exercise expenditure of 500 calories per day.

The first advice sheet is discussed together with its underlying philosophy of limiting or removing the cues for inappropriate eating. Often members will have suggestions which can usually be considered by the group and perhaps added to the sheets. The second sheet is distributed at the end of the session.

Week 5

This is devoted to monitoring progress and adjusting the diet and exercise programmes, discussing difficulties and distributing the final advice sheet which explores cues and methods for obtaining reinforcement for an appropriate life-style.

The question of relabelling emotions can be usefully considered at this session. It appears that many overweight people misinterpret emotions such as boredom, anxiety and tiredness as hunger. They can usefully be trained to ask themselves if there is an alternative explanation when they think that they feel hungry. Negative thoughts about such subjects as lack of willpower, relative inability to lose weight and excuses for not doing so are discussed in the group. These 'negative monologues' (Mahoney and Mahoney 1976) can be answered by 'appropriate monologues' in much the same way as negative automatic thoughts are answered by rational alternatives in the cognitive therapy of depression (Beck *et al.* 1979, see Chapter Nine). For example:

Situation	Negative Monologues	Appropriate Monologue
Seeking excuses	My family are all overweight.	With the right eating habits everyone can lose weight.
Too impatient	I shall never get rid of it.	

Support from other group members is extremely useful in finding appropriate alternatives.

Deep muscle relaxation which has been considered in detail in Chapter Six can usefully be taught at this point as an alternative response to eating which can be used to cope with anxiety, anger or frustration.

Week 6

After the usual assessment and adjustment, this session is used to determine which environmental cues each client finds most appropriate for him or herself and which emotions he or she may mislabel as hunger. As this is the last session of the intensive programme it is a good idea to suggest that the group takes a meal out together. This is a pleasant and appropriate setting to discuss the possible problems of public meals and hospitality.

Monthly Meetings

These have no formal structure apart from progress monitoring and the discussion of difficulties and negative monologues. They are incorporated to continue group support and to enable long term target weights to be reached.

Final Meeting

The difficulties of continuing without the support of the group are discussed and the problems of maintaining the changed pattern permanently. Each member is encouraged to write down for themselves what they have discovered to be useful either inside or outside the group. Another technique which is worth mentioning is to reintroduce the full monitored programme for one month in every six as a refresher course.

PATIENT INFORMATION SHEETS

TO HELP YOU TO MAKE YOUR DIET WORK I

Eat all meals at a formally prepared table in one room. Concentrate on the meal and never do anything else, such as read or watch TV at the same time as eating.

- Use a smaller plate than usual.

- Concentrate on chewing food slowly. Try to be the last to finish. Have a salad before the meal to take the edge off your appetite. Try a drink of water or unsweetened fruit juice before a meal to see if it reduces your appetite.

- Do your shopping from a list and only take enough money to cover the things on that list.

- Shop immediately after a meal when you are not hungry.

- Avoid buying prepared high calorie foods, such as biscuits, crisps or pies. Equally see that any high calorie foods you do buy need preparation and cooking. If possible keep them deep frozen.

TO HELP YOU MAKE YOUR DIET WORK II

Get your family and others around you to:

(1) Provide, or help you provide, suitable meals.

(2) Help you keep a check on what you eat and encourage you when you are doing well.

- Serve your food on to your plate before the meal – not from dishes on the table.

- Leave the table as soon as you have finished. Never leave food out in view after meals.

- Spread small portions over the plate making them look larger. Eat three meals a day at planned intervals, never miss one.

- Never get overtired.

- Have something to do at all times, for example, book, records, gardening, sewing to distract you from eating through boredom.

- Try practising leaving food on your plate and throwing it away. (Make it a rule never to leave a clean plate.)

TO HELP YOU MAKE YOUR DIET WORK III

Learn the full range and quantities of non-fattening foods from your chart and use them to give variety. Include occasional small quantities of fattening food to avoid craving.

Learn the amount of each which can be eaten so that portion size becomes second nature.

Have a reserve supply of non-fattening foods, for example apples, tomatoes, beef extract for snacks or save something from a previous meal.

Appendix 2: BULIMIA FACT SHEET

(1) Dieting is a response to bingeing but it also encourages bingeing by inducing the body and mind changes of starvation.

(2) Self induced vomiting and to a lesser extent use of laxatives and diuretics encourage binge eating because they seem to provide a 'way out' or escape from the unpleasant consequences of bingeing. Laxatives (and colonic irrigation) do not promote weight loss as they only eliminate body waste. Excess use of slimming aids may also encourage binge eating.

(3) Over-concern about shape and weight makes you diet and keeps the eating problem going. This is particularly true when you think that you must be a certain size and shape in order to be a worthwhile person.

(4) Too much worry about shape and weight is often associated with feelings of being ineffective and worthless.

GETTING TO GRIPS WITH THE PROBLEM THEREFORE DEPENDS ON CHANGING BOTH WHAT YOU DO AND WHAT YOU THINK.

Monitor your eating on the record sheet provided. This will be used to get a baseline and judge the effectiveness of the techniques used.

Appendix 3: SUMMARY OF A GROUP NON-SMOKING PROGRAMME

The group leader agrees to provide the materials necessary for the programme. He or she co-ordinates the group's discussions and provides support to members during various difficulties that may occur.

Material Requirements

(1) A Carbon Monoxide Monitoring apparatus.

(2) One pack per client containing:

    (a) A specimen Daily Smoking Record Chart which can be copied to provide charts for each day until the Quitting Date.

    (b) An ARU (Addiction Research Unit) Smoking Questionnaire (see end of Chapter). This gives a comprehensive account of smoking behaviour and attitudes.

    (c) Contract Sheet if required.

    (d) Summary Progress Chart.

    (e) Three advice sheets which may be retained by the leader for distribution later in the programme.

Timetable for the Group

Week 1

The outline of the programme is explained. The optional quitting date is discussed. Carbon Monoxide (CO) is monitored. The purpose of the ARU Questionnaire and the Daily Chart is explained together with using the Desire Rating. Summary and Contract Forms are given out with Stop Smoking leaflets. Those attending the first session are under no obligation to return but it is hoped that those attending for the second meeting will endeavour to attend the rest of the course.

Week 2

The returning participants are congratulated upon their decision and welcomed. CO is monitored. Completed Contracts, ARU Questionnaires and Daily Charts are discussed. The option of rapid quitting and the use of nicotine patches and chewing gum is considered. Group partners (buddies) are selected with the object of providing each member with a kindred spirit who can be contacted if the going gets tough. The details of the money deposits and destiny of forfeits are settled.

Week 3

Daily Charts, progress and difficulties are discussed. Deposits are collected and the arrangements checked. CO is monitored. The first hand-out, *The Smoker's Habits*, is distributed.

Week 4

Ways of helping to stop are discussed amongst the group. CO is monitored. If wanted and available, an outside speaker can be asked to talk about how he or she stopped. *Lengthening the Chain* is distributed.

Week 5

It is hoped that many will have stopped by this session. Usually those still attending will have done so but some time can be taken strengthening the resolve of any stragglers. CO is monitored. Methods of helping the new non-smoker avoid excessive weight gain are considered. Negative thoughts and difficult situations are discussed in order to generate relapse prevention strategies (Marlatt and George 1984). The hand-outs on *Withdrawal Symptoms* and *Remaining a Non-smoker* are distributed.

Week 6

The success rate is discussed and any special tips or difficulties. This meeting produced 'The Dottle Bottle' which is an extremely simple portable aversion therapy apparatus. It consists of the contents of a bar ashtray after a busy evening emptied into a wide-neck bottle and macerated with a little water. Carried in the pocket, it can be opened and smelt every time the desire to smoke is felt. At first suggested by a group member as a joke it was later adopted widely as a serious aid. If time permits a film may be shown and the venue for the bar or pub meeting decided.

Week 7

Final meeting of the intensive series is held in a bar or a pub. This is to enable the members to experience a normally difficult, high-probability smoking situation whilst still having the support of the group. Relapse prevention is discussed.

Extended Meetings

These may be held every month up to six months. The money deposit can be continued to be collected at the same rate but now four weeks at a time. It is repaid in the predetermined manner at the final meeting after six months. The purpose of these extended meetings is to protect against the danger period for restarting which seems to be at its height between six weeks and six months.

Running groups of this sort is a time-consuming and quite demanding pastime. It does, however, have a number of rewards and can be enjoyable. It is a moot point whether the use of professional time is cost effective when only small groups of up to sixteen people can be involved at one time and as stated above outcome research has not been encouraging. Professional resources may be saved by handing over the running of subsequent groups to 'lay graduates' of the earlier ones.

In addition running cognitive behavioural groups of any sort and collecting data leads to new hypotheses and ideas for revision of management with the development of new and more effective treatment plans so this protocol may be helpful if just used as a starting point.

PATIENT INFORMATION SHEETS

THE SMOKER'S HABITS

Study your Daily Smoking Record Chart. Make a note of particular activities associated with particular cigarettes. There may be coffee cigarettes, the after meal cigarettes, driving cigarettes, telephone cigarettes and so on. Each of these cigarettes has the same Desire Rating each day. Work through the week blocking out one or more extra habit cigarettes in each Desire Rating group each day. For example, on Monday you knock out the coffee cigarettes, Tuesday you knock out the coffee and the after breakfast cigarettes, Wednesday you knock out the coffee, the after breakfast and the telephone cigarettes and so on.

The following tips may be helpful:

The Coffee Cigarette – many smokers have the first cigarette with the first cup of coffee in the morning and all cups of coffee may carry a high probability rating. To beat it:

- change to tea or some other drink
- change your way of flavouring coffee, for example drink it without sugar if you have been used to sugar in the past or
- munch a tea biscuit or anything else you fancy.

The After Breakfast Cigarette – this could be a coffee cigarette or it could simply be a cigarette smoked while having a think about the day ahead. To beat it, change your habit by:

- going for a quick walk or jog
- if you are not athletic carry a paperback and have a quick read or
- use any other method you can think of to prevent 'dead time' developing: try to eat at breakfast time – however little.

The Driver's Cigarette – some drivers believe that a cigarette helps them to relax at the wheel and makes them a better driver. There is no basis for this, in fact smoking whilst driving is actually dangerous. To beat it:

- turn on and concentrate on the car radio
- try to carry a passenger so that you can talk
- chew gum or a hard sweet
- listen to tapes.

The Waiting Cigarette – read, exercise or chew a sweet. Watch others smoking and list your benefits from stopping, which they lack.

The Telephone Cigarette – to avoid this:

- doodle on a pad
- answer the phone in a different physical position
- play with an 'executive toy'
- don't keep cigarettes near the telephone.

The After Lunch Cigarette – like the after breakfast cigarette, try to eliminate the dead time by changing your routine. Take walks, read the paper or write an advice sheet on stopping smoking.

The Drinking Cigarette – this is often the toughest one to beat, particularly because your inhibitions and self-control are reduced when you drink. To avoid this:

- never carry your cigarettes or matches with you to a party – take only your rating form. If you allow yourself a cigarette you must cadge both it and a light
- telephone your partner (buddy) before any drinking session or during its early stages
- if you are fairly sure that there will be something to eat at the party, eat nothing beforehand and nibble often as you drink
- if all else fails, give up alcoholic drinks for a few months. This is hard but it may be the only way.

WITHDRAWAL SYMPTOMS

Weight gain – although not strictly a withdrawal symptom, this can be a problem. Try to increase the amount of exercise that you take, it will also help your efforts to remain a non-smoker and prove to you that you are fitter than before. Find something that you enjoy – it is much more fun and you are more likely to keep it up. Sugar reduced sweets and drinks can be helpful.

Other Symptoms – most other symptoms are mild and seldom last longer than a week. You may experience some of the following:

(1) Occasional dizziness because more oxygen is reaching your system.

(2) Headache.

(3) Hunger.

(4) Constipation. Drink extra water or fruit juice each day.

(5) Trembling and sweating. Both will subside as the body gets used to the non-smoking habit.

(6) Insomnia. You may actually need less sleep. Go to bed later and only when you feel tired (see notes on sleeping – Appendix 4, Chapter Six).

(7) Nervousness or irritability. This is due to increased energy and is best dealt with by increasing activities.

(8) Smokers cough may be worse initially as the lungs clear themselves out.

You may also notice slower breathing, slower pulse and better taste and smell – all of which should be benefits.

LENGTHENING THE CHAIN

Smoking requires a series of physical movements which are often half-conscious and semi-automatic. For example you keep your cigarette in a certain place and find them in a certain way, you use the same method of lighting-up and you hold and smoke the cigarette in a particular way which you have been doing for years.

These movements form a chain which must be first studied and then lengthened or broken to lose the habit. Deliberately alter every part of the chain of habits that you can. For example:

Change brands – choose a brand as different as possible from your normal brand.

Buy cigarettes in a new place – never again use the familiar machine, garage or sweet shop. Get them in a shop you have never used before.

Keep your cigarettes in a new place – if they have been in a pocket or a handbag, keep them on a shelf or in the desk drawer.

Make it hard to get to the packet and get a cigarette – wrap your rating form round the packet with tight rubber bands. Ideally lock the packet in the boot of the car and put the key in a locked locker two blocks away.

Change your way of lighting-up – if you use a lighter, change to matches and vice-versa. Light-up left handed which will be awkward. This is the main idea.

REMAINING A NON-SMOKER

(1) Never offer cigarettes to anybody else, for example, at a party.

(2) Never buy or carry cigarettes for anybody else.

(3) Never light a cigarette for anybody else. Say in your most charming way 'I'm sorry but I'm a non-smoker' **not** 'I've given up' or worse 'I'm trying to give up'.

(4) Don't keep ashtrays in view around your house. Only produce them if you see somebody lighting up.

(5) Never give an ashtray, lighter or any other smoking equipment as a present.

(6) If you wish you can ban all smoking from the house and car.

(7) Never buy duty-free cigarettes for people when you go abroad.

ALWAYS CALL YOURSELF A NON-SMOKER NOT AN EX-SMOKER.

Appendix 4: HINTS FOR REDUCING DRINKING

(1) Wait when you feel that you would like or need a drink.

(2) Sip more slowly, putting the glass down between sips.

(3) Change your habits – the bar, the type of drink and the company.

(4) Concentrate on smell and taste. Few expert wine tasters have a drink problem.

(5) Learn and practise what to say when refusing drinks.

(6) Make a choice of non-alcoholic drinks and use them as spacers.

(7) Make a point of not drinking for two days each week 'back to back'.

(8) Monitor your weekly total in units.

(9) Find other, non-drinking, activities.

Appendix 5: THE DRUG USER'S LANGUAGE
Acorn Community Drug and Alcohol Services
Information For GPs and Primary Health Care Teams

Ever thought that illicit drugs users speak a different language? They do! Here are some common words that might help you understand it.

DRUGS IN GENERAL: *Gear, Deal, tackle, score, stash.*

HEROIN (Diamorphine Hydrochloride): *skag, smack, H, Henry, Horse, brown, junk, dry amps.*

COCAINE: *Coke, Charlie, C, Snow. Crack (smokeable cocaine): rocks, ice.*

AMPHETAMINE: *Speed, whizz, Billy, sulphate, Dexies, uppers, Pink champagne.*

ECSTASY: *E, Doves, Pills, tabs.*

LSD: *acid, trips, tabs, blotters, microdots.*

CANNABIS: *(general), puff, blow, draw, dope. (specific), resin, grass, weed, Rocky, Afghan, Leb, Skunkweed, homegrown, slate, oil, sinsi, Thai-grass and many more.*

METHADONE: *linctus, juice, green, mixture, meth, (Injectable), Amps, Phy, Phialls.*

TYPES OF USAGE:

    INJECTING: *Fixing, cranking, jacking up, hitting up, shooting up, mainlining, skin popping, poking, spiking, jabbing, frontloading, backloading, stacking (steroids).*

    SNIFFING: *Snorting, doing a line, snorting a line.*

    SMOKING: *Chasing, tooting, toking.*

INTOXICATED BY DRUGS: *Stoned, wasted, spaced out, buzzing, high, out of my head, got a hit.*

MISCELLANEOUS:

*Mazzies, eggs, Hippos, Temazzies = **Temazepan.***

*Chillum, bong, bucket = **Cannabis pipes.***

*Blagging = **Deceiving (especially Doctors).***

*Poppers, Amyl = **Amyl nitrate.***

*Skins = **Rolling paper.***

*Reefer, joint, jay, spliff = **Cannabis cigarette.***

*Dikies = **Diconal.***

*Chill out = **Take it easy/a break (from dancing).***

*Special K = **Ketamine.***

*Munchies = **Drug induced appetite.***

*Speedball, snowball = **Heroin/Cocaine mix.***

*Clucking, turkeying = **Withdrawing from opiates.***

*Gouching out, gouching = **In a semi-conscious opiate-induced state.***

*Roach = **Filter for cannabis cigarette.***

*Downers, Tranx = **Benzodiazepeines or Barbiturates.***

*Shrooms, Silly Simons = **Magic Mushrooms.***

*Head, Freak = **Regular drug user (usually prefixed by drug of choice e.g. speed-freak).***

(Reproduced by kind permission of Alistair Sutherland, Acorn Drug and Alcohol Services, Frimley, Surrey GU16 5AD.)

Appendix 6: DRUG PRESCRIBING CONTRACT
Acorn Community Drug and Alcohol Services
Contract

CONTRACT FOR ....

I understand and agree to the following:-

1.   That I will be prescribed Methadone Mixture (1mg/1ml) DTF   mls.

2.   I will receive fortnightly prescriptions.

3.   I will see my GP and will keep all my appointments unless by prior agreement.

4.   I will see my GP Liaison Worker and keep all my appointments unless by prior agreement.

5.   My GP and GP Liaison Worker have the right to discuss my case and may see me together if this is felt appropriate.

6.   We need to have a urine test result in order to prescribe effectively. We expect you to provide these samples to ensure that our prescribing is appropriate.

7.   We may have to speak with the dispensing chemist.
      We also have to inform the Home Office for notification purposes when receiving a methadone prescription.

8.   If I miss two appointments, one after the other. with my GP Liaison Worker my prescription will be reviewed.

9.   If I continue to use street drugs inappropriately on top of my prescription there will be a review of my case. This could result in a change in what is being prescribed.

10.   My medication and any changes in dosage will be decided with my GP Liaison Worker and the doctor.

11.   Any attempt to obtain extra drugs from my GP, or any other doctor, will immediately cause a review of my treatment and loss of my prescription. If I am having problems with my prescription I should contact my GP Liaison Worker and GP in order to review my medication.

12.   If I go on holiday I will need to give two weeks notice so that my prescription can be prepared. (Please note certain restrictions apply to taking prescribed medications out of the county).

13.   If I am not in a fit state my GP and GP Liaison Worker have the right to refuse to see me.

14.   I am responsible for any drugs/prescriptions which I am issued and if I should lose them they will not be replaced.

WARNING: Opiates such as methadone, DF118, (dihydrocodeine) and heroin cause drowsiness as do benzodiazepines such as Temazepam and Valium (diazepam),
We advise against driving or operating dangerous machinery whilst using the above.
The dangers of alcohol whilst taking methadone and other drugs have been explained to me.
It is a criminal offence to alter a prescription, even if there is an error on the prescription.

Client   ....   Date ....

GP   ....   Date ....

GP Liaison Worker ....   Date ....

TERMINATION OF CONTRACT: It is at the discretion of the GP whether or not to continue to prescribe to a client. Any abuse or non-compliance with this Contract will result in a review of the situation.

(Reproduced by kind permission of Helen Tarbatt, Acorn Drug and Alcohol Services, Frimley, Surrey GU16 5AD.)

Chapter Nine
The Management of Depression

The psychological treatment of depression has pride of place in the cognitive behavioural field. The early work of Beck and his colleagues (Beck *et al.* 1979) was devoted to the management of depression and it was from a solid basis of groundwork in this field that the principles of CBT were gradually extended into other areas. Unlike most of the other problem areas that we are covering, however, there is respected and effective pharmacological treatment for depression, and it may seem rather luxurious to suggest that the primary care worker needs to be concerned with psychological methods as well. It is not our contention that anti-depressant drug treatment should be abandoned in favour of an exclusively psychological approach, rather that consideration of cognitive processes is essential for the proper management of depression by whatever means and that there are several important advantages in being able to combine the two approaches or in having a choice of therapies.

Amongst many patients and the news media, drug treatment of all forms of psychiatric disorder is always being questioned and criticised. Whilst anxiety over benzodiazepines seems well-founded, it seems illogical and dangerous to tar antidepressants with the same brush. Ill-informed criticism may actually prevent depressed patients receiving the treatment that they need and deserve. Drug treatment is, however, likely to be more convincing and logical to the patient if it forms part of a regime that recognises that the patient's self-image and way of life outside the consulting room are important and shows concern for his thoughts and behaviour. When the whole problem is being tackled, the drugs may seem more acceptable and the oft-heard criticism 'I went to my doctor but all he did was to give me tablets' can be avoided.

History of Cognitive Behaviour Therapy for Depression

In 1974 Seligman and his co-workers described changes in animals subjected to uncontrollable shock and other aversive events (Seligman 1975). These animals developed lack of motivation to initiate escape and were slow to learn control when it became available. They also developed stomach ulcers and other evidence of emotional change. To explain these changes, Seligman proposed the theory of 'learned helplessness' which, he suggested, occurred when an organism had no control over outcome of unpleasant events.

The practical application of this theoretical work was provided by Beck and his colleagues (Beck *et al.* 1979, Beck 1990) who in successive publications have developed systems of treatment based on the modification of activities and thoughts of depressed patients known as Cognitive Behaviour Therapy (CBT). As first presented, these systems were seen as alternatives to drugs and required extensive therapist training and many hours of treatment. Following this pioneer work Blackburn and her colleagues (Blackburn *et al.* 1981) in Scotland have shown advantages in combined drug and CBT in hospital outpatients. A GP patient group in the same study did equally well on the combination and CBT alone, both being superior to drugs alone. Many workers are now interested in separating out the essential elements of the CBT package with a view to much shorter, simpler interventions which would be suitable for use in the consulting room as an adjunct to traditional methods of treatment (Teasdale 1985).

Principles of Effective Treatment

Depression may be seen as a response to current experiences perceived as highly aversive and uncontrollable. The depression itself then modifies perceptions of current events, recall of memories and significance of symptoms in such a way that the negative aspects are selected, thereby increasing the depression by a vicious circle feedback. Negative aspects are regarded by the depressed patient as being due to global, permanent defects and inadequacies in himself as a person. The positive aspects of life, if noticed at all, will be attributed to transient chance external circumstances.

The factors operating to maintain depression once it is established include:

(1) Major life difficulties and stressors – which would be aversive for anybody whether depressed or not.

(2) Minor life problems such as domestic, child rearing and work difficulties which seem highly aversive and uncontrollable to the depressed person but not to the non-depressed.

(3) Memories of past depressing experiences which surface in the form of depressive ruminations if the depressed person is not otherwise occupied.

(4) The depressed state itself.

Different techniques may be required to treat each of these but the last, i.e. depression about depression, is probably the most important target for psychological approaches. First, in order to counteract the prevailing view that the depression is due to personal inadequacy, information must be given explaining the symptoms as those of a well-understood psychological state. This state is experienced by many and occurs as a natural reaction to certain circumstances affecting behaviour, thoughts, mood and bodily functions. It can be reduced by learning certain techniques which are under the patient's own control.

Second, a structured framework must be provided in which the patient learns and practises the appropriate coping techniques.

Third, the programme should provide ample feedback and monitoring so that the patient recognises the effects of his acquired skills.

By these steps the 'depression about depression' is reduced and a sense of control over his problem is returned to the patient.

In addition to these steps the first three factors may require additional techniques. These include the development of problem-solving skills and help in specific areas where difficulties exist such as in marriage or in employment.

The elements above as described by Teasdale seem to be common to the effective psychological treatments for depression. The theory and practice which are now described in detail are adapted to the requirements of primary care from all the work of Beck (Beck *et al.* 1979) and his co-workers.

The Cognitive Theory of Depression

This depends upon three components:

(1) *The cognitive triad of negative automatic thoughts* concerning the depressive himself (for example, 'I'm no good at anything'), the environment he lives in (for example, 'Nobody can get a job in this place') and the future (for example, 'It will never get any better').

(2) *Thinking errors* – examples include *all or nothing thinking* (for example, 'If I don't get this contract I'm a total failure'), *overgeneralisation* (for example, 'I'm always miserable at weekends'), *discounting the positive* (for example, 'Nothing went right today'), *jumping to conclusions* (for example, 'Other mothers never find it difficult to keep their children

happy'), *catastrophising* (for example, 'Even if I do win the lottery my ticket won't be valid'), *global judgements* (for example, 'I got that wrong so I must be useless'), and *personalisation* (for example, 'Everybody in my house always gets ill').

(3) *Assumptions or schemata* – these are underlying attitudes which are organised from past experience and produced to influence the way in which new situations and pieces of information are handled. They include the 'shoulds' and 'ought tos', the 'I must have...' or 'I need...' and the 'would be terrible if...' statements. The assumptions often imply unrecognised or half-recognised values which none the less exert a very powerful and restricting influence on a person's thinking.

Assessment

Before depression can be assessed it must be recognised so the first essential is for the clinician to put himself in the position to detect the true problem which may be obsured by somatic symptoms and social problems. It has been shown that a number of consulting behaviours significantly improve recognition. These are listed in detail in Goldberg and Huxley (1980).

When detecting depression it is important to be aware of specially vulnerable groups which include:

- postnatal women
- mothers of young children
- adolescents
- disabled and families of the disabled
- victims of life events – surgery, divorce, redundancy and bereavement
- learning impaired patients – one third also have mental illness, usually depression, which is particularly likely to go unrecognised
- the patient in later life who may present a difficult differential diagnosis of dementia and depression and co-existing states.

As we will point out later therapy begins during the assessment stage and the patients perceptions, interpretations and personal rules must be considered from the outset. More specifically the assessment can be based on the following:

Structured Short Interview

('The Eight Questions')

(1) What exactly is the current problem(s)?

(2) What disability is it causing?

(3) What makes it better or worse?

(4) When does it happen?

(5) What does the patient think it is due to?

(6) What does (s)he believe can be done about it?

(7) What would be a satisfactory outcome?

(8) What effect would that outcome have on him/her or other people?

This information can then be supplemented by a short screening check list based on the Diagnostic and Statsitical Manual of the American Psychiatric Association, 4th edition (DSMIV IV) (APA1994) diagnostic criteria. Many of these areas will have already have been covered and need not of course be repeated but it important to see that nothing important is left out.

Enquiry is made about low moods and weeping and their associated thoughts and images and then about loss of enjoyment and interest in almost all activities. These two are the key areas one or other of which must be present for depression to be diagnosed.

Subsidiary areas are then covered:

- Appetite loss/Weight loss.
- Sleep loss/Hypersomnia.
- Tiredness.
- Indecisiveness.
- Guilt (self blame)/Worthlessness.
- Activity (Retardation/Agitation).
- Loss of Concentration.
- Suicidal thoughts/Plans/Actions.

An estimate should by this time have been obtained about:

(1) The chief symptoms including obvious distorted or negative thoughts and images giving evidence of the cognitive triad.

(2) The effect of the depressed state on work, home and family.

(3) Other problems which may be contributing to the total picture.

(4) Some idea of rigid obstructive life rules.

From this information a problem list can be drawn up. The patient is then consulted as to which problem seems most important or urgent.

An explanation of the approach is given with, if possible, a simple experiment to show how thoughts can affect mood. This can be done by getting the patient first to think about a recent depressing time or experience, describe his mood and then transfer to a neutral or pleasant activity such as describing sights seen from the window, demonstrating that the mood will usually change with this distraction.

Assessment of initial severity is aided by getting the patient to complete the Beck Depression Inventory (see Materials at the end of this chapter) at the first visit; this is then repeated regularly in order to monitor progress. The BDI consists of 21 items each containing four or five alternative statements. It can easily be completed in a few minutes before or during a session. The maximum score is 63, mild depression scores 1–20, moderate 21–26, severe over 26. It should not be used to diagnose depression but only to estimate severity.

Planning Treatment

Cognitive behavioural management of depression does not start with elaborate specialised techniques but begins in the earliest stages of assessment. In fact the management may be regarded as having four stages all of which have a cognitive behavioural component and each stage overlaps the one before and the one afterwards as follows:

- ° Stage 1 – Assessment
- ° Stage 2 – Rationale and Drug Treatment
- ° Stage 3 – Behavioural Strategies
- ° Stage 4 – Cognitive Techniques.

If at first it seems paradoxical to refer to *assessment* as *management* this may become clearer as each stage is considered.

Assessment

Principally of course this is concerned, as explained above, with obtaining a full picture of the problem but it does more than that as is shown below.

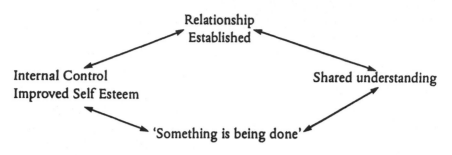

The establishment of a relationship may improve self esteem and shared understanding and may remove the sense of isolation that depressives often feel. There is a feeling that 'something is being done' and control over the problem has partly been handed back, or at least perceived to have been handed back to the patient All of these elements involve and promote cognitive change and should be taken into account by the therapist during the assessment stage.

Rationale and Drug Treatment

The rationale of how depression comes about and how it can be treated often brings hope, although initially accepted somewhat sceptically by the patient. Some sort of explanation that clinical depression is different from 'the blues' is needed. This may be in the form of a pre-prepared booklet (see Books for Patients) or a short typed or printed explanation along the following lines:

Patient Information on Depression

'Being depressed involves feeling low, being tearful and loss of enjoyment but also changes many bodily functions including appetite, sleep, energy levels and interest. Sufferers often blame themselves for their misfortune. They slow up physically, find it hard to concentrate and may even lose the will to live. Thus feelings, thoughts, physical well-being and daily activities may all be involved. Misfortunes, losses and other set-backs in everyday life may partially account for this but often there is no apparent reason which the sufferer finds even more puzzling and distressing.

Research has shown that there are chemical changes at the nerve junctions which occur when people become depressed and these can be corrected by treatment. This is quite different from treatment with tranquillisers and there is no danger of getting "hooked".'

Some advice as to how to get the best out of drug treatment is then provided (see below).

Drug treatment however is not enough by itself and encouragement and help will also be given to help the patient do more, enjoy life more and change some of the damaging thinking patterns that stoke the depression.

Try to use some examples from the sufferer's own experience to flesh out the explanation.

Obvious social factors may also be addressed at this stage. Work by Brown (1978) and others has demonstrated how important these are but unfortunately their modification is often beyond the powers of the therapist. Nonetheless headteachers, bank managers, solicitors and the Citizens Advice Bureau may all have a role to play as well of course as the professional social services.

There are still more issues involving thoughts and beliefs to be addressed when considering drug treatment which may be listed as follows:

Cognitive Factors in Introducing Drug Treatment

- Explanation of the nature of problem.
- Description of neurotransmission.
- Explain combined psycho-social and drug approach.
- How long drugs take to work.
- Possible side effects and how they fit in.
- Importance of coming back.
- Why doses may change.
- The how and when of stopping treatment.

Several of these factors have already been mentioned but it is important to consider some of the others in the context of the depressed patient's thought patterns and the cognitive triad of depressed thinking. For example, the patient may think that any side effects are evidence of failure of treatment and any delay from starting medication to onset of action or dose increases indicate that he is a hopeless case who will never respond to any treatment. The largely justifiable reaction against tranquillisers has resulted in a less reasonable loss of faith in antidepressant therapy as well. Given all these factors it is not surprising that over half of the patients prescribed antidepressants stop taking them prematurely (Johnson 1981). A close attention to the above factors should improve adherence to treatment and in order to achieve this planned follow-up is essential and repeat prescribing should normally be avoided.

Often it is possible to begin to work on the third (behavioural) element at the same time or very soon after drug therapy is started.

Behavioural Strategies

The objective is to record the patient's present activity level and to expand the patient's positive activities by carefully graded tasks. This is known as *activity scheduling* and the steps are as follows:

(1) Taking stock of the present activity level by a baseline chart (Weekly Activity Schedule WAS).

(2) Rating present activities for; A = Achievement and P = Pleasure (each out of 5) for all cells on the WAS.

(3) Discouraging records which are too detailed or too short.

(4) Working to expand activities, particularly those with promising A and P ratings (see Figure 9.1).

It is important to gauge the current level of the patient's activities and to find out what he has given up that he previously found satisfying and enjoyable. The severely depressed patient may find taking a bath or making a pot of tea a challenging task. Even simple activities must often be broken down into shorter, simpler components so that success, which is vital, can be achieved. For the first week or so he is merely asked to fill in a record sheet showing how he spends each hour of the day. Using this record as a baseline it is then possible to agree, week by week, gradually more extensive positive target activities, always advancing slowly enough to see that the targets are met. If a target is not met, it is put to the patient that this is not a 'failure' but merely a useful opportunity of gaining more information which will be of help in the future.

As soon as the records are understood and are being properly completed a second stage is introduced whereby each activity is rated on a 1–5 scale for Achievement and Pleasure. Other terms closer to the normal language of the patient such as Competence and Satisfaction may be substituted if necessary. The attention of the patient is drawn to the more positive aspects of his activities which can be used to provide evidence that he is selectively attending to the negative and discounting the positive. If the assessments are clearly too low or apparently inaccurate these can be challenged.

Experience gained from activity scheduling can be used to plan a timetable which increases the opportunity for satisfying events or reintro-

Name: John Smith   Week beginning: 10/2/92

	Mon	Tues	Wed	Thurs	Fri	Sat	Sun
9–10	Watch TV A=0 P=2	Slept late A=0 P=1					
10–11	Had coffee – radio on A=0 P=1	Read paper (jobs) A=3 P=3					
11–12	Looked at paper (jobs) A=1 P=0	Went to job centre A=1 P=0					
12–1	Went for walk A=2 P=4	Looked at TV A=0 P=3					
1–2	Helped get lunch A=3 P=2	Helped get lunch A=2 P=1					
2–3	Washed up A=2 P=0	Washed up A=2 P=0					
3–4	Mended plug A=4 P=4	Met children A=2 P=4					
4–5	Gave children tea A=3 P=5	Gave children tea A=3 P=5					
5–6	Children's video A=1 P=4	Watched TV A=0 P=2					
6–7	Made a model box A=4 P=4	Wrote to Jose A=3 P=3					
7–8	Children's bedtime A=3 P=4	Children's bedtime A=3 P=4					
8–12	Watched TV A=0 P=2	Watched TV A=0 P=2					

Figure 9.1 Weekly activity schedule

duces those which were previously satisfying but which have been allowed to lapse. These changes are not too time-consuming as much of the work is done by the patient at home. They should, however, be carefully negotiated as sometimes previous enthusiasms have become associated with the onset of depression and their reintroduction may not be feasible or therapeutic. Under these circumstances an alternative is to look to those subjects in which he has in the past been only mildly interested or to those that seem attractive but have never been explored.

As much time as is available during the session should be used in dealing with the blocks to progress. These may be chiefly of two types: (i) thoughts getting in the way of carrying out assignments, which can be explored and if possible dealt with in advance; and (ii) upsets during the homework period preventing progress, such as rows at home, unexpected adverse events, drinking bouts and so on. It may be powerfully helpful to suggest to the patient in advance that some such difficulties may be expected and to rehearse his possible response to them. Activity schedules and later automatic thought diaries can be adapted if they prove difficult to use in the standard lay-out.

Cognitive Techniques

This is the final and perhaps most sophisticated stage of the package but it should not prove too daunting as many of the strategies fit well into the primary care consultation and the principles will be familiar from earlier sections. The objectives are to recognise and modify;

(1) Negative and distorted thinking patterns.

(2) Rigid and unhelpful life rules and assumptions.

Recognising and Recording Negative Automatic Thoughts

As a preliminary it is necessary to emphasise that thinking patterns and interpretation of events affect mood. A simple example might be that emotion caused by finding a letter from the Tax Authorities in your post is greatly influenced by whether you are expecting a rebate or a demand. The depressed patient will always assume that it is a demand. A start is then made on training the patient to identify, count and challenge negative automatic thoughts. These thoughts are automatic, unreasonable, plausible and involuntary (Beck 1979). They may be recognised by replay rehearsal of a particular scene in the consultation and by asking the question 'What is going through your (my) mind at this moment?' Often they will be fleeting and although they are powerful enough to affect mood they may be forgotten soon after the event. Once spotted they are recorded by means of a record of *negative automatic thoughts* (NATS) (Figure 9.3) on which is written the date and time, the emotion or feeling, the situation and the automatic thoughts associated with that situation.

Date/ Time	Emotion(s) *What do you feel? How bad is it (0–100)?*	Situation *What were you doing or thinking about?*	Automatic thoughts *What exactly were your thoughts? How far do you believe them (0–100)?*
13/2 9.00 am	Sadness 90%	Received job refusal letter	I will never get another job 80%
15/2 4.00pm	Guilt 100%	Unable to give money for children's new blazers	I'm hopeless as a father 70% They should be able to depend on me 80%

Figure 9.2 Short daily record

These thoughts may be hard to recognise at first and occur as images or meanings as well as words. Often considerable practise is required by the patient in the actual situation before thoughts can be accurately identified. Paradoxically they may have become so much a normal part of the patient's thinking that he fails to recognise them as a separate phenomenon. Once recognised, these thoughts can be counted and the patient will often come to realise that the more of them he has in a particular day the worse he feels. Practise at acknowledging them as NATs and then dismissing them can follow. The most important stage, however, is to learn to challenge the validity and usefulness of the NATs.

Answering and Challenging Thoughts

Once a reliable record of thoughts is being produced, a start can be made with challenging and answering them. Again a chart is used but this time there are two further columns to allow for the recording of *Answering Thought* and *Outcome*.

Date	Emotion(s) *What do you feel? How bad was it (0–100)?*	Situation *What were you doing or thinking about?*	Automatic thoughts *What exactly were your thoughts? How far did you believe each of them (0–100)?*	Rational Response *What are your rational answers to the automatic thoughts? How far do you believe each of them (0–100)?*	Outcome *1. How far do you now believe the thoughts (0–100)? 2. How do you feel (0–100)? 3. What can you do now?*
13/2/92 9.00am	Sadness 90%	Received job refusal letter	I will never get another job 80%	There is a recession. Most people have to apply more than once 70%	30% Sad 70% Apply as often as possible
15/2/92	Guilt 100%	Unable to give money for children's new blazers	I'm hopeless as a father 70% They should be able to depend on me 80%	They know I love them and don't notice old clothes 60% They can depend on me for many things 90%	30% Guilt 50% Show them I love them in other ways

Figure 9.3 Daily record of automatic thoughts (full thought record)

This again is done largely between sessions but guidance as to the procedure used will be needed. There are a number of different techniques that can be used but most revolve round four groups of questions:

(1) Does the evidence support the way you think or is it against it? What objective evidence do you have to back it up? Would somebody else accept that evidence?

Example:

Date/ Time	Situation	Feelings	Immediate Thought	Answer
10/3 9 am	Office – Jim didn't say 'Good Morning'	Worthless	He must think I'm useless and has gone off me.	Perhaps he didn't notice or was concentrating on the balance sheet.

This is also an example of jumping to conclusions. Depressed people assume without any evidence that people are thinking critically about them (thought reading).

(2) What alternatives are there to the explanation (usually negative) that you have given? Is there another more positive alternative?
Example:

Date/ Time	Situation	Feelings	Immediate Thought	Answer
11/8 6 pm	Girl friend refused to go for a drink	Sad	It's all over, I'm not attractive to women.	Perhaps she had to finish her report and she will come out later in the week.

This is also an example of thinking in all-or-nothing terms and catastrophising (see thinking errors-below).

(3) What is the effect of thinking in this way? Does it help the situation? Does it help you get what you want out of life or is it getting in your way? Is there a more constructive way of thinking?
Example:

> *Thought* – I must always know all the answers and be able to show the juniors how to do it.
>
> *Advantage* – Enjoying feeling more knowledgeable than younger colleagues.
>
> *Disadvantage* – There's bound to come a time when I don't know all the answers and then I'll feel worthless. Nobody can know everything all the time.

Brooding over meaningless questions like 'Why is life so unfair?' 'Why didn't I make a different decision in the past?' 'Why do these things always happen to me?' is bound to be depressing as these questions have no useful answer and cannot help the solution of current problems.

(4) What thinking errors are you making? Some of these have been mentioned above. Others include:

  (a) condemning yourself on the basis of a single mistake 'I forgot Sue's birthday so I must be a hopeless husband'

  (b) taking personally casual happenings 'They always run out of corn flakes at the supermarket the day I need them' or

(c)   concentrating on the things which have gone wrong 'That was a really terrible day because the car wouldn't start'

(d)   not noticing or acknowledging good things like the boss congratulating you on your hard work on the new contract and Tracy winning the music prize.

Example:

Date/ Time	Situation	Feelings	Immediate Thought	Answer
11/2 11 am	Boss said to be sure to finish the job	Anxious	I've got it wrong again. I'll be made redundant.	It's an important job. He must think I'm reliable or he would have given it to one of the others.

Thinking errors fall into a number of different categories for example;

Thinking Errors

- *All or Nothing Thinking* – 'If I don't get this right I'm a complete waste of time'.
- *Overgeneralisation* – 'I'm always making mistakes'.
- *Mental Filter* – 'Nothing ever goes right at work'.
- *Discounting the Positive* – 'She was only feeling sorry for me'.
- *Mind Reading* – 'Everybody thinks I am a wimp'.
- *Catastrophising* – 'Failing the driving test will be the end of everything'.
- *Global Judgements* – 'I didn't get the job so I'm useless'.
- *Personalisation* – 'they always pick on me for the night shift'.

Challenging distorted thinking is done by *Socratic Questioning*. The therapist asks questions which lead the patient to examine the evidence himself. There are an infinite number of possible lines of questioning but some of the most promising are:

Challenging Negative Automatic Thoughts

- What is the evidence?
- Is that logical?
- Am I assuming thoughts are facts?

- ◦ Am I overestimating the probability?
- ◦ Am I underestimating my resources?
- ◦ Am I assuming every situation is the same?
- ◦ What would I think if I wasn't depressed (or next year)?
- ◦ What would another person think?
- ◦ What are the advantages and disadvantages of thinking like this?

(Relate these questions to the list of thinking errors)

When examining faulty thinking the technique of *distancing* is easily learned and particularly helpful. Distancing may be spatial in which case the patient is asked to imagine his reactions to another person in the situation which he is facing, or it may be temporal in which case he is asked to imagine his own reactions during a previous (or future) period of his life.

For Example:

'Would you regard your friend Bill as a total failure as a husband if he forgot his wife's birthday?' This may lead to an exploration of the double standard used by the patient in evaluating his own actions and those of others.

'If you had this bump with the car a year ago how would you have dealt with it?' It may turn out that the same event in a previous time would have produced a very different reaction.

'How would you have felt if you had not been depressed?' may also be a useful line of questioning.

The attitude to exploring thinking errors must be one of experimental co-operation rather than didactic instruction. Not all the hypotheses tried will be valid and there must be a readiness to reformulate ideas in the light of new data.

CBT in Primary Care

Although it may seem that this approach is too complex and time-consuming to be easily adaptable to the primary care setting, there are several compensating advantages (Paykel and Priest 1992):

(1) The techniques are easily broken down for use in very short contact sessions. One thought, thinking error or assumption can be examined at a time.

(2) The individual techniques can be usefully employed without a commitment to the whole package being necessary.

With the severe depressive much time may have to be spent in activity recording, and scheduling. The cognitive elements of thought spotting and the correction of thinking errors, however, can often be introduced much more rapidly with the mild depression often seen in primary care.

(3) Much of the work is done by the patient himself between sessions.

The Use of Homework

The behavioural element of the treatment requires that the Weekly Activity Schedule is completed at home. Initially this simply records activities but subsequently it is used to plan new ones, first by increasing components giving higher scores in achievement or pleasure and then by including new confidence-building items. Session time can be used to rehearse the problems which may be encountered in carrying out these schedules and discussing ways round those difficulties actually experienced in the previous week.

Progress in spotting, counting and challenging negative automatic thoughts and rating belief in them is more reliably assessed in homework where the patient is on his own away from the influence of the therapist.

An extremely important element of homework is the construction of experiments to test the validity of predictions. A depressed mother may believe she is a total failure 'because all the other mothers I know get their children to go to bed without a fuss but I can't'. After discussing the evidence for this assertion an experiment may be set up whereby the patient asks other mothers of her acquaintance whether they ever experience such difficulties. It may be that the patient will be much more relieved to find that they do. Even if it turns out that they don't it may become obvious that they do have problems in other areas of child rearing.

Experiments testing predictions should if possible be of the 'no-lose' variety so that even if the patient's negative prediction is supported the information can be used to help in further treatment. The negative results of a first experiment can be used to explore further thinking errors and once a different method of thinking is found a further experiment may be arranged, this time, possibly, with more positive results.

Assumptions

These form the third element of the cognitive model presented earlier. They are the information processing templates and life rules which we all have learnt. These basic beliefs are often useful but if they are too rigid and extreme they may predispose us to depression and other problems. They can often be recognised when the patient talks about 'should' and 'must' or 'always' or 'never', indicating that contact is being made with underlying belief systems. Their origins often lie deep in childhood-learning, when we first began to organise information about the world and set standards.

These are often tackled last, after symptoms have improved, mainly with the object of helping to prevent recurrence. Some arise out of the identifiable folklore of childhood, for example 'you must finish all your jobs or mummy won't like you', 'you shouldn't answer back', 'nice girls don't do that' or 'you must work hard and pass all your exams'. Built in to all these examples is the idea that if you fail in any of these respects you are in some way worthless. Other assumptions come from more sophisticated and less overt learning by modelling or reinforcement. As well as 'shoulds' and 'musts' they include statements about the catastrophic or awful effects of events, ideas of human worth rated on some internal absolute scale and the necessity of certain things if any sort of happiness is to be found.

Dysfunctional assumptions or schemata have the following characteristics:

(1) They are *untrue* or *irrational* – exaggerated, not supported by evidence or unreal.

(2) They are *commands* – not conditional or relative. Demands versus wishes, shoulds versus preferences, needs versus wants.

(3) They *disturb emotions* by being extreme and overwhelming. Depression versus unhappiness, anger versus irritation, anxiety versus concern.

(4) They *do not* help *attain goals* as they perpetually get in the way.

Beck (1979) specified some of the assumptions frequently found in depression:

- 'In order to be happy, I have to be successful in whatever I undertake'.
- 'To be happy, I must be accepted by all people at all times'.
- 'If I make a mistake it means that I am inept'.
- 'I can't live without you'.
- 'If somebody disagrees with me, it means he doesn't like me.'
- 'My value as a person depends on what others think of me.'

Exposing the nature of these assumptions and the potential that they have for damage may in itself promote their change. More specifically, however, they may be tackled by the vertical arrow technique in which a statement is explored by examining the meaning to the patient at deeper and deeper levels until the underlying assumption is uncovered.

Example:
'I've had a row with my wife. I feel terrible'

↓

(What does that mean to you?)

↓

'It means I've upset her and she'll feel miserable'

↓

(If that's true what does it mean to you?)

↓

'It means I'm a lousy husband'

↓

(If that's true what does it say about you?)

↓

'A lousy husband is a worthless person'

In other words: 'My estimation of my worth as a person depends on success in every aspect of every relationship'.

Other techniques include experiments to see what happens if the patient for once does not follow his particular 'shoulds' or 'nevers' which will often reveal that no dire consequences result. These experiments may either be done in reality or rehearsal.

Long Term Effects of Cognitive Therapy for Depression

Whilst most research evidence shows cognitive therapy and pharma-cotherapy to be about equally effective there is currently no outcome research on the short contact combined approach outlined here. Interest recently has focused on the capacity for cognitive approaches to prevent long term relapse and treat more complex cases. It might be expected that cognitive techniques once learnt could be recalled in the case of later need. Evidence is beginning to accumulate that this is so (Paykel 1989). Scott (1995) found that long term outcome was best after cognitive therapy with patients with high dysfunctional attitudes but worst with those whose problems were com-pounded by personality disorders or learning difficulties. Miller (1995) found cognitive therapy more effective than pharmacotherapy in moderately but not severely depressed in-patients on follow up. It is a reflection of the different styles of health care management in the United States and Britain that in the USA patients with moderate depression (Hamilton Depression Rating Scale Scores of 17–22) may find themselves treated as in-patients. The jury is clearly still out on these issues and more information will become available as more long-term studies are reported. There is a great need for outcome and follow up studies of simple primary care interventions.

References

APA (1994) *Diagnostic and Statistical Manual of Mental Disorders: Fourth Edition*. Washington: American Psychiatric Association.

Beck, A.T. (1990) 'Cognitive therapy: a 30 year retrospective.' *American Psychologist 46*, 368–375.

Beck, A.T., Rush, A.J., Shaw, B.F. and Emery, G. (1979) *Cognitive Therapy of Depression*. Chichester: John Wiley.

Blackburn, I.M., Bishop, S., Glen, A.I., Whalley, I.J. and Christie, J.E. (1981) 'The efficacy of cognitive therapy in depression: A treatment trial using cognitive therapy and pharmacotherapy, each alone and in combination.' *British Journal of Psychiatry 139*, 181–9.

Brown, G.W. and Harris, T. *Social Origins of Depression*. London: Tavistock.

Goldberg, D.P. and Huxley, P. (1980) *Mental Illness in the Community*. London: Tavistock.

Johnson, D.A.W. (1981) 'Depression: treatment compliance in general practice.' *Acta Psychiatrica Scandinavica 63*, 290, 447–453.

Miller, I.W. (1995) 'Predictors of long-term treatment response in depressed inpatients.' Paper presented World Congress of Behavioural and Cognitive Therapies: Copenhagen.

Paykel, E.S. (1989) 'Treatment of depression: the relevance of research for clinical practice.' *British Journal of Psychiatry 155*, 754–63.

Paykel, E.S. and Priest, R.G. (1992) 'Recognition and management of depression in general practice: consensus statement.' *British Medical Journal 305*, 1198–1202.

Scott, J. (1995) 'Cognitive therapy with chronically depressed in-patients: A four year follow up study.' Paper presented World Congress of Behavioural and Cognitive Therapies. Copenhagen.

Seligman, M.E.P. (1975) *Hopelessness: On Depression, Development and Death*. San Fransisco: Freeman.

Teasdale, J. (1985) 'Psychological treatments for depression: How do they work?' *Behaviour Research and Therapy 23*, 157–65.

Materials:

Beck Depression Inventory published by The Psychological Corporation, Harcourt, Brace and Co. 24–28 Oval Road, London NW1 7DX. Tel.: (0171) 267 4466.

Recommended for Further Reading

Beck, A.T., Shaw, A.J., Rush, B.F. and Emery, G. (1979) *Cognitive Therapy of Depression*. Chichester: John Wiley.

Williams, J. and Mark, G. (1984, 2nd ed. 1994) *The Psychological Treatment of Depression; a Guide to the Theory and Practice of Cognitive Behaviour Therapy.* London and New York: Routledge.

Books for Patients (See also General Appendix for leaflet series)

Beck, A.T. and Greenberg, R.L. (1974) *Coping with Depression.* New York: Institute for Rational Living.
Goldberg, D.P.B. (1984) *Depression.* London: Churchill Livingston.
See also BABCP, Oxford and Royal College of Psychiatrists Leaflets in Appendix.

Videos

These tend to be made, or at least sponsored, by pharmaceutical companies and predictably are not strong on psychological treatments:

What You Really Need to Know about Depression – informative professional production made by Dr Rob Buckman and John Cleese. Reasonable mention of psychological treatments. Good address list on box. Lasts 30 minutes. Available from Pfizer Ltd, Sandwich, Kent CT13 9NG. Tel. (01304) 616161. Made by Videos for Patients.

Dealing with Depression – the Patient – much more sketchy particularly with regards to treatment. Lasts 20 minutes. Available from Smith Kline Beecham Pharmaceuticals, Mundells, Welwyn Garden City, Hertfordshire AL7 1EY. Tel. (01707) 325111.

Useful Addresses

Centre for Cognitive Therapy, 133 South 36th Street, Philadelphia, Pennsylvania 19104, USA.
Fellowship of Depressives Anonymous, 36 Chestnut Avenue, Beverley, North Humberside, HU17 9QU. Tel: 01482 860619.
Depressives Associated, PO Box 1022, LONDON, SE1 7QB. Tel: 0181760 0544.
The Samaritans can be found in all local directories.

Chapter Ten

Cognitions and Behaviour in Health Care

Thinking, Feeling, Acting and Surviving

At the outset there is a dilemma. This chapter and the next will consider the way in which cognitions, emotions and behaviour can influence and be influenced by, bodily health. In order to do this the dualism of Rene Descartes (Descartes (1912) translated by Haldane and Ross) – the mind and body divide – has to be operationally resurrected from the honourable burial to which modern holistic approaches have consigned it. The effect of the mind on the body cannot be considered unless it is accepted, at least initially, that a distinction can be drawn between the two.

It is particularly important to understand the interaction of physical, social and psychological factors and their impact, particularly on older patients and those with chronic physical illness. The assessment of functioning must cover chronic and acute health problems as well as loneliness, poverty, bereavement and immobility. Past functioning and coping must be investigated before leaping in with antidepressants or any rigid cognitive – behavioural intervention.

Beliefs, perceptions and behaviour may affect physical health in three main areas:

First, in the *use of services*, such as the decision who, when and where to consult, adherence to treatment regimes whether self-administered or pre-scribed by others and in the interactions with carers both professional and voluntary.

Second, in the regulation of *life style factors*, both self injurious such as unwise sexual behaviour, incautious driving or the misuse of tobacco, alcohol or other drugs and positive such as increasing exercise, improving diet and achieving a proper proportion of rest and recreation.

Third, the exciting but still somewhat obscure area of the *direct effect* of cognitive behavioural factors on bodily systems such as the heart and circulation, the gastrointestinal tract and the immune system.

This chapter in the main attempts to address the first two of these areas whilst the next will look chiefly at the third.

Communication, Understanding and the Recall of Information

Most clinicians think that they are good communicators. Most patients want to know as much as possible about their health and their treatment (Morris 1990). Criticism from patients is uncommon but in eleven general practice studies over twenty years a mean of 28 per cent of patients showed dissatisfaction with the information they had received (Ley 1988). The adequacy of information is closely correlated with consultation satisfaction; which in turn is closely correlated with regime adherence. In the relatively restricted and straightforward area of prescribing only a mean of 29.5 per cent of patients felt that they had been given enough information (Gibbs *et al.* 1990). There seem to be problems with particular types of patients. Couples, adolescents and medically trained people were all found difficult, by doctors themselves. Particular types of problem also seem to cause difficulties for both doctors and patients. Both groups were uncomfortable with sexual and drug abuse problems. Doctors tend to prefer somatic to psychological diagnoses which perhaps reflects the strong bias of medical teaching which still all too often stresses that psychological diagnosis should not be entertained until a physical one has been excluded. This is a spurious order of priorities and excludes the possibility of physical, psychological and social factors all being present.

Patients also prefer a 'somatic' ticket of entry into the system. One reason for this is a reflection of the doctor's own usual bias. Another is that patients fear to be thought weak or, even worse, mad, and treated accordingly with all the stigma perceived to be involved. The patient may also believe that co-existing physical conditions will be disregarded and not receive proper treatment.

The traditional scheme of medical interviewing taught to the clinician medical student on his first day on the wards is also to blame. It is rigid, highly physically biased and completely directed by the doctor who asks a set of routine questions (Byrne and Long 1976). Enquiries about family, home, job and the impact or interpretation of the problem are usually scanty or absent altogether. Although early reports suggested that new GPs, with the benefit of vocational training changed their personal attributes (Freeman and Byrne 1976), even the tri-axial emphasis of the MRCGP exam, which it should be noted is only just acquiring a practical clinical content, seems to have achieved few demonstrable changes in patient satisfaction (Ley 1988). It should be noted however that patient expectations may well have increased over a similar period and many consultations in primary care are now given by other team members besides GPs.

There are three main areas in which the consultation can be improved:

(1) Providing an interview that is satisfactory in the patient's estimation.

(2) Elucidating accurately the patient's problem(s).

(3) Giving information about management which is likely to be remembered.

Satisfaction with the Consultation

This can be secured in the following ways:

- A friendly rather than business manner on the part of the doctor.

- An understanding by the doctor of the patient's real concerns.

- A consultation that does not thwart the expectations of the patient. (Korsch et al. 1968)

Accurate Identification of Problems

Symptoms must be clarified beyond the mere label to find out what they actually mean, when and where they occur and what other factors affect them. Typical examples would be 'can't sleep' and 'giddy attacks' neither of which yields any useful information until it is explored further. This has already been discussed in detail in Chapter Three.

Goldberg and Huxley (1980, p.80) identified ten definable and teachable behaviours which predicted the family doctor's success as a case detector. These are, at the outset of an interview:

(1) Makes immediate eye contact.

(2) Clarifies the presenting complaint.

(3) Uses directive questions for physical complaints.

(4) Uses 'open to closed' line of questioning, i.e. the interview starts with open questions of the 'How have things been?' 'Are there any other worries?' 'How has this affected you?' type and then goes on to find out in detail what are the factors relevant to each symptom by closed, direct questioning of the more traditional kind.

(5) Empathetic style (frequency), i.e. how often the doctor appears to understand the patient's feelings or put himself in the patient's place by his comments or questions.

(6) Sensitive to verbal cues, i.e. he can change his line of enquiry in response to some half-dropped hint.

(7) Sensitive to non-verbal cues, i.e. as above but in response to a gesture or a grimace.

(8) Does not read notes or use the computer during the history. This is a very common vice and yet it is the simplest thing in the world to say politely to the patient 'Would you mind if I just had a minute to catch up on/remind myself of your records?'

(9) Can deal with over talkativeness. Being able to listen to the patient does not imply sitting in silence whilst the irrelevant complaints about distant relatives or domestic pets are described.

(10) Asks fewer questions about past history. We have stressed before the importance of a predominantly here-and-now approach although we do not deny that past history can be extremely relevant and important.

We would add to these that a question about how the patient sees his problem, and how it is affecting his daily life should be considered in every clinical interview. It is also important to check that the patient does under-stand the terms that the doctor uses. A number of studies have demonstrated that a substantial proportion of patients do not understand commonly used medical terms and even more patients have major misconceptions about common anatomy (Ley and Llewelyn 1995).

Management Information

Finally the patient must know what he has to do. First, is he able and willing to respond to the offered regime? Rheumatology and respiratory clinics advise patients to lose weight or stop smoking without any attempt to consider how they might do it. The patient must have the resources in his repertory or if not he must be helped to obtain them. It follows that any advice is much more likely to be effective if it is compatible with the patient's existing lifestyle or preferences. Second, the patient must remember the advice if he is to follow it. Much information given in consultations is forgotten. A number of factors may help to recall them (Becker and Rosenstock 1984):

(1) Important information should be stressed and given first.

(2) Instructions should be simple and given in plain language whether written or verbal. Newspapers are good at this; doctors and, sadly, psychologists often are not.

(3) Instructions can be repeated at the same or different consultations. The patient may be encouraged to go through them himself but his dignity should not be offended.

(4) Advice should be specific, fore example, 'Walk a mile a day' not 'take more exercise' or 'drink a half pint of water morning and evening' not 'have plenty of fluids'.

(5) Checks should be made that he has understood and should give him an opportunity to say if he has not.

(6) The advice should be arranged in a stated order, for example, 'I am going to tell you what is wrong, what I am going to do, what you should do and what I expect will happen. Now first, what's wrong....'.

Hospital advice often seems less well understood than primary care management and time can usefully be spent checking that hospital instructions have been understood when the patient returns to the primary care. This may become more necessary as treatment becomes more sophisticated.

Health Beliefs and Adherence to Treatment Regimes

Doctors find the failure of patients to follow their advice puzzling, frustrating and irritating. After all, why should a patient seek their help and fail to follow their advice? A number of studies, however, have rated non-adherence at between 40 per cent and 50 per cent for a wide range of treatments of many different conditions (Ley 1982a). What is more easily forgotten is that health professionals also often fail to adhere to known rules for optimum care (Ley 1988).

Why Do We Fail?

The reasons for this paradox are complex and have not been fully explored (Maguire 1984). Satisfaction with the consultation and understanding of the proposed management are, as has been discussed above, extremely important. More specifically:

(1) The patient may not understand the nature or the significance of the condition. For example, a woman with post-coital bleeding is less likely to follow advice to see a gynaecologist if she believes the condition is due to muscle strain and is ignorant of the possibility of cancer.

(2) The patient may not understand the nature and effect of the treatment. A young woman needing hysterectomy for fibroids may refuse surgery

if she believes she will be spayed and has not been told her ovaries and their sex hormones will be conserved.

(3) The patient may expect adverse effects from treatment. A depressed patient is less likely to take antidepressants if he thinks they are tranquillisers which he has been led to believe from the media are addictive.

(4) The patient may be unprepared for the complexities of the advice given. A patient who feels tired and is asking for a tonic may genuinely expect a 'magic bullet' which will cure her at once. She may be unprepared for the suggestion that her problems have many factors. These may involve her children, job, husband, lifestyle and menstrual pattern which will all need to be considered if rational answers are to be found.

(5) The same patient in the previous example may understand the advice but be completely without the resources to carry it out for lack of mobility, money or housing.

(6) In their thinking doctors recognise two types of patient, those that follow their advice and get better or at least benefit and those who reject it and remain ill or get worse. They are much less ready to come to terms with the other two possible groups; those who follow advice and don't benefit, and those who reject it and still get better. A moment's reflection is enough to realise that both these groups are sizeable. Operant theory, which has been discussed in Chapter Five, clearly indicates the importance of these groups. Co-operation is extinguished in the third group and non-co-operation reinforced in the fourth. Personal or hearsay experience in the first two groups will increase the likelihood of medical advice being followed. The opposite, of course, is true of the others. The man who is told his chest pain is indigestion and will respond to antacids is less likely to take them if his father received the same advice and dropped dead of a heart attack shortly afterwards.

These factors influencing treatment adherence are summarised in the Health Belief Model:

1. Belief about susceptibility to
   disease increases

2. Belief about the likely severity
   of disease increases   The likelihood
                                                           of adherence
3. Belief about the likely benefit of
   treatment increases

4. Belief about likely barriers to
   treatment decreases

(Source: Becker and Rosenstock 1984)

Several factors predict non-adherence:

∘ Duration and complexity of the regime.

∘ Patients' general dissatisfaction with the service.

∘ Lack of supportive follow-up.

An out-patient study in an hypertension clinic found that drop-out rate was related to waiting time and non-availability and variations in staff. There is no reason why these effects should not be the same in primary care. Increasing off duty and decreasing use of personal lists may well therefore be interfering with successful management.

Effects are not only clinical. A survey indicated that probably 20 to 25 per cent of all hospital admissions were due to lapses in treatment (Ausburn 1981). The cost is substantial.

In spite of the evidence, however, many clinicians still give the problem scant attention.

Possible Remedies

(1) Improvement in communication as outlined in the last section.
    Although immediately appealing as a remedy, experience and studies (Ley 1988) show that there is a considerable lack of adherence by medical staff to such principles of good practice. Either they are never learnt or if learnt are soon forgotten

(2) The use of written material. This may either be in the form of;

   (a)   general information leaflets about a particular condition or
         medical topic

(b)   specific warnings about health hazards such as those associated with smoking, alcohol or unsafe sex

(c)   drug leaflets included with prescribed or over the counter medicines warning of specific side effects or interactions.

General information is useful in clinical management and usually welcomed by clinician and patient alike. It is important that it is couched in simple, understandable language. The Flesch Formula for reading ease gives a useful way of measuring this (Flesch 1948). A limitation is the capacity of the primary care worker to store quantities of such material in such a way that it is accessible.

Specific warnings have been widely adopted with certain high profile health topics. Their effect has been hard to evaluate and outcome research presents difficulties. There would appear to be an extinction of the effect of such warnings with repeated exposure, lack of confirmatory evidence ('I smoked cigarettes and haven't got cancer') and possibly increasing age (Centre for Behaviour Research in Cancer 1992).

The Elderly Patient

There are a number of additional techniques which are particularly helpful with the elderly patient who may find remembering to follow instructions particularly difficult. These can also sometimes be used with the younger age group.

(1)   When remembering to take medicines, a container where the day's dose can be put into compartments marked 'breakfast', 'lunch', 'tea' and 'before bed' by the patient or a carer is extremely useful. Such containers are now widely available from pharmacies.

(2)   The doctor should try to give instructions to a relative or friend as well as the patient.

(3)   It is important to make sure the patient can take the form of medicine prescribed, i.e. open containers or swallow pills.

(4)   Patients should be encouraged to destroy or, preferably, return old medicines – many elderly patients' medicine cupboards contain truly horrifying quantities of unused drugs.

Coping Styles and the Preparation for Stressful Medical Procedures

The role of psychological preparation for stressful medical procedures has received a good deal of attention (Johnston and Wallace 1990, Mathews and Ridgeway 1984). Recent work has concentrated on monitoring (information seeking) and blunting (avoidance and distraction) coping styles and their possible relationship to endogenous opioid secretion (Bruhl *et al.* 1994). The questions that we must try and answer are:

(1) Is psychological preparation of use in the type of medical procedures undertaken by GPs and if so in which?

(2) Has the GP a role to play in the preparation for hospital treatment and if so, what role?

Almost all the research that has been undertaken to date has involved hospital populations and much of it has been done with patients about to undergo surgery, who form a reasonably homogenous group which can be studied with scientific rigour. There are, however, two problems for the clinician that arise with these studies. Any assessment and intervention by hospital teams must take place; (a) after the admission to hospital which may in itself be a more stressful event than the surgery; and (b) in the very limited time available between the admission and the operation.

It is, however, interesting to summarise these studies, which in themselves provide a number of important leads about the direction of possible future primary care research and interventions. The methods of preparation attempted, have included:

(1) Information about the procedure to be undertaken, i.e. what is done, who will do it and how it will be done. This appears to affect outcome only very weakly if at all.

(2) Information about the physical sensations to be experienced, i.e. 'you will feel sick, a burning pain' and so on.

(3) Information about outcome which is often not clearly given or clearly understood by the patient. A suitable framework to consider what is needed might be as follows:

- ○ Will life expectancy be more/ less?
- ○ Will function be worse/better?
- ○ Will pain be more /less?
- ○ Will there be more/less disfigurement?
- ○ Will more/less care be needed from others? (*Source:* Kincey 1995)

With the help of this information the patient is not only able to make an informed decision about consenting to surgery or other treatment but also if it is undertaken will be much more confident at the time of the procedure.

(4) Behavioural instruction, for example, 'you should walk 330 yds', 'hold your side when you cough', is helpful if given clearly.

(5) Relaxation, either general or cued to specific situations or symptoms, has been discussed in the previous sections and appears to produce rather equivocal results.

(6) Cognitive coping techniques which involve identifying any anxiety provoking thoughts and finding an answer to them. For example, 'I am afraid they will find cancer when they do the operation'. This might be answered with 'It's a common operation which several of my friends have had. None of them have had cancer so why should I have it'.

The consensus of opinion is that the last technique of preparation is the most effective and the most universally applicable. It is also unfortunately the most difficult to use as measures such as information booklets or tapes need very careful design.

It seems that the information techniques must be used with care as a percentage of patients cope well with stress naturally by avoidance and distraction. These patients will not be helped and may actually find it more difficult to cope if provided with unsolicited information.

The published work outside the hospital surgical setting has been mainly in connection with dentistry (Anderson and Masur 1983) apart from one paper where sensory and procedural information was given when IUCDs were fitted (Newton and Reading 1977). The outcome measures in these studies were mainly self-report scales of pain with the occasional physiological measure such as GSR (Galvanic Skin Response). There have been a number of papers reporting positive results. It would seem worthwhile to use these techniques, with evaluation, more extensively for primary care procedures such as injections of soft tissue and joints, vaginal examinations, IUCD fitting and possibly in obstetrics.

Another interesting area is that of providing training in coping techniques for hospital patients well before admission. This would seem to have two possible advantages. First the techniques could be practised before the distractions and anxieties of admission arrived, and secondly much more time would be available for their perfection. It might, however, be difficult to obtain co-operation from patients whose procedures were not imminent. Kincey (1995) and Kincey and Saltmore (1990) give an outline programme of psychological care of surgical patients which may be summarised as follows:

Pre-operative Stage

- ° The goals of surgery are clearly explained (see above).
- ° A check is made on the patient's level of knowledge and understanding.
- ° The clinician must discuss risk realising that the patient may have a different perception of the real meaning of the risk figures mentioned and be using different value systems.

An estimate may be made as to whether the patient employs an 'approach' or 'avoidant' style of coping. If information is sought it should be given. If it is not actively sought essential information should be given but the patient merely informed that more is available if needed.

Immediate Post-operative Stage (usually hospital)

- ° After general anaesthetics verbal feedback confirms that the planned procedure was performed.
- ° During local anaesthetics the surgeon and other staff must realise that casual remarks may be easily misinterpreted by a hypervigilant patient.
- ° Clear self-care information is given after the operation.

Later Post-operative Care

- ° The primary care worker reviews the patients reaction to the procedure and clarifies if further information need be sought from any specialist involved.
- ° The emotions of bereavement may appear after major surgery. Anger, anxiety and depression should be discussed and allowed.
- ° Lay support groups and professional aftercare services such as Stoma Care may be needed at this point.

The role of family coping in preparing children for stressful medical procedures is reviewed by Melamed (1993).

Pregnancy, Childbirth and the Puerperium

Our previous book (France and Robson 1986) stated that:

> 'The explosion of literature in the behavioural medicine field has left
> maternity care relatively untouched. The reasons for this are unclear
> but may be associated with the transient nature of pregnancy and the
> rigid stance of most obstetric units, both of which make research
> difficult. Change in the management of pregnancy involves attitudinal
> and behavioural modification in obstetric and midwifery hierarchies
> often more interested in their concepts of obstetric 'safety' than in the
> treatment of parturient women as intelligent and sensitive human
> beings. It is possible that only by demonstrating that obstetric safety
> is indeed affected by these considerations that progress will be made.'

It is good to report that during the decade since that was written the battle
appears to have been largely won. Midwife lead units are now the rule rather
than the exception and mothers are permitted to determine the place and
manner of their delivery to a much greater extent and the anxieties and
emotional needs of parturient women are much better appreciated (Department of Health 1993, Green et al. 1990). Some caution is, however, needed.
Scientific investigation of the prediction of birth outcomes is somewhat
confused (Lobel 1994). The pattern of care is still patchy with the more high
technology units being on the whole less psychologically aware and the
finding of post traumatic stress disorder in thirty women, out of a self-se-
lected sample of a hundred who had undergone distressing obstetric or
gynaecological procedures is alarming (Menage 1993). It is also sad that the
GP's role in intrapartum obstetric care has further diminished, thus removing
an important link with continuing family care. There is also evidence that
reducing professional contact during pregnancy according to a 'new style'
care schedule reduced understanding and satisfaction during pregnancy
(Sikorski et al. 1996).

The essential elements of primary maternity care are as follows:

During the Antenatal Period

(1) As much *information* as possible concerning the physiology and
    management of pregnancy, involving not only talks, films and
    question-and-answer sessions for both parents but also feed-back on
    the various procedures. These include allowing the mother to see the
    baby on a real-time ultrasound scanner with expert and sensitive
    comments (Reading and Cox 1982) on the features seen and an

explanation of the nature and purpose of blood tests, all in easily understood language.

(2) Dealing with *negative thoughts and feelings* about being able to cope with labour, motherhood or related subjects. The mother must be allowed an unhurried opportunity to express her ambivalent feelings which can then be addressed by further factual explanation and the usual cognitive strategies. Open questions such as 'How do you feel about having the baby?' 'Are there any worries or problems?' may be needed to start the discussion.

(3) *Physical relaxation training and familiarisation with surroundings* is routine in obstetric practices but it is important to consider with individual patients how they are going to use it in labour and also cue it to other sources of tension such as early difficulties in breast feeding. If hospital delivery is chosen, a very important way of decreasing mothers' anxiety is to expose them as much as possible to the labour ward or delivery suite during pregnancy. This will assist them in achieving a sense of control over the childbirth environment which is now recognised as being so important (Dept of Health 1993). It is a good desensitisation exercise, as there can be few things more anxiety-provoking than to find yourself in a vulnerable and highly apprehensive condition surrounded by unfamiliar sights and sounds loaded with personal threat.

(4) Other measures to increase perception of control over the pregnancy by both the mother herself and by her attendants. These include co-operation over various measures of antenatal care such as vaginal examinations, blood tests, scans and amniocentesis so that they are chosen by a fully informed patient, not inflicted on her. Various options about the management of labour should be discussed. Where is it to take place? Who is to help and be present? What are the preferred methods of pain relief and what is available? Are induction of labour and episiotomy likely to be used and, if so, does the patient understand them and has she strong feelings about them? Does she understand the various options for the position at delivery and does she have a preference?

During Labour and Delivery

If the measures suggested above have been taken during the antenatal period, there may be little to do in labour except implement and adjust them as circumstances dictate. If for any reason proper discussion has not taken place some of the choices will have to be made when labour has already started. This is second best, but much better than inflicting a state of helplessness upon the mother.

The involvement of local, primary health care based midwives and other staff; (i) ensures that decisions and discussions taken in the antenatal period have a direct bearing on the conduct of the labour; and (ii) secures the attendance of consistent staff known to the mother which we have seen is an important correlate of good communication.

During the Puerperium

Four factors have been identified as predictors of post natal depression (Elliot 1985):

(1) Past history of neurotic depression.

(2) Past history of post natal depression.

(3) Poor quality of the marital relationship.

(4) Anxiety during the first trimester of pregnancy.

Perhaps rather surprisingly, obstetric and demographic factors do not seem to have much influence but as has been shown above traumatic experiences at delivery may provoke PTSD. The degree to which we can modify post natal depression and possible PTSD by attention to these factors must remain an open question but it would seem logical to improve communication and pain relief whilst lessening anxiety. For the more usual and fortunate mother whose puerperium is only troubled by the third to sixth day 'blues' at the most, some attention should be given to the problems of *adjustment to the changed state*. A chance to discuss methods of adjusting to the altered environment for both mother and father brought about by the arrival of the baby may uncover practical, emotional and cognitive problems. Amongst the latter the idea that 'mother love' is instant and overwhelming is a common assumption of many mothers. They suffer severe distress and make extremely negative self-evaluations when it doesn't arrive. For example; 'If I am not overwhelmed by love for that screaming pink thing, wet at both ends, then I must be lacking in essential feelings. This makes me a useless mother, therefore a worthless woman, therefore a defective person, in other words some sort of monster'. These sorts of assumptions, which can be expressed by the vertical arrow technique (see Chapter Nine), are common in new mothers and much distress can be avoided if they are examined logically and put into context.

Anxiety about the health of the baby can also usefully be explored. Some problem-solving on practical questions like breast feeding, family planning and return to work may be necessary.

Abortion

Spontaneous abortions are a form of bereavement and it is surprising how long it has taken the medical profession and others to realise the seriousness of this personal tragedy. Many of the considerations dealt with under that heading will apply, with numbing, searching, anger and guilt being common. Induced abortions are also a form of more complex bereavement although if undertaken under the best possible conditions it seems that guilt and self-blame are more likely to be avoided. Important factors in minimising adverse reactions are:

(1) The mother should feel fully responsible for the decision. The wife who bows to the wishes of her husband or the teenager who obeys her parents' orders are particularly at risk.

(2) The termination is carried out as early as possible since emotional adjustments become more difficult later.

(3) The matter is considerately handled by primary care staff, surgeon and clinic or hospital staff. This should not need saying today but sadly, insensitive remarks particularly in general hospitals are still too often a source of guilt and distress. The best specialised units have high technical skill and a more sensitive approach.

Terminal Care

It is now generally accepted that the professional has a duty to tell the truth to the dying patient but unfortunately there has been little emphasis on the way in which this is done. The result is that many inexperienced doctors and other workers feel uncomfortable and blurt out the facts with apparent disregard for the patient's feelings. There are a number of ways in which the breaking of bad news can be improved and it is worth rapidly reviewing these here.

(1) Sufficient time must be allowed.

(2) The place must be selected carefully, for example home or surgery.

(3) Consideration should be given as to who besides the patient is present.

(4) The truth should be told but the clinician must indicate that he or she realises that the information may well effect the patient deeply.

(5) An approach which questions the patient and finds out what he wants to know and is ready to receive may be adopted.

(6) A follow-up consultation soon after the news is broken should be arranged to allow further questions and clarify anything which has not been understood.

(7) Once the initial discussion has taken place plans for the patient to use the rest of his life fruitfully may be made. These may include arrangements for his dependants but also some planned pleasurable activities.

Previous parts of this chapter have dealt with subjects where the practice manager and the midwife are likely to be the most concerned. In the care of the terminally ill, however, the district nursing sister and her specialist advisers are likely to carry most responsibility. The techniques and procedures described here can be seen as one aspect, or as an extension of, the nursing process. Much of the progress in the care of the terminally ill in recent years has been brought about by the hospice service. The methods described in this section were pioneered by Lunt (1978) and Lunt and Jenkins (1983) working in a hospice in Southampton. Very little adaptation is required to make them entirely suitable for use in the community as no special facilities are required.

In outline, the approach is based on the philosophy that the terminal period should be regarded as a part of life not merely as a preparation for death. The dying patient has a number of problems associated with a number of aspirations which, with help, can be converted in many cases into realistic goals. Not all problems will be associated with goals and not all goals will be realistic but even the impossible ones may be achievable in part, if they are broken down into components, as may be seen in Figure 10.1 below.

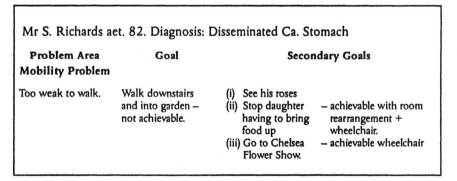

Mr S. Richards aet. 82. Diagnosis: Disseminated Ca. Stomach

Problem Area Mobility Problem	Goal	Secondary Goals	
Too weak to walk.	Walk downstairs and into garden – not achievable.	(i) See his roses (ii) Stop daughter having to bring food up (iii) Go to Chelsea Flower Show.	– achievable with room rearrangement + wheelchair. – achievable wheelchair

Figure 10.1 Goal setting

Assessment

This is carried out by means of an assessment form which groups the problems into various sections and then determines goal areas, priority, current status of problem and strengths and resources (see Figure 10.2).

Identified problems are listed in the various sections in the left hand column with goals in the next column. Priority is assessed as 1 or 2 (see below).

Problems	Goal Areas	Priority	Current Symptom Status	Strengths & Resources
Symptoms				
Self-care				
Mobility				
Sleep				
Recreation/Lei-sure				
Family				
Work/Employ-ment				
Financial				
Information on illness				
Other				
1 = attention now, or 2 = can be reviewed later.				

Figure 10.2: Assessment form

Current symptom status gives the original or baseline state which may be adequately described under the 'problem' heading or need amplification, for example: what does the weakness affect and what housework is impossible? Strengths and resources outline special factors such as motivation – Mr Richards in the example quoted was a life-long keen gardener – or special resources such as available friends, special equipment or skills (patient's or others').

Once the assessment has been completed a co-ordination meeting between the patient, the family or other home carers and the professional, such as a Macmillan nurse, district nursing sister and GP, at which resources and methods are discussed and an optional plan evolved. A patient's daily diary which can conveniently be written on the same form as the Weekly Activity Schedule (see Chapter Nine) is used to keep track of progress towards the goals. Assessments are made at agreed intervals, determined by the nature of the patient's illness. Progress is rated according to the following scale:

-2	-1	0	+1	+2
Much worse than expected	Worse than expected	Expected outcome	Better than expected	Much better than expected

In the light of these results, goals can be reset and new ones devised for as long as the illness lasts. There are a number of variations on the basic plan which can be used when the situation demands. For example, some of the goals may involve the aspirations of relatives, such as having a night out or taking a short holiday, as well as those of the patient. The above techniques may be useful in the management of any chronic illness or disablement.

Bereavement and Loss

Grief and loss in medical settings are usually thought of in terms of partners and close family members. Valency of loss, however, is a very individual thing, for loss of a pet may be more significant than the loss of a spouse and loss of status associated with a job or position may be more significant than either. It is a truism to say that to understand bereavement one has to understand the significance of the loss to the sufferer.

It is remarkable not so much that people need help but that so many manage without it. The primary care worker needs to keep an eye on his patients with recent loss and be prepared to step in when needed.

Who needs help?

It is particularly important to be aware of those whose loss may be unusual, unrecognised or somehow perceived as unimportant or disreputable. Amongst other circumstances which raise awareness are the sudden unexpected death, the death in the context of a previously poor, or worse, hostile relationship and the 'bad' death where there has been much suffering or real or perceived poor clinical management (Raphael 1978). The death of a child at any age may be particularly difficult for a parent and death without a body such as in a mid air disaster or far from home may presage pathological grief.

One loss affects many people and it is a common mistake to concentrate on the widow whilst neglecting the children and the friends. These mourners may feel that their job is to support the nearest relatives and that they do not have the right to grief – 'My job is to support my mother'.

When is help needed?

The primary care worker often has the responsibility of deciding whether to offer help in the absence of a specific request. This can only be done if he or she remains in contact with the mourner. Fortunately in primary care this is fairly easy.

How to intervene?

The most important function of the professional is to give permission to mourn. Many patients particularly young males do not have the vocabulary or verbal skills to express themselves in this emotionally charged situation. Modelling of words and expressions may be important. The components, no longer regarded as stages, of the grief reaction described by Parkes (1972) are still a useful guide. They are:

(1) *Shock*, which is associated with numbness, unreality and apathy.

(2) *Disorganisation*, which frequently follows the supreme effort of the funeral when the bereaved person may collapse into a state of helplessness.

(3) *Denial*, which is associated with searching for the dead person and the distressing idea that he is still present, provoked by the sights, such as a person in similar clothes in the street or sounds, like the noise of the dog in the kitchen interpreted as the dead husband making the tea. Although originally a defence mechanism, the continual correction of these false interpretations is often one of the most painful components of early grief.

(4) *Depression*, with feelings of pining and despair usually represents a progression to a more realistic phase and evidence that the 'work' of grieving is indeed being done as the person is coming face to face with the impossibility of bringing back the dead.

(5) *Guilt* often occurs, whether justified or not, with its concurrent obsessional thoughts of what might or should have been done for the dead person.

(6) *Anxiety* is caused by fears, sometimes realistic, of changed life circumstances, for example loneliness or finance problems. It may also be caused by a type of fear about fear for example of being unable to cope with the situation or of going mad.

(7) *Aggression* may take many forms. It may be directed against a friend or relatives who have 'not helped' or who still have spouses. It is commonly directed against those doctors or hospitals that cared for the dead person. In this context it presents special problems to the GP and his colleagues who may feel a considerable conflict of roles and interests. Finally it may be directed at the dead person – 'How dare he/she leave me like this to fend for myself!'

(8) *Resolution and Acceptance* occur when the farewells are finally said and the huge gap left by the dead person, like the wake of a ship, gradually fills. This allows the final battle phase of reintegration into a life without him or her to begin.

It is also useful to consider the modifications to Parke's model (1993) in which he elaborates grief as a psycho-social transition. Stroebe and Stroebe (1993a and 1993b) elaborate a useful model of oscillation between *loss-orientated* grief and re-building *restoration* activities. They have also found that men cope with bereavement by seeking distraction whereas women are more likely to express their emotions and confront their loss. Utrecht, Shut, de Keijser and van den Bout (1991) compared a programme of problem focused behaviour therapy with a programme of emotion focused client centred therapy. The results showed that the widows did better with problem solving and the widowers with emotional expression thus suggesting that supplying the deficient module may be important in resolving grief.

Management of normal grief is essentially passive and involves allowing time for the patient to work through his reaction with its sudden changes from component to component and then often back again. Patience is needed for the sometimes endless repetitive discussions of various aspects. A permissive approach is required to let the more sensitive issues like delusions of physical presence and fears of impending insanity to be raised. Ramsay (1977) has viewed grief as a special kind of specific fear or phobia. This model can be used in helping with normal bereavement as any tendency to avoidance can be countered by gentle persuasion to return to the real work which is to keep in contact with the feared stimulus, in other words the fact of loss.

As with other types of phobia, a graded approach may be used. This sets progressively more difficult goals, week by week, repeating them until they can be done without undue discomfort. For example, one week's goal might be to contact a mutual friend not seen since the bereavement, the next to tidy out a room with memories and a third to look at a photograph of the dead person.

In summary the primary care worker whether health visitor, district nursing sister or GP should:

(1) Be aware of the risk factors leading to morbid grief.

(2) When dealing with normal grief remain largely a permissive listener but be aware that they are involved in a process where avoidance and exposure both play a part.

(3) Be prepared to assist the mourner in finding practical solutions and in expressing painful emotions when necessary.

(4) Be prepared to direct the mourner to voluntary bodies such as Cruse or refer to more specialised resources when necessary.

There is also a useful work book for patient use by Street (1993).

Involving Patients in Their Own Care

In cognitive behaviour therapy the approach is always a collaborative one so that it is axiomatic that patients are partners in therapy. In more everyday medical management particularly in chronic conditions, there is much to be said for empowering the patient to take charge of as much as possible of his management. The diabetic and the asthmatic readily become experts in their own conditions and as well as ensuring higher quality management this sense of internal control (Rotter 1966) is a powerful restorative of self-esteem which may have been damaged when the diagnosis was made. The patient may be made responsible for his own medical records, may carry out his own monitoring tests and, where feasible, make his own treatment choices. He will be encouraged to read and research extensively about his condition and his advice may be sought during clinical interviews.

On a wider front patient groups are now often involved in the activities of their primary health care centres. Sadly this is still perceived as threatening by some workers. Even the most sceptical GP, however, may be won over when he realises that as well as monitoring and, perhaps, criticising, patient groups can initiate services like prescription delivery, patient transport and fund raising for additional clinical services.

Looking After the Carers

Modern society seeks to avoid long term hospital care and most of us would, if we were afflicted by chronic or terminal illness like to be cared for at home. In the UK the move is towards a primary care lead health service but inevitably when care is at home much responsibility and stress rests on the carers. To look after someone with chronic or worse terminal illness imposes many practical physical strains on the carer as well as an enormous emotional burden. Whilst the patient's life deteriorates the carers life style becomes ever more restricted, isolated, desolate and weary. At the same time there may be guilt – 'It is mother who matters, I am selfish feeling like this.'

Gradually a loving relationship may deteriorate into a morbid struggle and guilt is added to the already considerable stress. Occasionally the outburst of anger will burst through followed by more grief, guilt and remorse. The job of the professional in support falls into three categories:

(1) To uncover, discuss and legitimise the grief, anger and guilt. These emotions are natural and human and this has to be said.

(2) To maintain the best social, psychological care for the patient.

(3) To assist in practical problem solving for the carer. Are there problems, for example financial, work orientated or in other relationships which need help.

(4) To be conscious of the need to give explanations of what is happening, what will happen and how it can be managed. Fear, guilt and embarrassment form an enormous black cloud over carers and the professional carer must be prepared to discuss these feelings.

(5) To involve Macmillan nursing, Marie Curie nursing, Hospice outreach and any other service at an early stage before desperation sets in.

References

Anderson, K.O. and Masur, F.T. (1983) 'Psychological preparation for invasive medical and dental procedures.' *Journal of Behavioural Medicine 6*, 1, 1–40.

Auburn, L. (1981) 'Patient compliance with medication regimes.' In J.L. Shepherd (ed) *Advances in Behavioural Medicine Vol. I*. Sydney: Cumberland College.

Becker, M.H. and Rosenstock, I.M. (1984) 'Compliance with medical advice.' In A. Steptoe and A.M. Mathews (eds) *Health Care and Human Behaviour*. London: Academic Press.

Bruehl, S., McCubbin, J.A., Wilson, J.F., Montgomery, T., Ibarra, P. and Carlson, C.R. (1994) 'Coping styles, opioid blockade and cardiovascular response to stress.' *Journal of Behavioural Medicine 17*, 25–40.

Burne, P.S. and Long, B.E.L. (1976) *Doctors Talking to Patients*. London: HMSO.

Centre for Behaviour Research in Cancer (1992) *Health Warnings and Contents Labelling on Tobacco Products*. Melbourne: Centre for Behaviour Research in Cancer.

Department of Health (1993) *Changing Childbirth: The Report of the Expert Maternity Group*. London: HMSO.

Descartes, R. tr Haldane, E.S. and Ross, G.R.T. (1912) *Philosophical Works of Descartes*.

Elliot, S.A. (1985) 'Pregnancy and after.' In S. Rachman (ed) *Contributions to Medical Psychology Vol 3*. Oxford: Pergamon.

Flesch, R. (1948) 'A new readability yardstick.' *Journal of Applied Psychology 32*, 221–33.

France, R. and Robson, M. (1986) *Behaviour Therapy in Primary Care: A Practical Guide.* London: Chapman and Hall.

Freeman, J. and Byrne, P.S. (1976) *The Assessment of Post Graduate Training in General Practice.* Guilford: Society for Research into Higher Education.

Gibbs, S., Waters, W.E. and George, C.F. (1990) 'Communicating information to patients about medicine. Prescription information leaflets: a national survey.' *Journal of the Royal Society of Medicine 83,* 292–7.

Goldberg, D. and Huxley, P. (1980) *Mental Illness in the Community.* London: Tavistock.

Green, J.M., Coupland V.A. and Kitzinger, J.V. (1990) 'Expectations, experiences and psychological outcomes of childbirth: A prospective study of 825 women.' *Birth 17,* 1, 17–24.

Johnston, M. and Wallace, L. (eds) (1990) *Stress and Medical Procedures.* Oxford: Oxford University Press.

Kincey, J. (1995) 'Surgery.' In A. Broome and S. Llewwelyn (eds) *Health Psychology – Processes and Applications.* London: Chapman and Hall.

Kincey, J. and Saltmore, S. (1990) 'Stress and surgical treatments.' In M. Johnston and L. Wallace (eds) *Stress and Medical Procedures.* Oxford: Oxford University Press.

Ley, P. (1982) 'Understanding memory satisfaction and compliance.' *British Journal of Clinical Psychology 21,* 241–254.

Ley, P. (1988) *Communicating with Patients.* London: Croom Helm.

Ley, P. and Llewelyn, S. (1995) 'Improving patients' understanding, recall, satisfaction and compliance.' In A. Broome and S. Llewelyn (eds) *Health Psychology – Processes and Applications.* London: Chapman and Hall.

Lobel, M. (1994) 'Conceptualisations, measurement and effects of prenatal stress on birth outcomes.' *Journal of Behavioural Medicine 17,* 225–72.

Lunt, B. (1978) 'The goal setting approach in continuing care.' Paper presented at the Annual Therapeutic Conference, St. Christopher's Hospice, Sydenham, Novemeber 1978.

Lunt, B. and Jenkins, J. (1983) 'Goal setting in terminal care: a method of recording treatment, aims and priorities.' *Journal of Advanced Nursing 8,* 495–505.

Maguire, P. (1984) 'Communication Skills and Patient Care.' In A. Steptoe and A. Matthews (eds) *Health Care and Human Behaviour.* London: Academic Press.

Matthews, A. and Ridgeway, V. (1984) 'Psychological Preparation for Surgery.' In A. Steptoe and A. Matthews (eds) *Health Care and Human Behaviour.* London: Academic Press.

Melamed, B.G. (1993) 'Putting the family back into the child.' *Behaviour Research and Therapy 31,* 3, 239–247.

Menage, J. (1993) 'Post-traumatic stress disorder in women who have undergone obstetric and/or gynaecological procedures.' *Journal of Reproductive and Infant Psychology 11,* 221–228.

Morris, L.A. (1990) *Communicating Therapeutic Risks.* New York: Springer Verlag.

Newton, J.R. and Reading, A.E. (1977) 'The effects of psychological preparation on pain at intrauterine device insertion.' *Contraception 16,* 523–532.

Parkes, C.M. (1972) *Bereavement.* Harmondsworth: Penguin.

Parkes, C.M. (1993) 'Grief as a psychosocial transition: Process of adaptation to change.' In M. Stoebe, W. Stroebe and R.O. Hanson (eds) (1993) *Handbook of Bereavement: Theory, Research and Intervention.* New York: Cambridge University Press.

Raphael, B. (1978) 'Mourning and the prevention of melancholia.' *British Journal of Medical Psychology 51*, 303–10.

Reading, A.E. and Cox, D.N. (1984) 'The effects of ultrasound examination on maternal anxiety levels.' *Journal of Behavioural Medicine 5*, 237–247.

Rotter, J.B. (1966) 'General Expectations for Internal versus External Control of Reinforcement.' *Psychological Monographs: General and Applied 80* (Whole No.609).

Schut, H., de Keijser, J., Utrecht, T. and van den Bout, J. (1991) A controlled efficacy study into short-term individual grief counselling: Client variables. Paper presented at the 3rd International Conference on Grief and Bereavement in Contemporary Society Sydney, Australia.

Sikorski, J., Wilson, J., Clement, S., Das, S. and Smeeton, N. (1996) 'A randomised controlled trial comparing two schedules of antenatal visits: the antenatal care project.' *British Medical Journal 312*, 546–553.

Street, J. (1993) *Grief: A Healing Process.* Unpublished Workbook.

Stroebe, W. and Stroebe, M. (1993a) *Coping with Bereavement: The Dual Process Model.* Unpublished.

Stroebe, W. and Stroebe, M. (1993b) 'Determinants in adjustment to bereavement in younger widows and widowers.' In M. Stoebe, W. Stroebe and R.O. Hanson (eds) (1993) *Handbook of Bereavement: Theory, Research and Intervention.* New York: Cambridge University Press

Recommended for Further Reading:

Johnston, M. and Wallace, L. (eds) (1990) *Stress and Medical Procedures.* Oxford: Oxford University Press.

Liddell, A. (ed) (1984) *The Practice of Clinical Psychology in Great Britain.* Chichester: John Wiley.

Parkes, C.M. (1972) *Recovery from Bereavement.* London: Harper and Row.

Pendleton, D., Schofield, T., Tate, P. and Havelock P. (1984) *The Consultation. An Approach to Learning and Teaching.* Oxford: Oxford University Press.

Sackett, D.L. and Haynes, R. (1976) *Compliance with Therapeutic Regimes.* Baltimore: The Johns Hopkins University Press.

Stedeford, A. (1984) *Facing Death – Partners, Families and Professionals.* London: Heinemann.

Useful Addresses

Association for Post-Natal Illness, 25 Jerdan Place, London SW6 1BE. Tel: 0171 386 0868.

CRUSE Helpline 0181 332 7227 or see local telephone book for branches.

Lesbian and Gay Bereavement Project, Vaughan M. Williams Centre, Colindale Hospital, London NW9 5HG.

Chapter Eleven

The Management of Specific Medical Problems

Psychological interventions have been found to have a place in the management of medical disorders at three separate but inter-related levels. First, they can be used to increase the effectiveness of conventional treatment, for example, by improving adherence, treatment effects and communication. Second, they may be used to modify the psycho–social effect of various conditions and, third, they may be used as an alternative to more traditional kinds of therapy. This chapter considers the second and third levels in connection with a number of specific problems. In many conditions the final arbiter of success of therapy may well be the quality of life of the patient, a theory which has been the subject of much recent attention (O'Boyle 1996). This is difficult to assess, as the goals and values of individuals may be very different.

Cardiovascular Disorders – Essential Hypertension

Efforts to reduce blood pressure by cognitive behavioural methods have concentrated on two areas (Johnston and Steptoe 1989):

(1) The modification of behaviour associated with physical risk factors of raised blood pressure (Alderman 1994).

(2) The modification of stress related behaviour.

Physical Risk Factors

The perceived importance of various physical risk factors has waxed and waned over the years and there may be further shifts in the future. The following are thought to be currently the most important:

(1) *Body Weight* – even modest reductions in weight in the obese can have beneficial effects on blood pressure (Jeffrey 1991). The techniques to

achieve this are discussed in Chapter Eight. It is possible to achieve good results in patients with mild to moderate hypertension.

(2) *Alcohol Consumption* – a small amount of alcohol, particularly of red wine, may confer benefits on cardiovascular status. There is no doubt, however, that consumption of over twenty units a week contributes to hypertension and also raises cholesterol thus adding a further risk factor. Methods for helping to reduce drinking are discussed in Chapter Eight.

(3) *Salt Consumption* – this is a controversial area. Salt reduction has been shown to be highly effective but this involves the use of special salt-free foods and a sacrifice of flavour that many will find unacceptable. Modest reductions have not shown clear benefits although advice to add less salt to food at table may be sensible.

(4) *Physical Exercise* – increased physical exercise has been shown to reduce blood pressure (Nelson *et al.* 1986, Siegel and Blumental 1991)) as well as lowering sudden cardiac death rates from all causes (Kannel *et al.* 1985). It is important, however, that it should be consistent and maintained. To this end it is wise for the patient to choose a form of exercise which is achievable and pleasurable (Kimberley *et al.* 1995).

Stress Management Programmes

Attempts to alter stress responses may operate in three ways.

(1) *Removal or Reduction of Stressors* – it would seem to be common sense that if occupational or domestic life can be altered to remove or reduce the stressful conditions, it should be done. In practice many experienced primary care workers do address these issues. In research terms this is a largely unexplored area because of the difficulty of mounting appropriate studies. Some work has indicated a positive effect of increased control at work and improved marital interactions on risky life styles (Wickrama *et al.* 1995).

(2) *Reformulating Stressors* – the re-evaluation of stressors by identifying and re-interpreting negative thinking so that they are no longer seen as stressful is a promising area of research but has not yet been related to the management of hypertension.

(3) *Modifying the Response to Stress* – it is in this area of simply reducing stress responses that most work has been done. Patel (Patel and Marmot 1988) has worked extensively with relaxation and meditation programmes linked to biofeedback and has produced some very

promising results which indicate some continuation of the lowered blood pressure after the patient has discontinued active practice (Patel *et al.* 1985).

(Source: Johnston 1992)

A primary care stress management group (France 1993) may be used to train hypertensive patients along with others in the techniques described above.

Cardiovascular Disorders – Coronary Heart Disease

Cognitive behavioural measures in connection with ischaemic heart disease are appropriate before, during and after the myocardial infarct.

Primary Prevention

It is widely believed that coronary heart disease (CHD) is largely preventable and indeed the dramatic fall in mortality in the USA is probably due more to life style changes than improved treatment. Risk factors for CHD are reasonably well understood and the circumscribed primary health care service in the UK with its identified lists of patients would seem an ideal context for intervention. Unfortunately the results to date have not been encouraging. Even the expensive and well-publicised health promotion measures in the UK health 'reforms' of 1989–90 have been widely seen to have been unresearched, ill thought-out and crudely applied. The failure of these measures which have been subjected to constant change before being allowed to wither away may well have set the case of health promotion in the UK back many years. Better designed life style interventions too have had generally modest results (Elder 1985) although the most intensive in a triple programme study (Lovibond *et al.* 1986) produced a 41 per cent reduction in current overall risk of CHD.

Current thinking suggests that awareness programmes and low contact – high number interventions directed at the known coronary risk factors are worthwhile (see Appendix 1). 'Opportunist' advice about smoking, diet or life-style during a consultation for another problem is useful. Groups aimed at the correction of specific problems also have a place. In both these circumstances advice can be made effective if its importance is emphasised and coupled to some suggestions as to how it might be more easily put into practice. The overweight, under-exercised, two-packets-a-day business man might be helped by a programme to cut down or stop smoking and buy a bicycle to travel to work or the station. The savings on smoking would pay for the bicycle. The ride would help reduce weight, increase exercise and demonstrate increased lung function thus providing three potential areas of reinforcement. Naturally such a programme must be negotiated, not imposed. If, however, the patient finds it acceptable, he is likely to be favourably influenced by his doctor's practical involvement with the details of the scheme.

It is certain, however, that these factors alone are insufficient to explain all the variance found in coronary proneness studies (The Japanese are increasing their hard fat intake and smoke heavily but maintain a low CHD incidence). Much has been made of the role of Type A behaviour pattern (Friedman and Rosenham 1974). This has been succinctly defined by Johnston (1982) as 'being characterised by a chronic struggle to achieve more and more in less and less time'. The Type A person is thrusting, ambitious, time-pressured, decisive and becomes readily hostile when thwarted. There is a strong but unproven suspicion that such behaviour is actually reinforced and shaped-up by life in western urban societies, which may be one reason for the present epidemic of CHD. The significance of Type A behaviour is still by no means clear and a good deal of criticism of the model has filled research columns since it was first presented (Deffenbacher 1994)). Currently there is controversy as to whether CHD is prevented more by expressing anger ('anger-out') or suppressing it ('anger-in') and even this may depend upon other variables in the situation (Faber and Burns 1996, Denollet 1993). It has been shown that CHD predictive hostility can be modified in non-clinical populations (Gidron and Davidson 1996) but as yet there is no prospective research or work on clinical populations. A Stress Management Group in the practice armamentarium may be the most useful resource or transcendental meditation (Alexander *et al.* 1996) which has been used successfully to reduce cardiovascular risk factors.

Care During the Attack

About 40 per cent of the patients suffering from a myocardial infarction have clinically significant levels of anxiety and depression about half of which was present before the incident. There is no significant association between the psychological reaction to a myocardial infarct and its severity (Lewin 1995). In almost every case today immediate care will be in hospital rather than by the community team but the PHCT will be involved in the after effects of this care. It is worth noting, therefore, that amongst other findings, the extensive Vanderbilt/Holy Cross project in the USA (Cromwell *et al.* 1977) found that outcome was influenced best if patients received a lot of *information* about their condition but only if this was coupled with high *participation* in the form of monitoring their own ECGs, doing isometric exercises and generally being encouraged to take part in their own management, or high *distraction* in the form of TV, books, visiting and so on. Better informed patients actually did worse if they could not share in their own management. A sub-group of patients, however, cope by denial and do not accept information or even the diagnosis readily. This group should be allowed access to information only on request.

Aftercare and Rehabilitation

There has been much consideration of whether survivors cope by *attention* or *avoidance*. Although avoidance is associated with higher distress this is now thought to be the cause of the avoidance rather than the result. Patients use more attention coping during myocardial infarction but more avoidant coping later on (Johnston and Johnston 1996).

This is where most practical work has been done. Coronary rehabilitation programmes (Laerum *et al.* 1988, Denollet 1993, Hevey *et al.* 1996) are now available in many places and are often run by interested primary care workers. They usually consist of three main elements:

(1) Monitoring the physical condition, which has the additional psychological function of providing feedback and increasing confidence.

(2) Graded physical exercise, which as well as restoring physical fitness also helps rebuild confidence and the sense of control over the problem.

(3) Offering a counselling service that is overtly psychological.

This service includes:

  ◦ life-style advice to eliminate risk factors
  ◦ problem-solving related to the changed situation, including employment and hobbies
  ◦ allowing anxieties about the future to be expressed
  ◦ advising about the resumption of sexual activities which is often fraught with catastrophic images of sudden death in the minds of both partners
  ◦ advice on how to avoid over-protection by spouse, friend and doctor.

This last is particularly important as helplessness and its associated hopelessness is a predictor of poor survival rates after myocardial infarction (Cromwell *et al.* 1977, Wiklund *et al.* 1985) whereas overactivity seems to be relatively unimportant.

Neurological Disorders

Chronic neurological disorders present many opportunities for helping the patient with a cognitive behavioural approach. Each disease or disability will present different problems and no two individuals with the same condition will react in the same way. The range of problems open to some form of cognitive behavioural assessment and management ranges from localised problems, such as tinnitus (Budd and Pugh 1996), to the long term disabling and life threatening conditions, such as multiple sclerosis (Roa 1986). Nevertheless there are sufficient common concerns to allow some generalisations to be made.

Assessment

This should be based on a problem list generated by the patient and his carers each problem can then be viewed from a variable perspective:

Table 11.1 Needs assessment checklist

Patient's Needs		
Activity	*Symptoms*	*Emotions*
What can he do?	Pain?	Depression?
What does he need to do?	Insomnia?	Anxiety?
What does he want to do?	Constipation?	Anger?
Can it be achieved differently?		
Is there a satisfactory alternative?		
Who else can help?		
Carers' Needs		
Rest & Relaxation	*Help*	*Emotional support*
Time off (Sitting)?	People – Nursing?	Talking – Self Help group
Holidays (Respite Care)?	– Domestic?	Friends and neighbours?
	– Services?	Professional counsellor etc.?
	(Laundry, shopping)	
Family's Needs		

A 37 year old woman with multiple sclerosis had enjoyed going to the London theatre with her friends. She was prevented from doing this by urinary frequency which she feared would lead to incontinence if she could not easily reach her adapted toilet. A substitute programme was organised whereby her friends visited the house to watch classic videos accompanied by an 'interval supper' arranged by them on a rota basis.

Many of the techniques described under Terminal Care in Chapter Fourteen will also be found useful in these problems. It is also important that the whole family unit is considered as well as the patient and the chief carer.

The approach used is essentially one of goal setting with graded activities and problem solving with the practical difficulties. Distorted thinking is very common and the therapist may be trapped into colluding with this and agreeing 'Yes, it is awful isn't it?' A useful technique is to ask the patient if a hundred people in his condition would think exactly the same about it. The answer will be that they wouldn't and this can lead to the examination of more flexible ways of thinking.

The Management of Pain

Pain may be defined as an unpleasant bodily sensation usually, but not always, associated with tissue damage. Early conceptualisations of pain regarded it as a simple response in which pain receptors activated fibres in the peripheral nerves which in turn conducted impulses through the central nervous system to be received in the cerebral cortex. A great deal of practical evidence, however, indicated the inadequacy of such an explanation. For example, soldiers in battle suffered ghastly injuries which went unnoticed by them until they left the battlefield. Many other examples from more everyday experience indicated that multiple factors influenced the amount of pain experienced. A one-to-one relationship with tissue damage could not be sustained. From 1963 onwards Melzack (Melzack 1973, Melzack and Wall 1985) studied these other factors and developed the 'gate-control model' to explain them. The model is a complex one but in essence suggests that nerve impulses from the tissues have to pass through a 'gate' situated in the dorsal horns of the spinal column, at which point they become modified by descending influences from the brain, some of which open and some of which close the postulated gate. These influences include:

(1) *Mood and Emotions* – depression, fear, sadness and anxiety lower the pain threshold and happiness, relaxation and feelings of well-being raise it.

(2) *Motivation* – striving to overcome the pain and find ways of coping will in itself raise the threshold.

(3) *Distraction* – this explains the battlefield phenomenon mentioned above. Powerful distractions have a profound effect on modifying the experience of pain although recent work (Eccleston 1995) questions the scientific basis for this and even suggests that focusing techniques may have a place.

(4) *Interpretation* – a patient having a splinter removed in a treatment room may suffer the same amount of tissue damage as a detainee having a nail removed by the secret police. It is likely that their experience of pain will be quite different.

(5) *Past Experience* – previous experience of the same kind of pain or injury and its outcome influence the reaction to the present situation.

(6) *Past Learning History* – individual or cultural. We model our own perceptions and behaviour on those around us and this has been shown experimentally to effect the amount of pain experienced.

Different cultures cope with pain in different ways which also affects the experience. The British require considerable quantities of analgesic drugs but are not expected to show much overt emotion when subjected to a painful experience. With the Italians, for example, the situation is reversed in that they mistrust the drugs but are encouraged to cry out and indulge in self-expression. Such factors will modify the amount of pain and the way it is experienced. Returning to the individual, the consequences of his reaction to pain will have a powerful operant effect. If, for example, attention and warm concern are offered by members of the family only in response to pain this will have a considerable influence in shaping up pain behaviour and also affect the amount of pain experienced

This list is by no means exhaustive but serves to indicate that pain is a multi-faceted problem.

Assessment

The interview should include special enquiry into the factors mentioned above. Baseline observation follows. This often includes a record of date and time, situation, intensity of pain rated out of 10 or 100, associated thoughts and feelings, medication and outcome. There are various ways of collecting this information which will depend on the type of pain. Sometimes a graph will serve best, sometimes a diary-record is needed.

Intervention

As always, the type of intervention must be determined by the assessment data and the initial hypothesis.

Acute Pain

Current theory, derived from measuring cardiovascular responses, suggests that coping for acute short term pain is principally mediated by endogenous opiates and that other strategies such as ignoring, re-interpreting sensations and diverting attention only become effective once endogenous opiates are blocked. Distraction, cue-controlled relaxation and re-interpretation are, however, employed by instinct in many painful situations and seem to be anecdotally effective.

Chronic Pain

There are a number cognitive behavioural approaches to pain which have been researched and used clinically (Turner and Chapman 1982). These are listed below.

Applied Relaxation

This is effective with specific painful situations such as dental extractions or injections. Instruction in general relaxation is given first as has been described previously. This is then adapted to differential relaxation, without a tension phase, which is first rehearsed in an imagined painful situation and finally used in the real life setting (Linton 1982). The same approach can be used with long-standing or chronic pain with a particular level of pain being the cue for the relaxation sequence. Electro-myographic feedback using a simple apparatus can be used to provide the patient with information about the state of muscular tension. We have found this to be particularly useful where the patient finds it difficult to accept the rationale of pain relief by muscular relaxation or where specific muscle groups such as the jaw, the back or the sterno-mastoid are involved. An extension of this method is to use hypnotism, but this lies outside the scope of our discussion here.

The Operant Approach

This approach was pioneered by Fordyce (1976). It concentrates on pain behaviour and there is still considerable discussion as to whether pain experience is actually affected. It seems that there probably is a modest reduction of the amount of pain felt but the main advantage of the approach is in enabling the patient to lead a more satisfying life.

The treatment plan contains the following elements:

(1) Analgesic medication is arranged on a time schedule not given p.r.n. With the patient's permission, medication may be given in a liquid form so that the active ingredient can be reduced without the patient's knowledge. This eliminates a certain amount of reactive anxiety.

(2) A graded exercise programme is devised in relation to the pain and disability experienced by the patient. The initial level is set well below the pre-treatment amount of activity and extremely small increments

are used. In this way confidence is built up and it is often possible to reach activity levels which would have been inconceivable at the outset. Reward rests are made contingent on target exercise periods being achieved and not, as previously, on complaints of pain.

(3) Relatives and friends are encouraged to reinforce progress, activity and 'up time', meaning the time spent out of bed engaged on activities. It is important to build steadily on activities always maintaining those that were performed the previous day otherwise a yo-yo of alternating good and bad days may impede progress. 'Up time' should be increased steadily but very gradually for example by 10–12 minutes every day.

One of the problems of this type of programme is that it has largely been used in hospital with professional staff. It is possible to adapt these techniques to the home but only if there is co-operation from the relatives in providing reinforcement for various 'well behaviours' and a neutral attitude to 'pain behaviours'. In many of these patients, pain complaints have often been substantially reinforced by sympathy, concern and offers of medication. In some cases this may be the patient's only enduring way of getting any attention at all and, therefore, changes are required of both the patient and his family for a new pattern to be established. These considerations limit the effectiveness of this type of programme in the home but the difficulties may be overcome by the active involvement of as many of the family members as possible in such tasks as charting 'up time', timing exercise sessions and arranging outings.

The Cognitive Method

It has been noted that such factors as distraction, interpretation and mood affect the way pain is experienced and to these must be added the fact that pain is reduced when the sufferer feels that he can exercise control over it. These observations have been employed by Meichenbaum and his colleagues to produce a treatment package which is a modification of their stress inoculation training. In summary, the patient first develops a number of coping strategies with the help of the therapist which might include:

(1) He uses distraction, very much as described in the chapter on anxiety management. The patient distracts himself from the pain by imagining himself in a situation incompatible with the pain experience such as lying on a beach in the sunshine. More simple distraction techniques such as reciting poetry, solving problems, listing the sports teams in a league have also been used. He may also concentrate on aspects of

people or things in his surroundings such as those wearing brown shoes, the number of cars in the road and so on.

(2) He focuses on his own sensations including the pain and analyses and measures it 'like a scientist'. This appears to increase the perception of control.

(3) He manipulates the imagery surrounding the experience of the pain. He may imagine his experience as part of a heroic battle or exciting adventure. More sophisticated methods involve reinterpreting the pain as trivial, for example, 'just cramp' or 'like tingling' or suggesting that it is unreal or a long way away. Finally the pain can be incorporated in elaborate fantasy exercises like spy stories or television adventures. This is particularly useful in children who have a rich fantasy life and will meet the therapist half way.

The coping strategies are then incorporated into a timetable for pain management:

(1) *Preparing for the Pain* – worry and fear of pain are used as triggers to rehearse coping techniques.

(2) *Confronting the Pain* – the onset of the pain is the cue to relax and put the chosen strategy into operation, together with some calming self-statements.

(3) *The Critical Moments* – the ability of the chosen strategy to control the pain is monitored. If needed, one strategy can be changed for another, such as swapping reciting Kubla Khan to escaping from a terrorist gang. Self-reminders are given that the object is to stay in control of the pain not eliminate it.

(4) *After the Pain Has Passed* – the way of coping with it is rehearsed and self-reinforcement statements like 'Well done – you managed it' are made. A written record of the experience is also useful as this can be used for self-reinforcement on the next occasion.

(Source: Turk *et al.* 1983)

Long Term Pain

Williams and Erskine (1990) give a plan for a cognitive behavioural intervention in long term pain which includes a very detailed assessment. The intervention outline forms a useful template for adaptation to primary care:

(1) *Education* – including the multi-faceted model of pain and the importance of function.

(2) *Improving Physical Condition* – gradually increased accessible exercise directed towards rewarding goals leading to:

(3) *Recovery of Activities* – both useful and pleasurable with the modification and selection of goals.

(4) *Medication Reduction* – on a time contingent scale with careful assessment of continuing effectiveness and need.

(5) *Improving Mood and Confidence* – employing strategies from the treatment of depression and health concerns (see Chapters Six and Nine).

(6) *Behaviour Change* – directed towards empowering the patient to take control of himself and move towards well behaviours.

(7) *Generalisation and Skill Maintenance* – the adoption of relapse prevention techniques and written plans adaptable for future use. Involvement of carers and celebration of achievements.

These packages may seem extremely complicated and sophisticated to be recommended for use in primary care but they do have a number of advantages over the others. First, unlike the operant programme, they do not required trained staff. Second, once he has got the idea, the patient is able to do much of the work for himself and hopefully enter into the self-help spirit of the exercise. Third, it is almost endlessly adaptable to suit most sorts of pain and the main principles can be incorporated in a hand-out that the patient can keep for reference and discuss when he attends. Fourth, simplifications are possible when all the packages are not required. Finally, the experimental evidence indicates that they are probably more effective than the alternatives (Flor *et al.* 1992).

It is deliberate that no mention has been made of the vexed question of outstanding compensation lawsuits for injury as reinforcers of pain behaviour. They are undoubtedly very powerful and it may be difficult to attempt any sort of programme whilst this factor is operating. Unfortunately it is outside our scope to modify it, which would involve some profound changes in the working of the legal system, for example, no-blame compensation and rapid provisional case settlement.

Specific Types of Pain

Headaches

Although more than fifteen types of headaches have been described, those most suitable for behavioural treatment may be divided into tension headaches and migraine.

Tension Headache

It was uncritically accepted for many years that tension headaches were associated with sustained contraction of skeletal muscles, in particular the frontalis and temporalis. Treatment was, therefore, given by encouraging EMG feedback-aided relaxation of these muscles which was often associated with subjective improvement. More recent work (Flor and Turk 1989, Pikoff 1984) indicates that definite EMG abnormalities can only be demonstrated in a minority of tension headache sufferers and that many of the improvements noted as a result of EMG feedback training were probably due to non-specific factors. Hatch and his colleagues (1992) conclude that stress and low mood as well as muscular hyperactivity are probably the chief factors causing this type of headache. They cannot be regarded as merely a manifestation of altered muscle potentials. For practical purposes EMG biofeedback from the frontalis muscle may be worth a try, where facilities exist, as a small number will derive a specific benefit. Stress reduction and anti-depressant measures may be worthwhile in the remainder, but the more general pain modification strategies should also be considered.

Migraine

This is classically described as a unilateral throbbing pain associated with visual distortion, nausea and vomiting. There are, however, many different types, some differing quite widely from the classical description. The distinction from tension and other types of headache is not always easy. The pathology of the condition indicates an initial vasoconstriction phase associated with the prodromal symptoms followed by a vasodilatation phase associated with the throbbing headache. The vascular aetiology of the condition produced an early enthusiasm for biofeedback therapy based on skin temperature or blood volume. Papers on these techniques continue to appear sporadically (Gauthier 1983) which show that these techniques are effective. Comparable results, however, can be obtained without expensive equipment by relaxation training coupled with anxiety management techniques. These deal with high stress trigger situations and assertion and inter-personal skills training may also be needed when these are deficient (Mitchell and White 1977).

Recurrent Non-infective Sore Throat

A group of recurrent sufferers from sore throats exist where there is no evidence of infection or other local lesion. They do appear to improve with specific throat relaxation exercises with or without the addition of EMG feedback from the sterno-mastoid area. It is proposed that high crico-pharyngeal muscle tone may be a factor in the throat discomfort which is then exacerbated by repetitive swallowing. Experimental evidence in support of this is lacking but a similar treatment has been shown to be effective in the much less common spasmodic torticollis involving muscles in the same area (Martin 1982). The problem is a relatively common one in primary care and further investigation has still to be undertaken.

Primary Dysmenorrhoea

Relaxation training associated with EMG biofeedback from the lower abdominal muscles has been shown to be more effective than relaxation alone in the treatment of this condition (Bennink *et al.* 1982). We have no experience of using these techniques in primary care but in view of the prevalence of the problem and the relative ineffectiveness and unpopularity of many drug treatments it would seem to be a promising area to explore.

Respiratory Conditions

The exact cause of the alarming increase in the incidence of bronchial asthma in recent years is still unclear. Atmospheric factors have supplanted psycho-somatic causes in the popular imagination but research evidence is still confused.

Early attempts at directly influencing airway reactivity have been largely abandoned and recent cognitive behavioural work has focused on stress reduction and self management. Courses to train Nurse-Specialists to work in primary care have added immensely to the scope and quality of asthma management in this setting. The UK National Asthma Campaign programme is based on the teaching of self-monitoring by Peak Expiratory Flow (PEF) and a simple assessment of symptoms such as cough, wheeze, breathlessness and tight chest. Control is divided into four zones; from 1 = under good control, to 4 = medical alert/emergency, with appropriate management indicated at each stage. An even simpler management plan along the same lines is produced by Baker Norton (see Materials and Addresses at end of Chapter).

Much more complex is the plan devised by Creer (1986) who has used a self-management package including the following elements:

(1) *Information Gathering* – monitoring and recording information related to asthma particularly precipitants of an attack summarised by the acronym CAPE:

     ° Collection of information.

     ° Analysis of the information.

- ° Problem detection.
- ° Evaluation of the problem and its potential solution.

(2) *Judgmental Processes*

- ° Setting personal standards of performance.
- ° Comparing them to the performance of others.
- ° Assessing the value of learning and performing self-management.
- ° Assessing the effects of self-management on performance.

(3) *Decision Making* –By problem solving (see Chapter Five).

(4) *Self Instruction.*

(5) *Stimulus Change* – avoiding triggers.

(6) *Response Change* – knowing when attacks are likely to occur and modifying behaviour, for example exercise accordingly.

(7) *Self Reaction* – reinforcement of continued practise by improved performance.

Although there is good research evidence of effectiveness, this programme might be seen to be over elaborate and recent work has suggested, unsurprising that it may increase distress by introspection (Hyland *et al.* 1995) unless distress reduction counselling is included. After all an asthmatic patient, particularly a child (and asthma is most prevalent in children), faces a major series of difficulties. He has a frightening, disabling illness which may strike embarrassingly and unexpectedly. It makes him different from other children, often dependent on medication and, not infrequently, periodic hospital admissions.

Many of the principles guiding self-management in asthma can be applied to the less reversible chronic obstructive airways disease occurring in later life.

Diabetes Mellitus

Profound and diverse psychological problems and challenges are more frequent in diabetes than in any other single medical condition. The young diabetic faces major problems in developing self-esteem, in schooling, in recreation and in family life. Although management of these cases will always require specialist help it may be preferable to attend clinics at least some of the time in the community, which may involve less labelling as 'sick' and be logistically easier. Problems may reach a peak when the challenges of adolescence and sexual development are already testing. Later the condition may profoundly affect interpersonal relationships, child-bearing and lead to the early onset of many of the involutional handicaps of later life.

The St Vincent Declaration in 1990 established the goals for improved diabetic care:

The Saint Vincent Declaration

General goals for people – children and adults – with diabetes

Sustained improvement in health experience and a life approaching normal expectation in quality and quantity.

Prevention and cure of diabetes and of its complications by intensifying research effort.

Five-year targets

Elaborate, initiate and evaluate comprehensive programmes for detection and control of diabetes and of its complications with self-care and community support as major components.

Raise awareness in the population and among health care professionals of the present opportunities and the future needs for prevention of the complications of diabetes and of diabetes itself.

Organise training and teaching in diabetes management and care for people of all ages with diabetes, for their families, friends and working associates and for the health care team.

Ensure that care for children with diabetes is provided by individuals and teams specialised both in the management of diabetes and of children, and that families with a diabetic child get the necessary social, economic and emotional support.

Reinforce existing centres of excellence in diabetes care, education and research. Create new centres where the need and potential exist.

Promote independence, equity and self-sufficiency for all people with diabetes; children, adolescents, those in the working years of life and the elderly.

Remove hindrances to the fullest possible integration of the diabetic citizen into society.

It will be seen that the recommendations have a high psychological content. A recent study (Diabetes Care Evaluation Team 1994) found, not surprisingly, that integration of diabetic care between hospitals and general practice was as effective as hospital care.

To enable the patient to survive these challenges help may be needed in a number of areas;

(1) *Prevention of an Unhealthy Life-style* – body weight, smoking, exercise and alcohol intake will all have enhanced effects for good or ill on the diabetic (see Chapter Eight).

(2) *Treatment Adherence* – this is fundamental if damage is to be avoided. This is best achieved by empowering the patient to take over control of his own management. Self-monitoring of blood glucose (SMBG) and more controversially the use of continuous subcutaneous insulin infusion (CSII) give the patient, if motivated and skilled, a large degree of control over insulin dependant diabetes. Education and techniques such as motivational interviewing (see Chapter Eight) may be helpful in this context. Experimental and practical education methods may be more effective than didactic ones. The diabetic with a health belief system based on self-efficacy and the value of good control has the foundation platform of satisfactory care (Kavanagh 1993). A thought and problem diary can be grafted onto the diabetic record to identify difficulties which can be tackled by cognitive techniques (see Chapter Five). The advent of the primary care Nurse Specialist has been very helpful in improving care and her role in the management of psychological issues can be expanded.

(3) *Stress Management* – diabetes causes stress and is effected by stress. Blood glucose has been found to be higher under high stress (Goetsch et al. 1994, Aikens et al. 1994)). Cognitive techniques, problem solving and time management may be more effective in diabetic stress than relaxation and biofeedback.

(4) *Prevention of Complications* – psychological complications such as depression and anxiety must be addressed in their own right (see Chapters Six and Nine). Activity scheduling and thinking diaries will reveal the content of the depressive situation and are a basis for formulating a management plan. Patients who develop physical complications may require psychological input.

HIV and AIDS

This is one of the most worrying and challenging diseases of our time with major psychological implications for prevention, detection and management (Antoni and Emmelcamp 1995).

The issue of HIV in primary care usually presents with a patient asking for an AIDS test. The first task is to discover why the patient has come. Generally they can be divided into five groups:

(1) Those whose requirements are purely *administrative* for travel or insurance. It is important to explain the significance of the test and explore briefly for deeper anxieties or psychological problems.

(2) Those with a *misconception* of the nature of AIDS. These patients require explanation and, once informed, often do not want to go ahead with the test.

(3) Those with moderate to severe health anxieties which currently focus on *morbid anxiety* about AIDS (see Hypochondriasis in Chapter Six).

(4) Those who have engaged in unsafe sex or are intravenous drug users. These patients are *at risk* and may have valid reasons to think that they may have become HIV positive.

(5) Young people anxious about a *new relationship* who may or may not have a substantial risk.

Time in assessment will be needed in all groups but particularly the third and fourth. Attention must be given to the cognitive, emotional, behavioural, social and physical factors determining the problems that each patient faces. We will attempt to highlight some of the most relevant primary care issues in each group.

The *administrative* group present fewest problems. It is important to see confidentiality is maintained at the highest level and to this end it may be worth passing all information regarding the test, if negative, to the patient so that nothing remains on the record that might lead to misunderstandings later or prove unfairly damaging in subsequent medical reports. Occasionally of course a test in this type of patient (and in types 2 and 3 will prove positive. This eventuality will be considered with Group 4).

Those suffering from *misconceptions* must be allowed time to explain their concerns and beliefs. These must then be corrected by a fully-informed professional. If the doctor or other primary care worker is unable to answer all the questions he must be prepared to pass the patient on to a specialised aids counsellor. These now exist in most areas.

Morbid anxiety about HIV and AIDS has become common enough in recent years to present frequently in GPs surgeries and may be the largest of the four groups. They can be very distressed people presenting formidable problems in management. Scrag (1995) considers that they lie between the hypochondriac who believes his fears to be realistic and does not resist them and the obsessive who employs a number of techniques in an attempt to suppress, ignore or neutralise his symptoms. Issues of guilt and responsibility also feature prominently.

Unfortunately, although there has been some research on possible formulations of this common problem, very little has been published about the outcome of interventions. It would appear that challenging distorted thinking, abandoning reassurance seeking behaviour (Warwick and Salkovskis 1985) and modifying unhelpful beliefs is the best avenue of management. It is usually unnecessary and may be harmful to refer patients from this group to AIDS specialists (see Hypochondriasis, Chapter Six).

With the *at risk* group a number of issues must be considered:

(1) The nature of the test and of AIDS/HIV to make sure the patient is fully informed.

(2) The pros and cons of having the test. Here the motivational interviewing techniques may be helpful (see Chapter Eight). A positive test has profound implications for life insurance, job prospects and for relationships. On the other hand knowing removes uncertainty and this, strangely enough, is often felt as a relief even in some positive cases. It also enables lifestyle changes to be planned more logically and fundamental decisions to be taken on an informed basis.

(3) How wider social relationships might be affected by a positive test. Friends are often horrified.

(4) Deciding who should be told and when should the test be positive. This would include consideration of partners, children, wider family and perhaps close friends.

(5) Should more specialised advice be offered? No primary care worker has the aids knowledge of the specialised centres and self-help groups and this should be acknowledged. Information on these centres should be available and referral made as appropriate.

These considerations may take time and thought and it is important that this should be allowed.

The Positive Patient

If the test proves positive a healthy patient may have to live with this information for years. Most will receive some specialist advice when inforemed of the result but many do not have, or want, continued specialist contact as long as they remain well. An informed and empathetic GP or primary care worker is, however, a valuable confidant. From time to time discussion or action will be needed on the following issues:

(1) Medical examination to reassure about current health.

(2) The marked differences in the individual course of the positive patient. The importance of maintaining good general health (see Appendix 1 permission needed).

(3) How the virus is transmitted (see Appendix 2).

(4) Safer sex – whether to tell their partner and risk rejection or face vituperation when the partner finds out anyway. How to approach the subject – simple truth soon after the discovery is usually best (see Appendix 3).

(5) Discussion of latest research findings.

(6) Dealing appropriately with concomitant depression and anxiety.

(7) Helping with social support (Zuckerman and Antoni 1995).

(8) Helping with practical problems (see Appendix 4).

The Ill Patient

The care of the ill patient will be shared with specialist services and his or her psychological needs approach those of any other patient with a fatal and subsequently terminal illness (see Chapter Twelve).

Skin Disorders

The emotional component in the aetiology of various skin disorders has been recognised for many years. There may be some question as to whether emotional factors are primary causes or secondary consequences of the eczema group of conditions, but the psychological effect of any disfiguring and uncomfortable condition is immense.

Many eczema sufferers are children and the first essential of management is education of both patient, if feasible, and parents. Explanation is needed of the nature of the condition, the likely causative factors, the natural history, any necessary or particular unnecessary restrictions, and finally what can, and cannot, be done in the way of treatment. Co-operation, understanding and agreement of parents about the treatment plan is even more necessary in these cases than in other medical conditions.

Many parents of eczema sufferers are anxious and sometimes feel guilty about their child's condition. This in turn may have an adverse effect on the clinical course by adding to the child's anxiety and thus his scratching. Specific anxiety-reduction measures for both parents and child may be needed but even more necessary is a tactful approach to the problem.

A number of specific measures have been applied. The most useful are; (i) the extinction of scratching coupled to the reinforcement of scratching-free periods which may be gradually lengthened; and (ii) stress management techniques in general and particularly relaxation, sometimes EMG assisted (Pinkerton *et al.* 1982), and habit reversal (Jaspers 1994). Skin sufferers tend to have rather low self-esteem and therefore adjuvant treatment in the form of assertiveness training, self-reinforcement or other cognitive measures may be added. It is particularly important that they are shown how to cope with embarrassment or teasing. A children's relaxation tape is available (see Tapes for Children at the end of this chapter).

Gastro-intestinal Problems

Anorexia, bulimia and encopresis are discussed elsewhere in this book. Interest in the psychological causes of peptic ulcer has receded as H. Pylori infection and other physical mechanisms have become better understood.

Irritable Bowel Syndrome

Patients presenting with gastro intestinal symptoms for which no pathology can be demonstrated remain a challenge. Many patients continue to have pain and disordered bowel habit following an infection although in some cases the onset is spontaneous.

Mechanism of onset or maintenance may involve:

(1)   Hyper-responsiveness of the bowel muscle.

(2)   Enhanced perception of muscle activity.

(3)   Greater exposure to stress.

(4)   Conditioning processes often involving illness behaviour.

Intervention involves exploring the patients own concerns and attributions and correcting misconceptions where necessary. This may be followed by life style management involving dietary modification and increasing exercise. Associated conditions in particular anxiety and depression which are both often present (Schwarz *et al.* 1993), are managed independently. More specifically, methods for changing reinforcement to reward 'well behaviour' the health anxiety techniques of Warwick and Salkovskis (1985), and practical coping strategies about how to leave a room without embarrassment and how to protect against possible soiling may be important. Direct biofeedback methods of bowel motility control have had their vogue but outcomes were unconvincing.

Stoma Patients

The psycho-social problems of this important group of patients have received a good deal of recent attention (Bekkers *et al.* 1995). These may be summarised under three headings:

(1) *Anxiety and Depression* – the incidence of these is highest immediately following the operation and is particularly common in those shown to be vulnerable in their past history. Appropriate management along normal lines should be considered (see Chapters Six and Nine).

(2) *Social, Recreational and Occupational Restriction* – this is common in 10 to 40 per cent of sufferers. Management consists of:

    (a)   Stoma care improvements.

    (b)   Cognitive challenge to distorted thinking and beliefs.

    (c)   Situational problem solving.

(3) *Sexual Problems* – these are particularly common in men under sixty. In primary care awareness is probably most important as good help can be obtained from the stoma associations.

Gynaecological problems

There are a number of specific problems involving womens' health which have received attention. Within a generation the free availability of oral contraception has revolutionised sexual behaviour in young people only to be currently threatened by the world increase of HIV/AIDS.

Dysmenorrhoea

This is now felt to be primarily a prostaglandin dysfunction but psychological processes must be involved. Treatment has essentially been by prostaglandin inhibitors but useful, and perhaps more permanent, measures address relaxation training, desensitisation and exercise. The research literature is scarce.

Premenstrual Syndrome

The aetiology of this distressing condition is confused. Many believe that a change in progesterone levels or ratios in the luteal phase of the month is central to the cause but research evidence is scanty and confusing. Recently the role of endorphins in determining which patients will suffer has been invoked. When it comes to treatment progesterone supplements and diuretics have had their enthusiasts but research support for either is conspicuous by its absence. Some dietary measures have also been tried. Psychological treatments have concentrated on stress management, other cognitive techniques and life style changes but, again, although enquiring enthusiasm has been shown, research evidence of effectiveness is lacking.

The Menopause

Whilst there is general agreement about the role of the menopause in causing vasomotor symptoms and atrophic vaginitis, the role of diminished oestrogens in the psychological changes associated with the menopause is increasingly disputed (Pearce *et al.* 1995). Alternative theories involving stress and perceptions of women's roles in life seem more convincing (Gannon 1989). The clinical impression of help from hormone replacement with these symptoms remains strong but evaluative studies in this field are dogged by confounding factors.

Hysterectomy

This is a topic surrounded by myth and folklore. Perhaps more than in other operations it is important that the patient is fully informed and has a chance to ask questions that she may feel are embarrassing or even stupid. Written information is helpful.

Urethral Syndrome

This is a distressing and fairly common female disorder. Recent work (Bernstein *et al.* 1992) discounts anxiety and depression as factors in aetiology and establishes demonstrable abnormalities of pelvic floor musculature which might be subject to re-training by relaxation techniques or pelvic floor exercises.

In-Vitro Fertilisation Failure

Approximately half the couples who attempt this procedure fail. Coping after this disappointment is related to previous distress and feelings of loss of control. Cognitive techniques already described combined with goal setting, life plans and sex therapy can be used as appropriate (see Chapter Seven).

Long Term Disability

The GP and other members of the PHCT have a central role in helping the chronically disabled as:

(1) Their relationship with the patient is likely to be an enduring one.

(2) They are able to direct the patient to specialised resources judged on the clinical picture at a periodic re-assessment and the patient's expressed needs. It is notable that today new advances are often seen by the patient on television or in the popular press before they come to the attention of the clinician.

Some knowledge, therefore, of the psychological adjustment and coping processes of the disabled belongs in this text. Wright (1983) considers the essential ingredients of adjustment to be as follows:

(1) Enlarging the scope of one's values.

(2) Containing the effects of disability.

(3) Transforming values based on comparison with others into values based on one's own assets and strengths.

The primary care clinician may help in a number of simple ways, for example, by suggesting disabled swimming or riding and by pointing out that those in wheel chairs can play many games and sports with the able-bodied.

Moos and Tsu (1977) found the following processes to be associated with adjustment:

(1) Changing one's beliefs and goals.

(2) Avoiding 'taking it out' on others.

(3) Abandoning fantasies of 'getting better'.

(4) Accepting responsibility for one's disability and not seeing oneself as a burden on others.

(5) Information seeking.

(6) Threat minimisation – keeping feelings to oneself.

These are appropriate for management in the surgery setting where they form a framework which can be tackled piecemeal over a period of time at several consultations.

In management Nerenz and Leventhal (1983) describe a self-regulation approach in the following stages:

(1)   The representation of the illness or disability involving information gathering and interpretation to estimate the risks and threats to health and well-being; this should lead to stage (2).

(2)   Action planning, involving the choice and trial of different coping strategies along problem solving lines.

(3)   Monitoring and appraisal of their effectiveness.

This model is easily adaptable to the high frequency, low contact consulting pattern of primary care and enables the clinician to plan a useful intervention. Johnston (1996) proposes a new model incorporating some aspects of Leventhal's but adding a number of cognitive factors. This may result in some therapeutic advantages.

In practical terms it is useful for patients to find new activities and goals which are useful and maintain self-esteem without feeling that they are always a compromise. Patients often describe increased abilities and sensitivities in previously untapped areas, for example creative activities like art, music or writing or perhaps sport. One patient was excited to get a leaflet about disabled golf through the letter box soon after an above knee amputation. He had never played golf before but the leaflet was a stimulus to take it up which he did very successfully.

References

Aikens, J.E., Wallander, J.L., Bell, D.S.H. and McNorton, A. (1994) 'A normothetic-idiographic study of daily psychological stress and blood glucose in women with Type 1 diabetes mellitus.' *Journal of Behavioural Medicine 17*, 6, 535–48.

Alderman, M.H. (1994) 'Non-pharmacological treatment of hypertension.' *Lancet 344*, 307–11.

Alexander, C.N., Schneider, R.H., Barnes, V.A., Rainforth, M.V., Newman, R.I., Davies, J.L., Chandler, H.M. and Robinson, P.M. (1996) 'The effects of transcendental meditation on the psychological risk factors, cardiovascular disease and all cause mortality: A review of meta-analyses and controlled clinical trials.' Paper presented at the 10th European Conference of Health Psychology, Dublin, September 1996.

Antoni, M.H. and Emmelcamp, P.M.G. (1995) 'Special issue on HIV/AIDS.' *Clinical Psychology and Psychotherapy 2*, 4, 199–284.

Bekkers, M.J.T.M., van Knippenberg, F.C.E., van den Borne, H.W., Poen, H., Bergsma, J. and vanBergeHenegouwen, G.P. (1995) 'Psychosocial adaptation to stoma surgery: a review.' *Journal of Behavioural Medicine 18*, 1, 1–31.

Bennink, C.D., Hulst, L.L. and Benthem, J.A. (1982) 'The effects of EM. biofeedback and relaxation training on primary dysmenorrhoea.' Journal of Behavioural Medicine 5, 329–41.

Bernstein, A.M., Philips, H.C., Linden, W. and Fenster, H. (1992) 'A psychological evaluation of female urethral syndrome: Evidence for a muscular abnormality.' Journal of Behavioural Medicine 15, 3, 299–312.

Budd, R.J. and Pugh, R. (1996) 'The relationship between coping style, tinnitus and emotional distress in a group of tinnitus sufferers.' British Journal of Health Psychology 1, 219–229.

Creer, T.L., Backial, M., Burns, K.L., Ullman, S. and Leung, P. (1986) Living with Asthma: Part 1 Manual for Teaching Parents the Self-management of Childhood Asthma. Part 2 Manual for Teaching Children the Self Management of Asthma. NIH Publication 86–2364 Washington DC: U.S. Department of Health and Human Sciences.

Cromwell, R.L., Butlerfield, E.C., Brayfield, F.M. and Curry, J.J. (1977) Acute Myocardial Infarction: Reaction and Recovery. St Louis: Mosby.

Deffenbacher, J.L. (1994) 'Anger reduction: Issues assessment and intervention strategies.' In A.W. Siegman and T.W. Smith (eds) Anger Hostility and the Heart. Hillsdale: NJ Erlbaum.

Denollet, J. (1993) 'Biobehavioral research on coronary heart disease: Where is the person?' Journal of Behavioural Medicine 16, 2, 115–141.

Diabetes Care Evaluation Team (1994) 'Integrated care for diabetes: clinical, psychosocial and economic evaluation.' British Medical Journal 308, 1208–12.

Eccleston, C. (1995) 'Chronic pain and distraction: An experimental investigation into the role of sustained and shifting attention in the processing of chronic pain.' Behaviour research and Therapy 33, 4, 391–405.

Elder, J.P. (1985) 'Applications of behaviour modification to community health education: the case of heart disease prevention.' Health Education Quarterly 12, 151–68.

Faber, S.D. and Burns, J.W. (1996) 'Anger management style, degree of expressed anger, and gender influence cardiovascular recovery from interpersonal harassment.' Journal of Behavioural Medicine 19, 31–53.

Flor, H., Fydrich, T. and Turck, D.C. (1992) 'Efficacy of multidisciplinary pain treatment centre: a meta-analytic review.' Pain 49, 221–30.

Flor, H. and Turk, D.C. (1989) 'Psychophysiology of chronic pain: Do chronic pain patients exhibit symptom-specific psychophysiological responses?' Psychological Bulletin 105, 215–59.

Fordyce, W.F. (1976) Behavioural Methods for Chronic Pain and Illness. St. Louis: Mosby.

France, R. (1993) 'Coping with stress – the Yateley Stress Group In Royal College of General Practitioners.' Stress Management in General Practice. Occasional Paper 61. London: RCGP Paper.

Friedman, M. and Rosenman. R.H. (1974) Type A Behavior and Your Heart. New York: Knopf.

Gannon, L. (1989) 'Dysmenorrhoea, pre-menstrual syndrome and the menopause.' In S. Pearce and J. Wardle (eds) The Practice of Behavioural Medicine. Leicester: British Psychological Society, p.208.

Gautier, J. (1983) 'Blood volume pulse biofeedback in the treatment of migraine headaches: a controlled evaluation.' Biofeedback and Self-Regulation 8, 427–42.

Gidron, Y. and Davidson, K. (1996) 'Development and preliminary testing of a brief intervention for modifying CHD-predictive hostility components.' Journal of Behavioural Medicine 19, 3, 203–19.

Goetsch, V.L., Abel, J.L. and Pope, M.K. (1994) 'The effects of stress, mood and coping on blood glucose in NIDDM: A prospective pilot evaluation.' *Behaviour research and Therapy 32*, 5, 503–10.

Hatch, J.P., Moore, P.J., Borcherding, S., Cyr-Provost, M., Boutros, N.N. and Seleshi, N.N. (1992) 'Electromyographic and affective responses of episodic tension-type headache patients and headache free controls during stressful task performance.' *Journal of Behavioural Medicine 15*, 1, 89–112.

Hevey, D., McGee, H. and Horgan, J.J. (1996) 'Evaluation of Psycho–Social outcomes of cardiac rehabilitation: a systematic overview.' Paper presented at the 10th European Conference of Health Psychology, Dublin, September 1996.

Hyland, M., Ley, A., Fisher, D. and Woodward, V. (1995) 'All about asthma bother.' *British Journal of Clinical Psychology 34*, 601–11.

Jaspers, J.P.C. (1994) 'Behaviour therapy in patients with chronic skin disease.' *Clinical Psychology and Psychotherapy 1*, 4, 202–9.

Jeffrey, R.W. (1991) 'Weight management and hypertension.' *Annals of Behavioural Medicine 13*, 18–22.

Johnston, D.W. (1982) 'Behavioural treatment in the reduction of coronary risk factors. Type A behaviour and blood pressure.' *British Journal of Clinical Psychology 21*, 281–94.

Johnston, D. (1992) 'The management of stress in the prevention of coronary heart disease.' *International Research of Health Psychology 1*, 57–83.

Johnston, D. and Steptoe, A. (1989) 'Hypertension (Passim).' In S. Pearce and J. Wardle (eds) *The Practice of Behavioural Medicine.* Leicester and Oxford: British Psychological Society and Oxford University Press.

Johnston, M. (1996) 'Models of disability.' *The Psychologist* May 1996, 205–210.

Johnston, M. and Johnston, D. (1996) 'Do coping styles predict distress in the year following myocardial infarction?' Paper presented at the 10th European Conference of Health Psychology, Dublin, September 1996.

Kanagh, D.L., Gooley, S. and Wilson, P.H. (1993) 'Prediction of adherence and control in diabetes.' *Journal of Behavioural Medicine 16*, 5, 509–22.

Kannel, W.B., Wilson, P. and Blair, S.N. (1985) 'Epidemiological assessment of the role of physical activity and fitness in the development of cardiovascular disease.' *American Heart Journal 109*, 820–825.

Kimberley, A., DuCharme and Brawley, L.R. (1995) 'Predicting the intentions and behavior of exercise initiates using two forms of self-efficacy.' *Journal of Behavioural Medicine 18*, 5, 479–497.

Laerum, E., Johnsen, N., Smith, P. and Larsen, S. (1988) 'Myocardial infarction may induce positive changes in life style and in the quality of life.' *Scandinavian Journal of Primary Health Care 6*, 67–71.

Linton, S.J. (1982) 'Applied relaxation as a method of coping with chronic pain: A therapist's guide.' *Scandinavian Journal of Behaviour Therapy 11*, 161–72.

Lovibond, S.H., Birrell, P. and Langeluddeckle, P. (1986) 'Changing coronary heart-disease risk factor status: the effects of three behavioural programmes.' *Journal of Behavioural Medicine 9*, 415–37.

Lewin, B. (1995) 'Cardiac disorders.' In A. Bloom and S. Llewelyn (eds) *Health Psychology.* London: Chapman hall (2nd Ed) p.150.

Martin, P.R. (1982) 'Spasmodic torticollis: A behavioural perspective.' *Journal of Behavioural Medicine 5*, 249–73.

Meichenbrum, D. (1977) *Cognitive Behavior Modification*. New York: Plenum, pp.143–182.

Melzack, R. (1973) *The Puzzle of Pain*. New York: Basic Books.

Melzack, R. and Wall, P.D. (1985) *The Challenge of Pain*. Harmondsworth: Penguin.

Mitchell, K.R. and White, R.G. (1977) 'Behavioural self-management: An application to the problem of migraine headaches.' *Behavioural Therapy 8*, 213–21.

Moos, R.H. and Tsu, V.D. (1977) 'The crisis of physical illness: an overview.' In R. Moss (ed) *Coping with Physical Illness*. New York: Plenum.

Nelson, L., Jennings, G.L., Esler, M.B. and Korner, P.I. (1986) 'The effect of changing levels of physical activity on blood pressure and haemodynamics in essential hypertension.' *Lancet 8505*, 473–476.

Nerenz, D.R. and Leventhal, H. (1983) 'Self-regulation therapy in chronic illness.' In T.G. Burrish and L.A. Bradley. *Coping with Chronic Diseases*. London: Academic Press.

O'Boyle, C.A. (1996) 'Quality of Life assessment: a paradigm shift.' Keynote address presented at the 10th European Conference of Health Psychology, Dublin, September 1996.

Patel, C. and Marmot, M. (1988) 'Can general practitioners use training in relaxation and management of stress to reduce mild hypertension?' *British Medical Journal 292*, 21–24.

Patel, C., Marmot, M.G., Terry, D.J., Carruthers, M., Hunt, B. and Patel, M. (1985) 'Trial of relaxation in reducing coronary risk: Four year follow-up.' *British Medical Journal 290*, 1103–1106.

Pearce, J., Hawton, K. and Blake, F. (1995) 'Psychological and sexual symptoms associated with the menopause and the effects of hormone replacement therapy.' *British Journal of Psychiatry 167*, 163–73.

Pikoff, K. (1984) 'Is the muscular model of headache still viable? A review of conflicting data.' *Headache 24*, 186–98.

Pinkerton, S., Hughes, H. and Wenrich, W.W. (1982) *Behavioural Medicine: Clinical Applications*. New York and Chichester: John Wiley.

Roa, S.M. (1986) 'Neuropsychology of multiple sclerosis: A critical review.' *Journal of Clinical and Experimental Neuropsychology 8*, 50, 503–542.

Scrag, P. (1995) 'A critical analysis of morbid fear of HIV/AIDS.' *Clinical Psychology and Psychotherapy 2*, 4, 278–84.

Schwarz, S.P., Blanchard, E.B., Berreman, C.F., Scharff, L., Taylor, A.E., Greene, B.R., Suls, J.M. and Malamood, H.S. (1993) 'Psychological aspects of irritable bowel syndrome: comparison with inflammatory bowel disease and non-patient controls.' *Behaviour Research and Therapy 31*, 297–304.

Siegel, and Blumenthal, J.A. (1991) 'The role of exercise in the prevention and treatment of hypertension.' *Annals of Behavioural Medicine 13*, 23–30.

Turner, J.A. and Chapman, C.R. (1982) 'Psychological interventions in chronic pain: a critical review I and II.' *Pain 12*, 1–146.

Turk, D.C., Meichenbrum, D and Genest, M. (1983) *Pain and Behavioural Medicine: A Cognitive Behavioural Perspective*. New York: Guildford.

Warwick, H.M.C. and Salkovskis, P. (1985) 'Reassurance.' *British Medical Journal 290*, 1028.

Wickrama, K., Conger, R.D. and Lorenz, F.O. (1995) 'Work, marriage, lifestyle and changes in men's physical health.' *Journal of Behavioural Medicine 182*, 97–109.

Wiklund, I., Sanne, H., Vedin. A. and Wilhelmsson, C. (1985) 'Coping with myocardial infarction: a model with clinical applications, a literature review.' *International Rehabilitation Medicine* 7, 167–75.

Williams, A.CdeC. and Erskine, A. (1990) 'Chronic pain.' In A. Bloom and S. Llewelyn (eds) *Health Psychology*. London: Chapman and Hall (2nd Ed), pp.368–71.

Wright (1983) *Psychological Aspects of Physical Disablement*. London: Harper and Rowe.

Zuckerman, M.J. and Antoni, M.H. (1995) 'Social support and its relationship to psychological, physical health and immune variables in HIV infection.' *Clinical Psychology and Psychotherapy* 2, 4, 210–9.

Materials and Addresses:

Asthma Management Plan – Baker Norton, Gemini House, Flex Meadow, Harlow, Essex, CM 19 5TJ.

Self-management and peak flow measurement – National Asthma Campaign, 300 Upper Street, London N1 2XX. Tel 0171 2262260.

The Terence Higgins Trust – Helpline 0171 242 1010.

Recommended for Further Reading:

Bradley, C. (1994) *Handbook of Psychology and Diabetes*. Reading: Harwood.

British Diabetic Association – Recommendations for the Management of Diabetes in Primary Care. BDA 10, Queen Anne Street, London W1M OBD.

Broome, A. and Llewelyn, S. (eds) (1995) *Health Psychology* (Second Edition). London: Chapman and Hall.

Broome, A. and Wallace, L. (eds) (1984) *Psychology and Gynaecological Problems*. London: Tavistock.

Clinical Psychology and Psychotherapy 2, 4. Special Issue HIV/Aids.

Christie, M. and French, D. (1995) *Assessment of Quality of Life in Childhood Asthma*. Reading: Harwood.

Fordyce W.E. (1976) *Behavioral Methods for Chronic Pain and Illness*. St Louis: Moseby.

Friedman, H.S. (1990) *The Self Healing Personality: Why Some People Achieve Health and Others Succumb to Illness*. New York: Henry Holt.

Green, J. and McCreaner, A. (eds) (1996) *Counselling in HIV Infection and Aids – Second Edition*. Oxford: Blackwell Scientific.

Melzack, R. (1973) *The Puzzle of Pain*. New York: Basic Books.

Pearce, S. and Wardle, W. *The Practice of Behavioural Medicine*. Leicester: British Psychological Society and Oxford: Oxford University Press.

Steptoe, A. and Mathews, A.M. (eds) (1984) *Health Care and Human Behaviour*. London: Academic Press.

Tapes for Patients:

I Can Relax (Childrens' Relaxation Tape) by Jane Madders from Relaxation for Living, 12 New Street, Chipping-Norton, Oxon OX7 5LG.

Appendix 1: POSITIVE HEALTH BEHAVIOURS

(1) Avoid other sexually transmitted diseases by following 'safer sex'. These may be co-factors, that is, they may worsen the prognosis.

(2) Some live vaccines should be avoided as they may act as co-factors. Check with your doctor who may consult a list published in the British National Formulary.

(3) Women should avoid pregnancy which is a risk to the child.

(4) Eat a balanced diet.

(5) Avoid uncooked, or partially cooked, meat or fish because of the risk of possible infection from other pathogens.

(6) Engage in appropriate exercise.

(7) Reduce use of recreational drugs, including alcohol to moderate levels.

(8) Reduce levels of stress.

(9) Engage in relaxation, muscular relaxation, yoga or meditation as you prefer.

(10) Increase the amount of pleasurable activities to maintain mood.

(*Source:* Green, J. (1989) 'Counselling in HIV and Aids.' In S. Pearce and J. Wardle. *The Practice of Behavioural Medicine.* Oxford: British Psychological Society. We gratefully acknowledge the permission of the publishers to reproduce this table and the assistance of the author in revising it.)

Appendix 2: ROUTES OF TRANSMISSION OF HIV

The following are known routes of transmission:

Blood and Blood Products: if infected blood from one person gets into the body of another person, the recipient may contract HIV infection. Many cases of infection have occurred worldwide in the past through whole blood transfusion (now screened in most countries) and through Factor VIII concentrate used in the treatment of haemophilia (now heat treated to inactivate the virus).

Injecting drug users can pass on HIV through blood by contaminating a syringe that is shared with others. They may inject themselves, pull blood back into the syringe and then re-inject it leading to particularly heavy contamination of the syringe. There is no evidence that infection can occur through blood contamination of intact skin but in very rare cases infected blood coming into contact with extensively damaged skin appears to have caused infection.

Tissue and Organ Transplants: similar considerations apply as for blood.

Semen: relatively large amounts of virus can be present in the semen of infected men. This can enter the sexual partner via the vagina, cervix and rectal mucosa, all areas that have cells related to T cells present. Damage to these areas is thought to aid transmission but not to be necessary for infection to occur.

Vaginal and Cervical Secretions: can contain relatively large amounts of virus. In female to male infections the virus probably passes across the glans rather than the shaft which is skin covered. Lesions to the penis are not necessary for transmission to occur.

Breast Milk: can contain considerable amounts of virus. Breast milk is now considered to provide a substantial additional risk of infection to the child and so breast feeding by an infected mother should be avoided where safe alternatives exist.

Other Materno-foetal transmission *in utero* and at birth occurs. The relative importance of these two is still not clear.

The following are **not** thought to be routes of transmission:

Saliva, Tears, Faeces and Sweat: the levels of virus found in these body fluids are extremely low and, in the case of saliva, there is some evidence that enzymes may inactivate the virus.

Overall: transmission of the virus is dependant, in practice, on two things. The first is the amount of virus present in the body fluid or tissue – the higher the concentration the greater the risk. The second is that the virus has to get *into* the body to cause infection. There is no evidence that it is able to cross intact skin, therefore the virus must come into contact with either non-skin surfaces like the vaginal and rectal linings, or be carried through the skin, as with blood transfusion.

Millions of people are infected worldwide. It is impossible to rule out very rare cases of unusual transmissions but there have been so many cases that we can be confident about how virus can and cannot be transmitted.

(*Source:* Green. J. (1996) Post-test counselling p.45. In J. Green and A. McCreaner (eds) *Counselling in HIV Infection and Aids.* Second Edition. Oxford: Blackwell Scientific. We gratefully acknowledge the permission of the author and publisher to reproduce this table.)

Appendix 3: CURRENT SAFER SEX ADVICE

Vaginal Intercourse: HIV is transmitted from male to female and female to male in vaginal sex. The only entirely safe approach is to avoid such sex entirely. However, a condom provides protection providing it is used properly and does not break. Condoms should be used with water based lubricants. Oil based lubricants will weaken condoms and therefore will lead to breakages. The effectiveness of the female condom in this context remains to be established. The use of spermicidal agents such as nonoxynol-9 for additional antivirus protection is not supported by the available evidence. Women should be advised to use a second method of contraception, such as the pill or diaphragm, in addition to the condom in order to provide better protection against pregnancy.

Anal Intercourse: the receptive partner is at high risk in anal sex. However, the risks to the insertive partner appear to be much lower, although some still exist. The use of condoms provides protection for both partners providing that there is no breakage. Breakages are probably more common in anal than vaginal intercourse, but if condoms are used with care and with liberal amounts of water based lubricant, such breakages can be kept to a minimum. As with vaginal sex, the only completely safe way is to avoid anal sex altogether.

Oral Sex: this remains an area of debate. The difficulty of finding individuals who have only ever had oral sex makes it difficult to assess the potential risk. In fellatio it is likely to be the receptive partner who is at risk and this risk is markedly reduced if intra-oral ejaculation is avoided. Any risks could be further reduced by the use of a condom. Many prostitutes use a condom for this purpose, but many other people find condoms unaesthetic. A handful of reports on possible transmission in cunnilingus are difficult to evaluate, hence the value of dental dams etc. is uncertain.

Sharing sex toys: for instance, dildos, vibrators. High risk and to be avoided.

Oral-anal contact (rimming): to be avoided because of the risk of transmission of pathogens from the gut. These may be a particular risk to immunocompromised individuals, such as those with HIV infection.

Inserting hand into rectum (fisting): can cause damage to anorectal area and, if followed up with anal sex, can potentially increase risk to both partners.

Water Sports (urinating on partners body): not a risk in itself.

Mutual Masturbation: safe. Can be engaged in with as many people as desired, as often as desired.

Body Rubbing (frottage): safe if kept to rubbing genitalia against skin.

Other Activities: the ingenuity of the human mind knows no bounds when it comes to sex. However, the risk of any behaviour can usually be assessed by analogy to one of the above items. Any activity involving contact between cervical or vaginal secretions, blood or semen and areas not covered by intact skin are probably best avoided.

Other Infections: the above advice is for protection against HIV. It is worth remembering that other sexually transmitted diseases can be transmitted in other ways and that these may act as co factors for HIV disease progression, as well as having adverse effects in their own right. While mutual masturbation and body rubbing are likely to be safe for more or less everything, other sexual behaviours carry different risks.

(*Source:* Green. J. (1996) Post-test counselling p.52. In J. Green and A. McCreaner (eds) *Counselling in HIV Infection and Aids.* Second Edition. Oxford: Blackwell Scientific. We gratefully acknowledge the permission of the author and publisher to reproduce this table.)

Appendix 4: SOME PRACTICAL ISSUES FOR THE PATIENT WITH AIDS

(1) *Loss of Income:* PWAs may lose their jobs through long spells off work or physical loss of ability to work.

(2) *Housing problems:* PWAs who lose income may be unable to continue to pay the mortgage or rent and may need assistance. They may be unable to cope with a large house or the stairs in a flat and may need to move elsewhere. They may be unable adequately to heat their property.

(3) *Loss of Social Life:* PWAs may no longer be able to go out as often as in the past for physical reasons or because they cannot afford it. they may need help to build up a social life appropriate to their capacities. Volunteers 'buddies' can play an important part in preventing isolation as can the groups run by organisations such as the Terence Higgins Trust, BM AIDS. London: WC1N 3XX.

(4) *Self Care:* PWAS may find that for financial or physical reasons they cannot cook the food that they need or clean their home. They may need help through other agencies in obtaining a range of social security benefits and services.

(5) *Travel Problems:* PWAs may be unable to drive, or to get about on public transport, and may need help from voluntary and statutory agencies in tavelling. For instance some local authorities will offer assistance with taxis through 'taxi card' schemes.

(6) Widespread prejudice and discrimination against those with AIDS.

(*Source:* Green, J. (1989) Counselling in HIV and Aids. In S. Pearce and J. Wardle. *The Practice of Behavioural Medicine.* Oxford: British Psychological Society. We gratefully acknowledge the permission of the publishers to reproduce this table and the assistance of the author in revising it.)

Chapter Twelve

Problems of Childhood and Adolescence

Many of the most effective behavioural interventions in primary care are with children. There are several reasons for this. First, children learn, unlearn and relearn with a rapidity that their elders envy. Second, a parent or teacher is almost always at hand to act as a co-therapist; and third, the reinforcers of a child's behaviour are much easier to control than those of an adult. The last is probably the most important factor but it also highlights a potential ethical problem as the very dependency of children on adults makes them particularly vulnerable to misdirected attempts at behaviour modification. For this reason the triangular nature of any therapy involving children must always be taken into account in a behavioural assessment. Otherwise, not only will the effectiveness of the intervention suffer but harm may occur through failure to distinguish parents' problems and needs from those of the child.

It is important to decide at the outset whether a problem exists at all. Many children are brought to the surgery by anxious parents with 'problems' which are in fact only less usual examples of the very wide variation of the normal. An explanation about the range of sleeping and eating patterns in infancy or rebellious behaviour in adolescence may be all that is needed. If a problem does exist, it is necessary to decide whether it belongs solely to parent, solely to the child or much more commonly, in varying proportions to each. A frequent example is the non-sleeping baby who may himself be miserable but is causing a far greater degree of distress to his fraught mother.

Once the nature, severity and functional determinants of the problem are plain, the advantages of treatment in primary care often become apparent, as it is possible to deal with problems away from school hours so that the intervention is kept as discreet and 'normal' as possible. Many problems with smaller children can receive attention before school age when the health visitor, with her knowledge of the home and family, is well placed to initiate or collaborate in treatment. This low-key approach enables potential problems to be recognised and helped at an early stage. This benefits both parent and child. However, if the problems give cause for greater concern then referral may be necessary and urgent and the workings of the Children's Act implemented (Herbert 1993).

In general, programmes for children need to be rigid enough to work but not so inflexible that they become punishing for both child and parents. Parents are often so exhausted and at the end of their tether that initial changes must be kept small and very gradual for them to be able to co-operate consistently. Extra care and imagination must be taken in specifying target behaviours in steps which are clearly understood and which are possible in the prevailing circumstances. The most carefully thought-out toiletting programme will come to nothing if the youngster is unable to reach the door handle of the lavatory which is always kept shut. A small boy may see older boys urinate standing up and adapt quickly standing up to urinate in a small bucket rather than being made to sit on a potty. These sorts of problem are sometimes difficult to spot if programmes are run from the surgery or office without home visits by at least one member of the team. It is important to see that a programme demands only behaviour that is age- and ability-appropriate and, if at all possible, already exists in the child's repertory. New behaviours can be built up by a variety of modelling, shaping and chaining procedures which have already been described in Chapter Five but the reinforcement of existing responses is clearly much more economical.

Most of the rest of this chapter will consider a number of specific problems which are amongst those most commonly seen in primary care. The techniques of assessment, data collection and basic methods of intervention have been described in Part One of this book. Some of the examples used there involve children. The reader is advised to refer back to these sections. Many of the chapters in Part Two, notably those on anxiety-related problems and habit disorders, contain much that is applicable to children as well as adults and may also be useful.

We will not deal specifically with classroom or institutional problems as these are outside our scope. It is, however, worth pointing out that a telephone call to the school is usually very rewarding when dealing with any school-aged patient. Some schools will cooperate to a limited extent, if approached tactfully, in such things as record keeping and data collection but it should always be remembered when asking for this that teachers have a heavy work load. We will not deal with the topical and delicate subjects of physical, sexual and emotional abuse of children. We realise these areas are important but feel that referral to expert agencies is always necessary both because of the seriousness of the problems and the likelihood that any attempt at primary care intervention may risk damage to the long-term professional relationship with the family. Although families will inevitably become involved in behavioural interventions with children, we do not feel competent to discuss formal family therapy and the interested reader is referred to specialised manuals.

Before dealing with some of the commonest specific problems, we are going to reconsider the concepts of reinforcement and Time-Out (from positive reinforcement) and the way in which they are used.

Reinforcement

The main principles governing the use of reinforcement as an instrument of behaviour change have been considered in Chapter Four. We return to it here not only because positive reinforcement is the most powerful instrument in changing children's behaviour but also because inappropriate reinforcement is often responsible for maintaining problems in the first place. Let us consider Kevin who is grizzling for sweets at the check-out of the supermarket. The most likely outcome is that sweets are given or are sometimes given. If Kevin never gets sweets in this situation he will soon realise that grizzling is unproductive. If sweets on the other hand are always forthcoming, Kevin is on a continuous schedule of positive reinforcement. If sweets are sometimes forthcoming, perhaps admixed with an occasional clip round the ear, he is on a variable ratio intermittent schedule of positive reinforcement which, as we have seen in Chapter Five, is more resistant to extinction than continuous schedules.

Two other points about this example are important. First, even if sweets are not gained, mother's attention (and probably the rest of the queue's) certainly has been. He is thus provided with social as well as material reinforcement for grizzling. Second, if she gives way and buys the sweets, mother is being negatively reinforced because Kevin shuts up. There are therefore a number of very powerful supporting factors strengthening this particular behaviour pattern.

Parental attention is the strongest and most pervasive reinforcer of children's behaviour even if that attention is critical or punishing. It is unfortunate but true that it is usually easier for a child to gain attention by hitting the baby, pulling the cat's tail or putting jam on the Hi-Fi than by playing quietly with toys. When the toddler is quiet, mother is likely to sigh with relief and get on her own activities. To improve the situation the contingencies of reinforcement must be altered so that playing quietly with the toys gets the attention and praise of mother and, as far as safety allows, other less desirable activities are ignored. This process is known as *Differential*

Reinforcement of Other Behaviour or DRO. If possible, the other behaviour should be incompatible with the problem; meaning it should be impossible for the two to co-exist. This is particularly important when seriously damaging activities like baby-hitting or fire-raising are involved as in these situations the reduction of behaviour by extinction, at least in its normal behavioural sense, is inappropriate.

It is important to look at the range of types of reinforcer that are available. It must be stressed that, with the exception of parental attention mentioned above which is virtually always effective, nothing can be assumed to be reinforcing until it has been tested in the situation under consideration. From the theoretical point of view it must be remembered that a reinforcer increases the likelihood or frequency of that behaviour occurring in the future. In practice this means that it is essential to discover what is in fact rewarding for the child in question *not* what the parent or the therapist thinks will be rewarding. Most of us can remember childhood 'treats' organised by well-meaning adults that were far from enjoyable to us.

There are some other general points. Parental praise and attention are very important. Some parents do not know how to give this and may need help with prompting and role play. This can present a problem in primary care where it is difficult for professionals to spend a lot of time in the patient's home. It is also very important to make sure that the child is able to perform the target behaviour. If not, he also will have to be taught perhaps using the methods described in Chapter Five. During assessment the distinction must, therefore, be drawn between skills deficits (i.e. not knowing) and performance deficits (i.e. knowing but not doing) in both child and parent.

A further problem with parental praise is that it can be overused. The first time somebody says 'well done – that's very good' is likely to be more effective than the fifteenth as anybody with a 'gushing' friend will agree. There is, therefore, a place for other rewards. The best are, of course, the natural consequence of the task, for example, the pleasure of making a toy or reading an exciting story, but these are often not available for manipulation. Other reinforcers may have to be linked to the behaviour and may be tangible, such as food or toys, or special treats or privileges, such as a game of football with father or half an hour's extra TV.

There are many varieties of points and token systems ranging from the common, and now sometimes overused, star-chart to sophisticated token economies where all goods and services must be bought by earnings. These programmes are really suitable for institutions but can be adapted for home use. Tokens are usually earned towards a 'back-up' reinforcer of which there are an infinite variety. The advantages of tokens are:

(1) They have great flexibility in that the ratio of tokens to the back-up reinforcer as well as the nature of the latter can be changed at will.

(2) They are more difficult to forget than social reinforcers, as the would-be recipient can prompt the deliverer.

(3) They are cheap per unit and always available.

It is useful to include other siblings in any sort of token system as this prevents disproportionate attention going to the identified problem child and also may produce all-round improvements in the way that the family functions.

Time-Out

For practical purposes, Time-Out represents the most commonly used means of reducing unwanted activities and is usually used in conjunction with differential reinforcement of other behaviour, which has just been discussed. The routine for applying Time-Out has been described in Chapter Five but there are some further aspects which can be considered here. There has been some press and public criticism of Time-Out as being too punishing and mechanical but this has usually been because it has been ill-applied or ill-understood by the critics. There is, after all, nothing very disturbing about removing a child from sources of reward for a short period of time. Many commonly used domestic punishments are much more severe, if less effective. The effectiveness of Time-Out, particularly when coupled with differential reinforcement means that in practice problems come quickly under control and the number of occasions on which it has been used usually decreases rapidly as long as the assessment has been correct. The following points should be borne in mind when using the technique:

(1) The procedure (see Chapter Five) should be meticulously followed and the Time-Out situation must really be non-reinforcing not, for example, a relief from more boring activities.

(2) An explanation of the rules for Time-Out (pp.50–51) is given when it is introduced. The reason for its use on a particular occasion is clearly, but briefly, stated both for the child's benefit and also to ensure that it is not used by the parent in a vague and slipshod manner.

(3) Relief does not take place until the behaviour (a tantrum for example) ceases or else relief may inadvertently act as a reinforcer.

(4) The timings given in Chapter Five represent a consensus of opinion but essentially it seems that as short a time as possible can be used initially and only increased if it proves insufficient. If shorter periods are

mixed with longer ones the former will be ineffective (Hobbs and Forehand 1977).

(5) Parents can be asked to rehearse the Time-Out procedure in the consulting room to make sure that they have understood it. The non-verbal part of the exercise in which the child is unemotionally but caringly removed from the problem situation to the Time-Out area, without shutting, slamming or locking of doors, is particularly important. It has been our experience that in simple family situations it may be enough to allow the child to release himself, without a fixed term, once the problem has ceased. This has not been experimentally tested. For example, the child may be carried to his bedroom and told that when he has calmed down he can come down stairs and have a story. If the child creates a mess in the Time-Out area while still in the throws of the tantrum, such as stripping the bed, this is best ignored once calm is restored rather than entering another battle ground.

Sleep Problems

About a quarter of young children have serious sleep disorder so the non-sleeping child presents as a common and distressing problem. Parents often fail to recognise the signs of the tired child who instead of becoming drowsy and sleepy becomes overactive, demanding and fractious. At this stage parents can reasonably think that the child needs more stimulation rather than more sleep. Adults and adolescents react to sleep loss or poor quality sleep by nodding off during the day or looking tired. Pre pubescent children react differently and may be irritable and overactive rather than drowsy. Failure to deal with the problem leaves the parent anxious, guilty and exhausted. Parents may suffer from lack of sleep themselves, feel perplexed, powerless and sometimes angry. Behind all this can be a host of negative thoughts and feelings that they must be defective as parents or, worse, that there is something the matter with their child. The first essential for GP or health visitor faced with this potentially explosive situation is to gain the confidence of the parents by listening to them and taking their problem seriously. Once trust has been established work can begin in earnest.

Assessment

The assessment phase starts with the behavioural analysis of the problem. A statement of the exact current difficulty is obtained together with details of the following:

(1) Bedtime and settling routine. Some parents have no consistent pattern and this is often associated with difficulties. They may have a different routine for the child first going to bed from that used in night waking.

(2) Night waking, including frequency, duration and what action is taken.

(3) Daytime naps if any.

(4) Whether help has previously been obtained from outside and how the couple have tried to cope with the problem themselves.

(5) Whether the child has any other problems.

(6) What the effect has been of the problem on the family as a whole.

An opportunity is then made for other family and emotional problems to be discussed with particular attention being given to any marital discord or sexual difficulties – a non-sleeping child is an excellent contraceptive.

The parents' attitude and feelings about the problem are then covered together with their expectations of the nature and effectiveness of various types of help. Parents may simply be seeking drugs for the child. The advantages and disadvantages of sedatives must be discussed before other techniques will be willingly accepted. Finally, as has been implied, the presence or at the very least the co-operation of both parents must be obtained as no intervention can succeed in the face of opposition or simply lack of understanding.

After the assessment, it should be possible to form a preliminary hypothesis of the factors maintaining the settling or waking problem which can be confirmed by a baseline recording in the form of a sleep diary noting:

- Time to bed and action taken.
- Time to sleep.
- Time(s) awake in the night, action taken and time to sleep again.
- Time of morning waking.
- Time of parents to bed.

With this information, a plan of intervention can be formulated with agreed targets. These must be settled with the parents, having due regard as to what is tolerable and acceptable to them. For example, six hours of sleep per night with not more than one waking three times a week might be acceptable to one set of parents but not to another. However, the parents cannot choose to be with the child to help him get to sleep in the evening then expect him to get to sleep on his own if he wakes in the middle of the night.

The approach to be adopted must be selected in accordance with the analysis of the problem. The following are amongst the techniques most often considered:

(1) *Punishment* – is used in various forms and the sleepless child is at some risk of being battered. As a method of achieving change it has nothing to recommend it, as it is unpleasant, weak and temporary. It is also usually applied inconsistently.

(2) *Extinction* (i.e. ignoring the crying and sleeplessness) – this can be employed and if used consistently it is quick and effective but should not be necessary. In any case most parents simply cannot listen to their child crying and there is always the risk that there is some unrelated reason for the crying that needs to be dealt with. Unsuccessful attempts with this method result in intermittent reinforcement as mother finds that she can stand the crying no longer and goes in. This is, as we have seen, a powerful way of strengthening behaviour. The assessment should show if extinction is a possibility by exploring both parents' attitude to listening to their child cry. If it is attempted, the rule for the parents must be *first time or not at all*, in other words they can go to the child as soon as he wakes but not after he has been crying for some time.

(3) *Positive Reinforcement* – usually of quiet night behaviour rather than sleeping itself, can work well for the slightly older child. One three-year-old improved quickly once a morning drink brought by father was made contingent upon rapid night settling. The usual rules for reinforcement (see Chapter Five) apply. It is important to define exactly what is to be reinforced, for example 'staying in your own room', 'staying in your own bed' (which is difficult to observe) or 'not coming into our bedroom'. It is also important to make sure that the reinforcer can be delivered first thing in the morning to keep the necessary interval between task and reinforcer as short as possible.

(4) *Graded Approaches* – these are usually the most useful as they do not require the parents, who are often exhausted and demoralised, to do anything that is too unpleasant or difficult. The child's behaviour is changed gradually in very small steps. Short wakings are normal for most children but some cannot go back to sleep unless mother is present. For these children this method is particularly suitable as long as the initial bed time routine is the same and involves the child learning to go to sleep on his own. Assessment will show the exact

requirements of the individual situation but a typical programme might involve:

   (a)   Mother sleeping in the child's bed holding his hand.

   (b)   Mother sleeping in the child's bed without contact.

   (c)   Mother in bed but Teddy in between.

   (d)   Mother in another bed alongside.

   (e)   Mother in chair alongside.

   (f)   Mother in chair at other side of room.

   (g)   Mother outside the door in chair.

   (h)   Mother looking in before her own bedtime.

The variations on this theme are infinite and the most important factor is achieving small enough steps. The use of a Teddy-bear or favourite toy during day time naps as at bedtime may help to wean the child off mother's presence by providing a substitute stimulus for settling: the same technique must be used in the day time, at bedtime when initial settling is a problem and at night wakings. In addition, if the actual bedtime needs adjusting it is first set at the normal time and is then progressively changed by fifteen minute intervals, in the required direction each night until a satisfactory time is achieved.

(5) *Bedtime Routines* – these are often absent or intermittent where children have difficulty in settling. Work to establish a regular programme is often helpful. A model sequence might be bath, cuddle, story, drink and settle. The cuddle should be placed early in the sequence if there is any fear that it is, or might become, the essential stimulus for settling (as described earlier).

(6) *Drugs* – these may be used with these programmes, particularly if parents' morale is very low. If possible, however, it is better to avoid them as they are often unpredictable, ineffective, difficult to stop and may increase thirst.
(*Source:* Douglas and Richman 1982)

Nightmares, Night Terrors and Sleep Walking

These parasomnias are all relatively common in children with onset usually before the age of ten, but complaints should be taken seriously. These parasomnias may occur in response to anxiety and may be more common when sleep schedules are irregular. The primary care worker's normal job is to provide reassurance, education and treatment and explain to the parents that no permanent harm is likely to result. If the symptoms continue to be very severe, distressing or dangerous to the child, then referral may be indicated.

Sleepwalkers should be made to sleep in a safe environment, with bars on windows and stair gates in doorways if doors are left open.

Night terrors often start with a terrifying scream, increased heart and respiration rate. They last from one to several minutes and are different from nightmares. In children a regular bedtime routine that encourages sufficient sleep usually leads to improvement.

Table 12.1 Coping with night terrors: a guide for parents

Normal sleep includes cycles of light sleep, deep sleep, and partial waking. Occasionally dreams, nightmares, and night terrors can disturb a child's sleep.

What are night terrors?

Night terrors are brief episodes (about 10–20 minutes) of partial waking that occur during deep sleep and are accompanied by thrashing, kicking, rolling movements, and unintelligible speech. The child does not respond to voice, touch or reassurance. They are most common among children aged 2–6 years and usually occur within the first two hours of going to sleep.

Important facts about night terrors

(1) The child will not remember it in the morning.

(2) Trying to wake the child during the night terror rarely shortens it.

(3) The child is not ill.

(4) Night terrors do not have any long term ill effects.

(5) They often occur only once a night, and not every night. Usually they will decrease and disappear three to four months after they start.

(6) Overtiredness and changes in routine will make them worse.

What parents can do

(1) Stay calm during the night terror.

(2) Restrain the child physically only to prevent self injury.

(3) Place anything breakable out of reach. If necessary lock doors and windows.

(4) Maintain the child's routine as far as possible, and encourage periods of rest after physical activity.

(5) Reassure siblings that the terrors will do no harm and will go away.(6) Remember that the child will have no memory of the incident the next day.

(7) Your reaction and that of siblings may upset the child who is having the night terrors; reassure the child.

(8) Try to find out if the child is worried about anything, and see if you can help.

(9) Consult your doctor if the type and frequency of night terrors changes, or if they occur for more than three months.

Feeding Difficulties

These are common and usually relatively easy to treat. Parents get extremely anxious when children refuse to eat and the child readily finds the coaxing and other bizarre attention very rewarding.

Assessment

This concentrates on:

(1) Inappropriate feeding – is the child getting the wrong food, too much food or food at the wrong time?

(2) Attitudes and assumptions of parent about feeding. Some parents assume that food fads and refusal carry a grave health risk to the child. They may be unaware of normal variations between children, and at different times within the development of the same child. In adolescence, both parents and peers influence eating behaviours (usually in conflicting ways) and this has implications for modification.

(3) The functional analysis of eating or what happens before, during and after meals using the ABC model described in Chapter Three. This will reveal ways in which the refusal or fads are currently being cued or reinforced.

Management

This follows on from the assessment. Usually it is sufficient to concentrate on eliminating the coaxing, anger and other disturbance caused by the problem. Parents are encouraged to serve food without fuss or comment and to remove it, also without comment, at the end of the meal if it has not been eaten. Praise and attention possibly with the help of tokens or stars, are given if the meal is eaten without disturbance. It is important to warn parents that fuss at meal times will increase before it diminishes (the extinction burst) and that this storm must be weathered calmly. Snacks and sweet drinks must be eliminated or used only as a reward after the meal has been finished.

Obesity is still a considerable problem amongst children seen in primary care although parents have become more conscious of the advantages of breast feeding followed by a rational diet. Some parents, however, still seem to be unable to grasp these concepts and these same parents often prove resistant to advice and education. Careful detailed instruction in food preparation from a dietician or health visitor coupled with a programmed increase in exercise seems to produce the best results. Many of the techniques described in the section on adult obesity (see Chapter Eight) may also be used with children.

Enuresis

Bed Wetting

This is also an extremely common childhood behaviour problem often presented to the GP or health visitor. It is fortunate that it also has one of the highest cure rates.

Assessment

This involves an accurate description of the duration and frequency of wetting and any factors making it better or worse. Special enquiry is made into stressful events such as birth of siblings, moving house or deaths of relatives or pets. These factors may have particular importance when wetting recurs after a period of dryness. Physical examination is essential both to discover the occasional relevant abnormality and as a prelude to explanation and reassurance. A mid stream specimen of urine should be taken as a minority of enuretics have urinary infections. Baseline recording is by a chart, often using stars or pictures, which the child fills in himself. This in itself is a powerful means of change and, in many cases, when coupled with parental praise may be sufficient to solve the problem.

Management

Management starts with a discussion with the parents of the nature of the problem and its background. Many parents request help too early and it is useful to point out that 7 per cent of children are still bed wetting at seven years old and as many as 11 per cent at five. Some may have misconceptions that the problem is due to serious disease, bladder weakness or the need for circumcision. These myths may be discussed and dispelled. Previous attempts at management may have included:

(1) Punishment, which is unkind and ineffective.

(2) Restricting fluids which may send the child to bed uncomfortably thirsty and produce an irritable concentrated urine. It also begs the essential question of getting the child to respond to a full bladder and then learning to tolerate it.

(3) Lifting, which is ineffective as it is not related to the full bladder stimulus.

All of these should be considered and tactfully dismissed.

Once the decision is taken to go further with a programme the following techniques may be used:

(1) Monitoring and reinforcement with a star chart linked to a small back up reward for a pre-arranged number of dry nights. This number can be varied as the programme advances.

(2) The buzzer, also known as the bell and pad or the Mowrer pad. A number of similar devices are available which make a loud noise or vibrate when activated by contact with urine. It is important to use an appliance that has adequate safety approval. Some of the best equipment uses a single pad with double aluminium tape. This has the advantage that it is easier for the child to reset in the night. Sets worn inside pants are also available. The same range also provides an extra loud alarm for the child who has difficulty in waking, a pillow rocker for the child sharing a room and an extension alarm to lead to another room should this be required (see Equipment at the end of chapter). The noise results in the child waking with a start that turns off the urine flow. The exact way in which this highly efficient apparatus works is unknown. It may make use of classical conditioning – pairing the full bladder sensation instead of the buzzer noise with waking. The negative reinforcement of avoiding the noise and the wet bed and positive reinforcement of being in a comfortable dry bed are also probably involved.

The procedure must be thoroughly rehearsed. First, an explanation of the equipment and procedure is given to the child in a way that he can understand according to his age. Second, he is shown how to assemble the apparatus in the order; (i) mattress; (ii) waterproof sheet; (iii) buzzer sheet – correct way round; (iv) top bed sheet. Third, the leads are connected to the buzzer which is switched on. Fourth, the buzzer is made to sound by pouring some salt water over the sheets. Fifth, he is shown how the buzzer is switched off. Sixth, he repeats all the steps himself with appropriate prompting and praise.

When he wakes in the night he switches off the buzzer, goes to the toilet 'to finish if possible', takes the dry sheets from a previously arranged place, remakes the bed, switches alarm on again and gets back into it. Parents guide and encourage these steps.

A chart is kept recording not only wet and dry beds but also the size of the wet patch (initially) and whether the correct procedure has been achieved. It is important that the whole programme should be made fun and small back-up rewards incorporated. A suitable target is fourteen consecutive dry nights. When this has been achieved relapse is minimised if an overlearning phase is incorporated. In this the child is given extra drinks at bedtime – one or two pints per night, according to age – and the routine continued until the target number of dry nights is again achieved. Surprisingly this usually happens quite quickly following the first phase.

Some snags may occur. The buzzer sheets get hard wear and particularly some types need frequent renewal if they are to work properly. Some children do not wake to the alarm in which case putting it in a tin will make it louder. Some turn it off before waking properly in which case it must be placed out of reach. If the child cannot turn off the urine stream when the alarm sounds, day time practise in the toilet stopping the stream when the buzzer sounds may help training. False alarms are sometimes a problem and as they are likely to weaken the programme every effort should be made to find the fault and stop them.

There is now available (Collier *et al.* 1996) an excellent interactive CD-Educational package about nocturnal enuresis developed by a multidisciplinary team at Nottingham University entitled *All About Enuresis*. Although designed for hospital clinic use this programme would serve excellently in primary care (details are given at the end of this Chapter).

Day Time Wetting

This is often associated with:

- failure to detect full bladder signals until it is too late
- inability to hold on once the signals are received
- excessive distraction by other activities
- unattractive or over-public lavatories at schools without locking doors.

Each of these situations requires its own management. Reception of bladder signals may be improved by practising waiting an extra five minutes after the urge is noticed. Holding on can be helped by waiting or stop–start exercises when passing water. Distraction may need concentration on discriminating bladder sensations by checking whether they are present at deliberately given intervals. A fixed timetable, for example at break, before lunch, after lunch and so on, with gradual lengthening of the intervals can be effective. The school lavatories may require a diplomatic approach to the head teacher, or a rehearsed coping strategy for the child. They may need to investigate which one to use and when, and to acquaint themselves with a particular place before the situation is urgent and anxiety provoking.

Soiling

This is, with a certain proviso, another extremely suitable problem for management in primary care as the behavioural and physical elements are often closely intertwined. The proviso is necessary as some soiling children have profound complicated emotional problems and for these intensive treatment may be needed. The most common type of soiling seen in primary care is retention of stools with overflow. This is caused by an initial failure to empty the bowel so that the rectum remains full although the urge passes. There may be many reasons for this – for example, hurry to do other things, a fissure *in ano* or the all too common unsuitable school lavatories. Once the urge has passed stool continues to accumulate so that the sphincter becomes overstretched and leaking takes place around the bolus. Any attempt to pass the stool mass is frustrated by painful overstretching or tearing.

The first step in management is to empty the rectum which usually requires an enema. This is followed by a high fibre diet and a suitable laxative agent such as docusate sodium syrup 25 mgms t.d.s (Dioctyl). From this point on the behavioural element of carefully charted regular toiletting with positive reinforcement from the parents takes over. The object is to train the child to detect when the rectum is full and go to the toilet immediately. This is then rewarded. It is important not to make 'clean pants' the target for reinforcement as this can promote a return to holding back.

Lack of control without retention is less common and may occur for a number of reasons. The very young child may simply not yet have learnt control or may temporarily have lost it. The occasional purely physical cause should not be ignored. Most serious are those children where persistent, usually secondary, encopresis is a symptom of personal or family stress. In these cases it is the under-lying problem which must receive attention.

Where reinforcement alone is ineffective, more intensive methods are available. Overcorrection requires thirty minutes after each soiling to be spent in the child washing himself, his clothes and anything else soiled and then hanging them out to dry. Positive practice requires him to sit alone in a quiet room for ten minutes followed by ten minutes 'trying to go'. This sequence is repeated three times. Both these methods seem to us fairly punitive and we have not found them to be necessary in primary care.

Disruptive Behaviour

Many children only get attention when they make a nuisance of themselves. The shock and horror on the faces of bystanders and the confused embarrassment of mother are powerful rewards for having a tantrum. The overall object of any treatment is, therefore, to turn the situation round so that co-operative behaviour is rewarded and disruption is extinguished. Tantrums, disobedience and aggression occur in different circumstances but have features in common in both their origins and their management.

Tantrums

These usually appear first and are so common as to be almost universal. The first question is to establish whether reassurance that they are within normal limits will solve the problem or whether something more is required.

Assessment

This follows the normal pattern (see Chapter Three). Special points of importance are:

(1) The sort of situations that trigger the tantrums. What sort of demands are being made on the child. Who is present? Where do they normally take place? A tantrum in a supermarket requires different handling from one in the kitchen.

(2) What does the child actually do during the tantrum? Can it be safely ignored or is there real danger? Screaming in the garden can be left; pulling the saucepans off the stove cannot.

(3) Exactly how does mother or do others react to the situation? How do they try to stop it? Does this method make matters better or worse?

Goals must be clear and achievable. In a severe case thirty minutes without a tantrum may be realistic initially. Baseline measurements produce a clearer perspective of the problem which often seems less overwhelming when accurately measured. They may also promote change by providing a calm alternative response for the mother. An ingenious variation on recording is for mother to write up the chart, which must be filled in, in detail *immediately* in the bedroom whilst Tommy is left to have his tantrum in the kitchen (Hill 1985).

Management

Management techniques include:

(1) Shaping and prompting mother's behaviour so that she can ignore (not reinforce) harmless tantrums and intervene firmly but calmly when this is necessary. Time often needs to be spent explaining that shouting or slapping can reinforce in that it provides attention.

(2) Identifying and shaping up activities that are incompatible with tantrum. These periods of quiet play are often seen by mother as 'an opportunity to get on' and the child is, therefore, ignored during them. The necessity of joining in with the games or admiring the drawings must be explained. Role play can be helpful as some parents are unused to giving praise and constructive comment.

(3) Initiating new activities which are incompatible with tantrums. A four-year-old master of supermarket tantrums was encouraged to draw dogs by copying the pictures on a well known brand of pet food. These were then praised and backed up by an ice cream for tea after a tantrum-free supermarket trip. This is an example of distraction and differential reinforcement of other behaviour (DRO). It is extremely simple to initiate quickly from the surgery.

(4) Time Out in the manner described in the beginning of this chapter and in Chapter Five.

Disobedience

This is also a frequent complaint and may be quite normal and require only reassurance or a review of the parents expectations in relation to the child's age and development. How much are they telling the child rather than asking the child to do things? Are all the demands really necessary? If the problem requires further attention it is important to focus on the frequency, consistency and type of commands which are being flouted. Direct observation is invaluable in these circumstances as self-report by the parents ('I always do that' or 'I never do that') is notoriously unreliable.

Observation in the home is ideal but often impracticable and a lot can be learnt by watching the mother and child in the surgery or clinic room when, for example, clearing up toys. A count can be made of the number of alpha commands, which are defined as clear requests which allow time for a definite response that the child could reasonably be expected to make, such as 'Stop pulling Tracy's hair'. Beta commands are those that are unclear, contradictory or countermanded before the child has a chance to comply, for example 'I told you, you couldn't have a biscuit – oh well, you might as well eat it now'. These are also counted. Observation will often show that compliance problems are most common where mother uses a lot of beta commands. Management involves modelling and prompting the mother's commands so that the beta commands become fewer and that alpha commands predomi- nate and are followed through so that obedience is obtained. Failure to obey may be managed by a period of Time Out if repeated clear requests are unsuccessful.

Aggression

Aggression must be carefully assessed in relation to the family background and the nature of the relationships involved. Assessment should particularly look at:

(1) Whether the child has been taught to be aggressive because mother or father are frequently aggressive themselves.

(2) Whether a degree of aggression is necessary to achieve anything in that particular school or household.

(3) Whether aggression on the part of the child is being met with more aggression on the part of the parents. This can lead to a vicious circle of coercive behaviour which can have two outcomes, both bad. The worst result is that the child is subjected to severe battering. The less bad, but also unfortunate, is that the parents give up, leaving the child in command of the situation. He has thus learnt that force is the best way of achieving results.

Intervention with these children relies heavily on the use of Time Out which is an effective but non-violent response. At the same time everything possible must be done to reinforce co-operative, constructive behaviour.

Fear and Anxiety in Childhood

As most of us can remember, childhood is a time of rapid learning and vulnerability which frequently contains many fearful experiences. Most of these are a normal and natural part of learning which equips us to cope with the dangers of the world. In some cases unreasonable fears arise which may in part be due to family patterns and parental modelling (Muris et al. 1996). This can be dealt with by the methods of exposure and anxiety management described in Chapter Six but it is important that parental anxiety should be considered at the same time.

There are, however, two problem areas which require special attention – fear of hospital admission and fear of school.

Fear of Hospital Admission

Methods of reducing adults' anxiety before admission to hospital have been covered in Chapter Nine. Children are even more vulnerable than adults in this respect, even though free visiting and the admission of parents to hospital with their children has in recent years done much to reduce the potential damage. Several techniques may be useful:

(1) Gradual exposure to the hospital by visits and explanation beforehand. This may be coupled with encouragement of 'the grown-up way the child behaves at the hospital' whilst at the same time allowing fears to be openly discussed.

(2) Films of children going through hospital treatment, meeting the pain and the uncertainties but overcoming them and leaving again better and happy. This presents a *coping model*, dealing with the experience to the child. This has been shown to be more effective than a mastery model which is one where no difficulty is experienced (Meichenbaum 1971). At present such films are rather hard to find but perhaps in the future they may be made available by health education agencies.

(3) Encouraging and teaching positive self-statements such as 'It will hurt a bit but I can look after myself and I will soon be better and back home' or 'It is one more bad sore throat but the nurses will help me and soon I'll be home with no more rotten throats.'

Melamed (1993) examines how the family's coping resources help the child to prepare for medical stress.

Fear of School

Many school phobias are initially reinforced by the parents who readily allow the child to stay at home on the smallest pretext. The GP who is unsure whether the child could be truly ill colludes in this. It follows that the GP is uniquely placed to nip the problem in the bud by being aware of incipient school fears and satisfying himself that there is no unnecessary absence.

Assessment

Investigation of the established problem must first decide whether the absence is due to true fear of school or the rival attractions of staying away (truancy). The nature of any possible rival attractions is explored and it is established whether the parents know that the child is staying away or not. Truancy can be dealt with rapidly by an explanation of the law concerning school attendance and if necessary referral to the school attendance officer.

True phobias require more delicate handling. The exact nature of the fear is established and explored. It will usually revolve round either anxiety about leaving home or worrying activities at school. Precipitating factors at home might include: bereavement, illness of child or others, divorce, separation, moving house or the birth of a new sibling. School factors might be change of school or class, loss of friend, bullying or ridicule, embarrassment at PE or shower time, learning problems or clashes with teacher. A phone call to the school will often throw light on these factors and pave the way for a joint approach.

Management

The main management may be undertaken with the help of the parents alone but co-operation between GP, health visitor, school teachers and educational psychologist is often necessary and desirable. The main tactics of management are:

(1) If possible deal with any problems in the home.

(2) By co-operation with the teachers make sure that the child is attending a school suited to his needs, for example not too academic or where the physical demands exceed his capacity.

(3) Arrange for a sympathetic reception at the school when he returns.

(4) Rehearse arrival at school by a gradual approach, perhaps first visiting the school at a week-end when it is empty. Rehearsal of the first conversation with friends is also valuable, for example 'I wasn't well but I'm better now'. After a long absence it is often valuable to return after a holiday or half term which causes less comment. An arrangement with the teacher for the child to go somewhere quiet, if distressed, without leaving the school may be helpful.

(5) Encourage the parents to remain calm and reward the child for success. At the same time attention should not be given to somatic complaints or 'bad days' at school. If for any reason the child does stay at home, there should be no TV or enjoyable activities.

(6) The child is escorted to school by, if possible, a parent. Failing this a friend or, at the last resort, a professional such as health visitor, social

worker, GP or psychologist may act as escort. It is important that the escort should be prepared and able to withstand tears and tantrums.

Follow up is important and particular care should be exercised following illness or any others life event which might act as a precipitating factor for further problems.

Tummy Ache

Recurrent abdominal pain in the five to twelve-year-old is an extremely common problem occurring at some time or another in nearly three-quarters of children. In an important minority it is due to a urinary tract infection and an urinalysis should always be performed. Most, however, are non-organic and form another example of a somatic reaction to stress similar to those reactions found in adults and described in Chapter Six. Children of this age seldom complain of headache and therefore abdominal pain becomes the chief somatic outlet of anxiety and tension.

Interview and baseline measurements focus on the problem in relation to school (in and out of class), sibling and parent relation-ships, recent bereavements (for example, grand parents or pets) and important child life events such as the beginning of the new school year and the approach of Christmas.

Management

Management involves:

(1) Physical examination and urine analysis as urinary tract infections are a possible cause.

(2) A sympathetic and assured diagnosis to both child and parents.

(3) An explanation of how stress can affect muscles, aided by a diagram of the abdomen.

(4) An exploration and, if possible, correction of contributory factors.

(5) A full discussion with the whole family of misattributions, such as appendicitis, twisted bowel or 'something seriously wrong' and a confident explanation that referral is not indicated.

(6) Advice about leading as normal a life as possible in spite of the pain.

(7) If essential, a prescription for an antispasmodic such as dicyclomine HCI whose effect may be as much placebo as pharmacological.

Common pitfalls to be avoided are:

(1) Increasing avoidance of normal life and school by the child 'because of the pain'. Once established this is hard to correct.

(2) A crescendo of family anxiety associated with lack of understanding of the true nature of the problem. This often leads to multiple negative investigations and a series of inconclusive referrals.

Bullying

Children who present with somatic symptoms or school refusal may be suffering the effects of bullying, teasing or victimisation at school. This victimisation may be physical or psychological such as exclusion from a valued peer group. This in particular leads to internalising in the form of anxiety and depression. Due to the loss of self esteem and feelings of failure children are often very secretive about this and tactful questioning is required to elicit pertinent facts.

An exact description of the bullying or teasing needs to be paired with a precise description of the victims response. Sometimes the problem can be cured by modifying the child's response and making it unrewarding for the perpetrator. This is particularly the case with teasing related to personal appearance or handicap where the child can learn to make light of the jibes, laugh at them, ignore them, agree with the statements or even turn the situation to their advantage. For example, to 'Your mother looks like a witch' the response from one child was 'I'll send her round at the weekend when she uses her broomstick and black magic'. Another child with no outer ears started to earn money by charging other children to try out his powerful hearing aids and the bullying ceased.

It is important the child uses his own words in any response and role plays a situation in the surgery setting to feel comfortable before trying it at school. He should be able to report back on the success or otherwise of the exercise as soon as possible (preferably with appointments outside school hours).

In cases of bullying incorporating violence, racism or extortion the parents or child should be encouraged to contact the school to find out their policy and ask for help and guidance. Specialist professional help may be advisable for a child who is or has been continuously or seriously bullied.

Stammer

Parents tend to be more distressed than children at the onset of stammer. At school age, however, children find the isolating effect of stammering accompanied by ignorance or mismanagement by teachers affects their ability to cope and may lead to negative long term effects. Assessment by a speech and language therapist is essential and it is never too early to ask for advice which initially may only consist of parental guidance. If early help is not available measures may be taken to reduce peer and parental pressure. Parents expectations of speech development may be too high and advising them to relax themselves and give the child time to think and speak may resolve the problem. An example of sibling pressure was noticed when a child only stammered in the school holidays. A problem solving approach led to the parents organising separate activities for the elder child which allowed the younger child to develop at his own pace and stop stammering.

Hyperactivity (Attention Deficit Hyperactivity Disorder)

This takes many forms and it is important to assess individual differences carefully (British Psychological Society 1996). The one most likely to present in the primary care is intermittent situation-specific hyperactivity where the child, usually a boy, is overactive and restless in some situations but not in others. This may be seen as a problem in developing an adequate concentration span rather than as a behavioural excess.

Management

Management may be by drugs or diet but these are the province of specialists and lie outside our scope. Behavioural management may include the following elements:

(1) Reinforcement of quiet sedentary activities, such as drawing or table games, with praise and attention. It is important that the children experience success.

(2) Provision of opportunities for structured quiet play – working the energy off by rushing about is ineffective.

(3) The parents responding to overactivity quietly, thus not providing overactive models themselves. Regular routine is reassuring and important.

(4) Finding and shaping up by praising the smallest amounts of quiet constructive play, thus developing a longer concentration span. It is important to break the cycle of abuse and punishment which is generally the result of these children's unattractive behaviour.

(5) Encouraging the child to 'save-up' demands or questions so they can be dealt with at a fixed time.

(6) Sleep may be a problem. Quiet wakefulness may have to be reinforced and other measures taken as mentioned earlier in this chapter.

(7) Parents should be consistent within themselves and with each other.

(8) The parents should feel free to bring appropriate day to day problems to the appropriate professional worker.

Parents should not expect recovery overnight and such unrealistic aspirations should be gently modified. Equally, they should not attempt to deal with all the child's problems at the same time but should concentrate on the most important.

In the context of homework difficulties in normal US school children from 7 to 10 years old Kahle and Kelly (1994) found that goal setting in small stages was more effective than training parents to set a routine. Such goal setting procedures would appear to be easily adaptable to ADHD.

Some of the ideas given above and much further information for both clinicians and families is available from the ADD-ADHD Family Support Group (see Useful Addresses).

If more unusual types of hyperactivity are suspected or the problem is beyond the resources at hand early referral to a child psychiatrist is advised.

Teenage Problems

Many of the problems of adolescence mirror those of childhood and adult life. Some aspects, however, deserve special consideration either because they are peculiar to adolescence or because they present different features in this age group.

Interpersonal Problems

It is not surprising that stress and functioning in adolescence has been shown to be closely related to family structure and communication skills (Weirson and Forehand 1992, Leppin 1996). This stress is most often manifest in rebellion and conflict. The teenager who refuses to comply with parental rules and requests appears frequently in primary care. More complicated disagreements must be seen in family terms and a joint interview with the whole family is an important part of the assessment. It is equally important to see the adolescent on their own so they have a chance to express their views without interruption or an atmosphere of disapproval and to investigate the possibility of depression, anxiety or other mental illness. An attempt has to be made to distinguish between dangerous or genuinely unreasonable behaviour on the part of the youngster and failure of the parents to realise that he is developing into an adult. The parental behaviour is sometimes inappropriate to the age of the child and despite telling the child to 'grow up' and 'take responsibility', they may continue to tell them when and what to eat and when to come home. In less complicated cases huge changes can be made by parents 'asking' the child rather than 'telling' them what and when to do things. If the child has made the decision he is much more likely to feel responsible for carrying it out.

The clinician acts as the 'honest broker' and must be careful to be seen to be fair to both sides. Problems are defined in terms acceptable to all, and everybody is allowed to state their personal goals. Acceptable joint goals are then developed. The most useful way of achieving this is by means of behavioural contracting in which the parties agree that a particular behaviour on the part of one will be met by a particular response. The rules for these contracts may be summarised as follows:

(1) Within a family, rewards and affection must be earned and cannot be expected by anyone as a right.

(2) Everybody must be fairly compensated for their contribution.

(3) The more positive reinforcement given, the more will be received in return.

(4) Rather than being restrictive, contracts in fact create freedom because all parties know exactly where they stand and inconsistencies are ruled out. (*Source:* Stuart 1971)

The most frequent problem in setting up contracts is to restrain the authoritarian demands of parents. They are good at generating long lists of requirements but rather poor in seeing that reciprocal services or privileges are due to the teenager. This situation demands considerable tact on the part of the clinician/negotiator. A useful start can be made with small relatively non-contentious items. In this way success is achieved and the principles understood before moving on to more difficult topics. For example, 'Feeding the cat each evening is to warrant a free hair cut' might be a useful initial contract. Later the real problem might be addressed with the more complicated 'Going out with friends in the evening receives agreement to come in at 10 p.m. on weekdays and midnight at weekends'. It is important to check repeatedly that the terms of any proposed contract are seen as fair by all parties and are reasonably close to the behaviour of their peers. To this end it may be necessary to work on the ability of the family members to state their wishes clearly, clarify the wishes of others and provide feedback information on how the behaviour of others affects them. Such skills may well be lacking in families with communication problems.

Depression

Depression in teenagers may be peculiarly difficult to diagnose as it often presents (if it presents at all) with a hostile taciturn patient whose problems at first seem far removed from the normal picture of clinical depression. Particular leads may be some of the following:

- Separation anxiety in relation to parents.
- Anti-social behaviour.
- Running away from home.
- Poor school performance.
- Hypochondriasis.
- Weight gain.

Cognitive therapy is a definite option for such patients and is now being developed for use even with young children (Kendall 1991). Antidepressant drugs can be used very successfully in this age group although many GPs seem reluctant to try. This is a pity in view of the paucity of adolescent psychiatric services. It is important, however, to remember that suicide is an ever present danger in this group and therefore the SSRI group which have much lower toxicity are to be preferred in a combined approach. Some if not all cognitive techniques can be used with older teenagers in both depression and anxiety as well as interpersonal and other problems. Much stress and anxiety is induced by parental expectations and peer group relationships (Albano 1995) which can lead to dysfunctional assumptions and low self esteem (see Chapter Nine).

The excess use of alcohol and taking of 'recreational' drugs is very common in this age group and in certain sub-cultures is almost universal. These problems have been addressed in Chapter Eight but it should always be remembered that they may be a factor in other problems such as panic, study difficulties and depression. These and gambling such as fruit machine addiction can, if not too severe or in the early stages, be modified with a mixture of self help and supervision of the programme by the primary care staff.

Homesickness is a commonly experienced state of distress in this age group amongst those who have left home temporarily or permanently or suffered a broken home. It can often be the cause of depressed mood and a variety of somatic complaints. Research evidence suggests it can have far reaching negative effects on health status. Intervention will depend on the reasons for the move or migration and a full functional analysis will help to formulate the problem in each individual case.

Anxiety about parental separation and divorce can lead to psychological distress with components of guilt, feeling used, trapped or responsible. Often the effects are not clear to the sufferer or their confidante until they first leave home and notice the degree of distress or the paradox of feeling homesick having left an unhappy situation.

Anxiety

This is frequently related to social appraisal and this has been mentioned earlier (Albano 1995) Role play and video review are useful techniques in tackling this problem together with the other measures mentioned in Chapter Six. There is now considerable evidence that general anxiety and panic disorder occur in adolescents although they may be interpreted slightly differently (King et al. 1993). After carefully building a relationship which may present particular difficulties with this age group intervention should be along the lines already described in Chapter Six.

References

Albano, A.M. (1995) 'Treatment of social anxiety in adolescents.' *Cognitive and Behavioural Practice 2*, 271–298.

British Psychological Society (1996) 'Attention deficit hyperactivity disorder: Summary of the report of the society's working party.' *The Psychologist 9*, 10, 435–436.

Collier, J., Crook, I., Garrud, P., MacKinlay, D. and Redsell, S. (1996) 'Improving children's knowledge of their medical condition: an interactive multi-media package on enuresis.' Paper presented at the 10th European Conference of Health Psychology, Dublin, September 1996.

Douglas, J. and Richman, N. (1982) *Sleep Management Manual.* London: Department of Psychological Medicine, The Hospital for Sick Children.

Herbert, M. (1993) *Working with the Childrens Act.* Leicester: British Psychological Society.

Hill, P. (1985) Personal Communication.

Hobbs, S.A. and Forehand, R. (1977) 'Important parameters in the use of time out with children: A re-examination.' *Journal of Behaviour Therapy and Experimental Psychiatry 8*, 365–70.

Kahle, A.L. and Kelley, M.L. (1994) 'Children's homework problems: A comparison of goal setting and parent training.' *Behavior Therapy 25*, 275–290.

Kendall, P.C. (ed) (1991) *Child and Adolescent Therapy: Cognitive-Behavioural Procedures.* New York: Guilford.

King, N.J., Gullone, E., Tonge, B.J. and Ollendick, T.H. (1993) 'Self reports of panic attacks and manifest anxiety in adolescents.' *Behavioural Research and Therapy 31*, 1, 111–116.

Leppin, A. (1996) 'Significant others and the self; social and personal resources as predictors for health related behaviours and cognitions in adolescents.' Paper presented at the 10th European Conference of Health Psychology, Dublin, September 1996.

Melamed, B.G. (1993) 'Putting the family back into the child.' *Behaviour Research and Therapy 31*, 3, 239–247.

Meichenbaum, D. (1971) 'Examination of model characteristics in reducing avoidance behaviour.' *Journal of Personality and Social Pathology 17*, 298–307.

Muris, P., Steerneman, P., Merckelbach, H. and Meesters, C. (1996) 'The role of parental fearfulness and modelling in children's fear.' *Behavioural Research and Therapy 34*, 3, 265–268.

Stuart, R.B. (1971) 'Behavioral contracting with families of delinquents.' *Journal of Behaviour Therapy and Experimental Psychiatry 2*, 1–11.

Weirson, M. and Forehand, R. (1992) 'Family stressors and adolescent functioning: A consideration of models for early and middle adolescents.' *Behavior Therapy 23*, 671–688.

Recommended for Further Reading:

Herbert, M. (1987) *Conduct Disorders of Childhood and Adolescence: a Social Learning Perspective*, (2ndEd). Chichester: Wiley.

Herbert, M. PACTS (Parent, Adolescent and Child Training Skills) a series of Handbooks for Therapists Published by the British Psychological Society, 48 Princes Road East, Leicester LE1 7DR.

Hill, P. (1989) *Adolescent Psychiatry: Current Reviews in Psychiatry*. Edinburgh: Livingston.

Morgan, R. (1981) *Childhood Incontinence*. London: Disabled Living Foundation.

Ross, A.D. (1981) *Child Behavior Therapy*. New York and Chichester: John Wiley.

Books for Patients and Parents:

Herbert, M. (1989) *Discipline – A Positive Guide for Parents*. London: Ponting-Green.

Myers, R.J. (1996) *Parenting Teenagers*. London: Jessica Kingsley Publishers.

Multi-Media Programme:

All About Enuresis obtainable via Dr Jacqueline Collier, Lecturer in Behavioural Sciences, A Floor, South Block, Queen's Medical Centre, Nottingham, NG7 2DZ. Tel: +44 113 9709119 Fax: +44 113 9709495.
email: jacqueline.collier@nottingham.ac.uk

Equipment:

Enuresis Alarms (as described) available from: Headingly Scientific Services, 45 Westcombe Avenue, Leeds LSA 2BS.

Useful Addresses:

ADD-ADHD Family Support Group, Mrs. Gill Mead, 1a The High street, Dilton Marsh, Wiltshire. Tel: 01373 826045.

Chapter Thirteen

Study and Employment

The problems considered in this chapter may at first glance seem rather remote from the content of normal primary medical care. They are included for four reasons. First, the GP and his colleagues are often the only independent people who can be approached when psychological, physical or practical difficulties arise. Second, the more common clinical problems including anxiety, depression and psychosomatic disorders often have their origins in the life transitions associated with learning, working or ceasing to work. Third, increased insecurity and financial problems associated with both study, employment and unemployment create prolonged stress as do many of the organisational changes imposed in the workplace. Fourth, in our experience, cognitive behavioural methods offered in limited appointment times can be extremely effective in alleviating these types of stress.

We shall not concern ourselves with institutional or organisational aspects such as classroom behaviour, job applicant selection and industrial planning which, although highly important, are beyond our competence and scope. Our interest is in problems affecting the individual which may become apparent in the consulting room. A number of threads run through the chapter. Amongst these are ways of coping with stress induced by the outside world, the setting of realistic goals and the need for cognitive change to develop tolerance to imperfect situations.

The referral of these problems to specialists is surprisingly difficult. University counselling services and personal tutors are often hard to find with the recent increase in student numbers. They may, however, be a starting point from which local services can be accessed and give practical help relating to missed work or other problems directly associated with a student's course. The educational psychology service in schools, at least in the UK, is usually too overloaded with other tasks to be readily accessible to this sort of problem. For the most part industrial psychologists seem more involved with organisational problems than the individual needs of workers, although there is some evidence that this is changing.

Study and Examination Difficulties

Study problems present frequently to family doctors particularly around the school and college examination months. Often they simply take the form of a request for medication but a little further investigation may reveal depression, anxiety or other problems many of which are amenable to cognitive behavioural intervention.

Examinations present a high degree of stress, and some associated anxiety is both useful and universal. Fear related to such fundamentally threatening evaluations can, however, easily become excessive, and all the anxiety management techniques previously discussed may be useful.

There are, however, some aspects which deserve special consideration and these will be discussed below.

Concentration Problems in Reading and Revision

Students commonly complain that concentration and memory have become impaired. Analysis of the problems and or physical symptoms is important as they may be indicative of depressive illness or specific anxiety. It may be continuous or restricted solely to the examination or test situation itself.

As well as concentration and memory impairment, eczema, eye problems and headaches are further symptoms. Hyperventilation frequently accompanies anxiety and severe and unpleasant physical sensations can often be traced to this source.

Some students need to learn revision skills, others may need to adopt a more active or novel approach to working practices if struggling against concomitant depression or stimulus situations which are conditioned to anxiety. Discussion of the maintaining factors and maintenance of a baseline study diary will often show that concentration is not so much lost as simply diverted onto less threatening or more interesting activities. Alternatively, high levels of anxiety may prevent learning because of distracting worrying thoughts.

In order to counteract this some or all of the following strategies may be helpful:

(1) Limit study to short bursts of, say, 30 minutes interspersed with equally short breaks. Periods should end once the mind begins to wander but every effort should be made to complete a small section successfully and then get ready for the next by deciding on what to

do and preparing the relevant books and notes. Topics covered need to be recorded to check against a master list and see that no topic is being neglected.

(2) The work area should be as appealing as possible with a varied supply of paper, pens, highlighters, chewing gum, cards, staplers etc.

(3) If possible work should be done at a table with pleasant but adequate lighting.

(4) If the student is easily distracted or associates certain places and times with failure or anxiety, new venues can be tried for working such as the public library, a friend's house, working with a friend or a side table in a large canteen. Panic is contagious and if the student appears to be unduly anxious because of contact with peers, it may be advisable to avoid work in college and go instead to a public place.

(5) It is essential to keep a sense of perspective and not allow the significance and consequences of the work in hand to grow out of proportion. on the whole importance and possible consequences of the work.

(6) Reading should be tackled in an organised logical sequence. A useful scheme is to; (i) *survey* the material rapidly; (ii) formulate a *question* that might be asked or set on the subject; (iii) *read* the passage fully; (iv) *recite* the answer to the question; and (v) *review* the important points of the material. This can be memorised as SQ3R (Beneke and Harris 1972)

(7) Sleeping routine should be properly organised. Most people have a preference for studying early in the morning or late into the night but it is inadvisable for this to be taken to extremes as students may become overtired or sleep during the day. Conditioning is such that a person who regularly takes an afternoon nap and then has to tackle an afternoon exam may find it hard to stay awake for long enough to finish the paper. Students should stop studying and change to another activity for at least thirty minutes or so before going to bed. If studying in the bedroom it is advisable to tidy work up neatly ready for the morning or even cover it over if the mere sight of books or computer is uncomfortable. Strategies for sleep disorders described in Chapter Eight may also be helpful.

(8) The use of breaks should be planned. These may be used to have a hot drink, make a phone call, do household chores or take exercise. Particularly when examinations are near, many students take very little

physical exercise but a swim, run, game of squash or trip to the gym need not be too time consuming and can be very effective in dissipating anxiety and agitation.

Note Taking

This generally develops along idiosyncratic lines during the course of school and college life, but difficulties can arise particularly in the transition from school lessons to college lectures and the need to take notes from books. In lectures it is important to sit near the front and have a separate book or folder for each subject. Note taking may be restricted to picking out important facts or alternatively an attempt may be made to record everything, which is then checked over and reduced to the main points soon afterwards. Many of the more conscientious students make far too many notes, losing sight of the aim of the reading and ending up with merely a precis of the printed text. Wherever possible, apart from quotations, notes should be made in the student's own words as this forces him to work out and re-express the meaning. He can then understand, memorise and use the material. It is hard to learn and adapt another author's vocabulary and sentence structure.

Essay Writing

Essay writing for course work is another skill and differs from writing exam essay answers. The starting point should be an essay plan which can be a guide to reading and a source of questions to be answered in the note taking phase. Students who develop writing blocks at any stage of an essay can move to another section first or try talking the essay into a tape recorder as if giving a seminar or explanation to a fellow student. Many students falter as they try to turn the essay into the definitive work on a subject.

The Revision Period and Examination Problems

Examination difficulties may present as a phobia of the actual test situation itself or as anxiety related to lack of skill, parental pressure, or personal cognitions which need modification.

The examination phobic may suffer from worrying thoughts about the coming ordeal, provoking severe panic during the revision period and physiological disturbances such as sleepless nights. These may be treated by imaginal desensitisation (described in Chapter Six) aided by coping self-statements. The hierarchy used in this situation might include items like:

(1) Thinking about the exam.

(2) The night before.

(3) The morning before.

(4) Entering the exam room.

The student should be relaxed, presented with the scene and then asked to switch to positive coping statements such as:

- ○ I have worked steadily, I know enough to pass.
- ○ If I panic I will only have to take them at another time.
- ○ If I remain fairly calm, I shall do better.
- ○ I must concentrate on controlling my breathing and the tension in my arms.

In some cases anxiety about examinations leads to overbreathing and related symptoms of fainting, sickness and general panic which can be managed by demonstrating the linking relationship and teaching controlled breathing as described in Chapter Six. It is important that all these techniques are practised sitting in an upright chair similar to the examination setting.

This technique is not time consuming. The student can learn the relaxation techniques at home. Time can be saved and the therapeutic impact increased if the desensitisation session is taped and can be replayed frequently.

Anxiety Related to Lack of Skill may be realistic in students who have not taken examinations before or who have always repeated similar mistakes without attempts at correction. In these cases help may be needed with:

(1)   Revision techniques.

(2)   Practising timed question in various situations.

Revision requires an extension of the study methods already covered. It should aim for a gradual condensing of information from copious notes to a single page per topic and then perhaps to a few key points. If these are well learnt they are not easily forgotten in a panic and can act as cues to further details once writing has started. Practice timed questions can be answered at home with, perhaps, a relative acting as invigilator. First attempts should be at an easy question, then a more difficult one and finally a simulated hurried final question with only twenty minutes left. Practise should stress the importance of getting down facts and arguments without lengthy introductions and conclusions. Good literary essay writers often find this difficult. Later practise might include; (i) a very difficult question; (ii) a question on a topic not revised; (iii) starting one question and then being asked to change to another; (iv) making very brief notes in case time runs out. Many students still have to be reminded of the importance of attempting each question. Beta blockers are the drugs of choice if needed to supplement these techniques or in last minute emergency. Comfort is also gained from having a good supply of pens, pencils, sweets, drinks and smokers may benefit from Nicorette gum to chew in a long exam.

The Driving Test

Intended driving test candidates often attend the surgery asking for tranquillisers to help them overcome nervousness. Most commonly they are older people who have never experienced, or have got out of the habit of, taking tests. To provide tranquillisers for this purpose is dangerous and to take them without careful preparation is probably illegal.

Beta blockers, however, can be used without drowsiness in this and other examinations. It is often enough for a candidate to have a few in his pocket 'in case' although if they are likely to be used they should be tried beforehand to check their efficacy and inspire confidence. A simple desensitisation programme to the test circumstances and many repeated practice tests with the usual instructor, including making and mentally dismissing mistakes, will often achieve good results and render any drugs unnecessary.

Problems at Work

Although sometimes the presenting complaint, work problems more usually come to light when enquiring into the circumstances surrounding tiredness, snappiness or too frequent physical illnesses. They are commonly related to interpersonal problems with colleagues, restructuring of the organisation, overwork or poor time management.

Interpersonal Problems

These may occur with bosses, peers or subordinates. Assessment should try to pinpoint clearly the behaviour causing the difficulty. Who is doing what to whom? Where and how often? What triggers the problem? Who benefits from the present situation and how could it be altered? What would be the result of that alteration? All of these must be established clearly out of the pervading sense of injustice that usually surrounds these problems. Further information is then obtained by a baseline record which can contain any items thought to be relevant. A useful starting point is to ask the patient to record anything which irritates him at work, how it started, who was there, what action he took and what the result was. This may be enough to form an hypothesis or may indicate where further information is needed.

Employer Problems

When problems arise with bosses, there is frequently a sense of helplessness on the part of the junior and an assumption that nothing can be done. In fact few bosses are as unreasonable as they may seem. They are often content, however, to continue with the *status quo* (including their own bad habits) either because there is a hidden reward or because they are unaware of the consequences like staff inefficiency or dissatisfaction. To take an example: Peter a section leader, is criticised by Mr Power, the works director, for not having drawings for the biscuit plant ready on time. Peter knows the reasons for this are; (i) the commission for the plans sat on Mr Power's desk for two weeks before being passed to Peter; and (ii) that an experienced draughtsman in his section had just been replaced by a junior with no training in this type of project. Peter says nothing about it because, in spite of a feeling of injustice and frustration, he thinks that it is his job to 'deliver the goods' and not to 'whine to the bosses'.

Analysis of the problem showed; (i) communication failure between Peter and Mr Power; (ii) submissive attitudes and behaviour by Peter; (iii) Mr Power's behaviour inappropriately reinforced, as he was able to get on with other work, go to the gym or take days off without any apparent penalty for failing to pass the commission on to Peter.

Peter originally consulted his GP wanting tranquillisers for tiredness and edginess. After this analysis, he booked an interview with Mr Power at which, maintaining good eye contact, he asked for his boss's experience and help in dealing with some problems (thereby reinforcing Mr Power's status). He explained how tight time was on certain jobs (prompting quicker delivery of commissions from Mr Power) and said that this was particularly true with inexperienced staff. He asked if Mr Power could use his influence in getting preliminary training for new draughtsmen. This Mr Power promised to do and added his own suggestion that if this proved impossible, extra time must be allowed for jobs in those sections with inexperienced staff.

Future commissions were passed on promptly. When Peter delivered the drawings back on time, he always remarked to Mr Power that is was easier to do the work now that he had enough time (reinforcing Mr Power's new behaviour). Staff pre-training was instituted.

It should be noted that in this example the subordinate has got the desired change without being critical, aggressive or servile. He has merely spoken his own opinions clearly and encouraged the behaviour he wanted. This sort of programme takes a little longer than the five-minute consultation but can be very productive and avoid requests for psychotropic drugs. It is also more rewarding for the doctor. Sadly there are cases of harassment and bullying which cannot be resolved so easily. The same monitoring is needed to obtain the real facts of the situation and although some change may be possible the patient may need strategies to survive in the organisation while given the confidence and support to look elsewhere for work.

Thought records and thought challenging can be used to great effect in order to relieve the feelings of helplessness, loss of control and personal blame and prevent taking prolonged sick leave or premature resignation. The first of these makes it hard to return, the second makes it difficult to obtain further employment. An unpleasant or stressful work environment can also be made more tolerable simply by better organisation and time management by, for example, taking breaks when allowed, leaving the premises whenever possible. The breaks may be used for interesting activities, exercise or meeting friends. The self employed are particularly vulnerable to being taken over by work and establishing time boundaries and the use of an answerphone at set times of day can reduce the pressure considerably.

Peer Group Problems

Problems with the peer group in work may be concerned with social skills difficulties (see Chapter Seven) or involve unrealistic goals or unhelpful assumptions. A young woman working with entirely male colleagues in a male-dominated engineering field became tense and exhausted. Assessment of thoughts showed that she believed that she must be perfect at every part of her job or the men would say that a woman was unsuitable for the work. Exploring this attitude showed that, although there was some truth in it, the men would not assume her gender accounted for every minor lapse and that thinking in this way was unhelpful as perfection was impossible. The cognitive change combined with cue controlled shoulder relaxation produced a marked improvement in her work and physical and mental state.

Promotion

Promotion brings special problems particularly in its requirements for more strategic planning, delegation and different modes of communication. A recently promoted sales manager was depressed as he found himself edgy and overstressed. He concluded that he had reached his potential as a (very good) sales representative and that his promotion had been a mistake. This added to his depression. Assessment showed that he was attempting to do both jobs – his present and former one – and as a result had had no chance to plan the strategy of his new responsibilities and thus was staggering from crisis to crisis.

The first stage of intervention was to list the things he might leave subordinates to do by themselves and the possible consequences either for good or bad. In fact nothing further was needed from the GP as the patient saw what was happening, began delegating tasks and found time for planning. He carried out the whole programme with no further prompting. This case was a striking example of the rule that if behavioural assessment is adequate, change can often be obtained with little further trouble.

Job Burn-Out

We use this term a little reluctantly both because it is a fashionable label and because it really only groups together a number of problem features of work which are far from new. Everyone has the occasional bad day at work, but when that day turns into weeks and months a pattern of symptoms emerges. These are loss of drive, dissatisfaction, depression, increased liability to illness and absenteeism and increasing inefficiency leading finally to crisis and need for escape. Commonly the person is able and enthusiastic in the early stages of his career. He finds himself becoming increasingly dissatisfied with the job, exhausted physically and despondent and cynical psychologically. Pessimism and self doubts grow and eventually he becomes obsessed with his frustrations and the need to find a 'way out'. Sometimes this 'way out' will be a change of job or environment and the problems may improve but, unfortunately, often this adaptive solution seems impossible and 'the way out' will be alcohol, depressive illness, drugs, suicide or coronary thrombosis.

Additional circumstances such as family demands or environmental pressures such as poor housing, financial difficulties or excessive commuting predispose to burn-out but relaxations such as sport or hobbies will protect against it. Triggers often come from within work itself such as missed promotion or difficult colleagues or unrealistic career goals. Equally damaging can be changes in the firm such as mergers, contractions or altered management structure when known and trusted colleagues are replaced by threatening unknowns.

Assessment will consist of an interview determining the factors discussed above and a stress diary recording all events felt to be disturbing for, say, one week. Cognitive factors are important in modifying goals to more realistic levels and in modifying how work situations are perceived.

A work stress checklist will help to identify the most troublesome areas (Veninga and Spradley 1981):

---

(1) Threats to health and safety.

(2) Work overload: imposed or self induced.

(3) Threats to job security real or imagined legal and illegal.

(4) Time pressures.

(5) Working under load and boredom.

(6) Stressful interpersonal relationships.

(7) Perception of the job as 'dead-end'.

(8) Threats from the boss or bullying.

The first stage of behavioural management overlaps assessment and consists of understanding and monitoring the problem. As with many problems, change is much easier to obtain early before the worst features of the downward spiral have developed. Thus early problem recognition is particularly important. If more is needed, the following strategies may be useful:

(1) Attempt to modify the environment if possible, with attention to such factors as additional office space, more staff, change of job, improved travel, flexitime (however see later warning) or job sharing.

(2) Attend to unhelpful thoughts and attitudes by listing them and then attempting to answer or modify them (as with depression see Chapter Nine). For example: Thought: 'This is a nothing job – dead end and worthless.' Logical Answer: 'It is boring a lot of the time but I have some good friends and the odd joke. It's better then nothing – stick to it and perhaps I can change later. I can concentrate on hobbies for now.'

(3) Challenge perfectionist attitudes and learn to tolerate an imperfect self in an imperfect world.

(4) Invest physically and mentally in outside interests.

(5) Modify the timetable by allowing more time in the morning, cutting overtime or extra work and incorporating reward breaks in the day.

Changing Jobs and Redundancy and Unemployment

These are deliberately grouped together as redundancy may be perceived as a change of occupation or the loss of it and the fear and possibility of long term unemployment or early retirement must be addressed. Unemployment is generally 'bad' in terms of mental health but can be an improvement for a limited number of people. Many factors are thought to have effects on mental health both at the immediate transition from work and in the long period of joblessness. Warr (1991) suggests a nine factor framework for examining employment and unemployment and this is a useful guide in assessing a patient's distress:

(1) The opportunity for control of activities and events.

(2) The opportunity to use or extend a person's skills.

(3) The task demands of the job and extrinsic demands (how the job fits in to domestic life and leisure).

(4) The variety in the work.

(5) Environmental clarity – what is required, feedback on performance, predictability of the future.

(6) Availability of money, satisfaction and perceived fairness of pay.

(7) Physical security, working conditions.

(8) Opportunities for interpersonal contact, making friends, support and achieving personal space.

(9) Social status and self-esteem.

By considering these points in a functional analysis, an individual programme for change can be developed. In addition, a list of assets and liabilities can be drawn up and a problem-solving approach used to minimise the drawbacks of the employment situation and to take advantage of the assets. This can then be converted into a task list including items dealing with financial requirements, conditions for work or leisure and the availability of resources such as job vacancies, job finding clubs or agencies and adult classes. The patient can be advised to set a specified time aside each day to attend to applications and collect information on alternative plans. Cognitive techniques and recording can be used to prepare for the inevitable rejections and for confidence building for interviews and telephone enquiries be they for jobs or leisure pursuits. By using these techniques the multiple problems associated with redundancy or unemployment may seem a little less dire. Social and financial problems can be addressed in the first instance by a visit to the citizens advice bureau which may hold sessions in the practice premises. In the long term, support from job-finders clubs can augment the individual efforts.

Shift Work and Flexitime

Shift work is a common cause of multiple problems including sleep and eating disorders, digestive troubles, fatigue and irritability which are probably associated with disturbance of the normal twenty-four-hour pattern known as the *circadian rhythm*. In addition there are further problems associated with disruption of family, social and leisure activities. Night work appears to have a more adverse effect on physical health whereas afternoon and evening shifts disrupt home and recreation. The fixed-shift worker usually adapts to his changed circumstances in both body and life-style whereas the unfortunate rotating shift worker is denied this opportunity with a consequent higher incidence of stress-related problems (Landy 1985). Interventions may be directed to changing the working pattern with its associated difficulties or to modifying its adverse effects by using stress control techniques already discussed.

Flexitime implies a variable working week usually incorporating a core of obligatory hours with the rest to be made up at the worker's discretion. Although not possible in all types of work, it does give the worker a greater degree of control over his life and avoids, to some extent, the problem of incompatible timetables between spouses. The disadvantages of it are that it may obliterate the normal breaks in the day, perhaps allowing no time for lunch or a walk but more time to flop in front of the television or worry about the day's activities and current personal problems. In patients where flexitime is contributing to stress these breaks can be used to reduce pressure. The working week can be designed to incorporate a variety of breaks for rest or pleasurable and constructive pastimes.

References

Deneke, W. and Harris, M (1972) 'Teaching self control of study behaviour.' *Behaviour Research and Therapy 10*, 35–41.
Landy, F. (1985) *Psychology of Work Behaviour.* Homewood, Illinois: Dorsey Press.
Veninga, R. and Spradley, J. (1981) *The Work Stress Connection.* Boston: Little Brown.
Warr, P. (ed) (1991) *Psychology at Work.* Harmondsworth: Penguin.

Further Reading

ISCO (1995) *Twelve week study skills programme.* Camberley: ISCO Publications.
McKenna, E. (1994) *Business Psychology and Organisational Behaviour: A Students Handbook.* Chapter on Health and Work Stress. New York: L. Erlbaum Assoc.
Veninga, R. and Spradley, J. (1981) *The Work Stress Connection.* Boston: Little Brown.
Warr, P. (ed) (1991) *Psychology at Work.* Harmondsworth: Penguin.

Self Help Books

Smith, M. and Smith, G. (1994) *A Study Skills Handbook.* Oxford: Oxford University Press.

Chapter Fourteen

Problems of Later Life

Previous generations have, for better or worse, had more clear cut definitions of old age. Women at sixty and men at sixty-five were acknowledged by the state to have reached pensionable age. Various positive and negative consequences ensued notably the label of 'geriatric' or a person on the 'scrap heap' but with a bus pass and a lot of free time.

There is now a much wider age range during which people can suddenly or gradually be propelled into 'later life' states by retirement (early or later), redundancy or physical incapacity. For many women, HRT has blurred the physical transition into middle age and beyond.

Many of the problems presenting at the GP's consulting room by the elderly population require the same cognitive behavioural analysis, skills and treatment as those of younger patients. However, the formulation and treatment plan should acknowledge any specifically age related handicaps due to physical ill health, reduced mobility and social opportunities.

Several topics specific to later life feature prominently in GP or health visitor consultations and these will be dealt with separately in this section even though there is obvious overlap with other chapters in the book.

In general, assessment and functional analysis can be carried out with the person in the surgery, but perhaps in this group especially there is benefit from a home visit or from going into the environment in which the difficulties arise so that the effects of that environment on their behaviour can be seen and modified.

Monitoring or time sampling (see Chapter Four) can be set up if necessary. For example, an elderly person who is confused may find that all the doors on the landing look the same and keep wandering into the 'wrong' room. Clear cue cards on the doors and low intensity lighting at night may be all that is required to put matters right.

Elderly people living on their own can become very anxious about minor day-to-day problems. Problem solving techniques such as listing all potential solutions and finding the most practical and appropriate, can be immensely helpful. For example, a lady was terrified of the dark when alone at night, having read about attacks on elderly people at home. The fear was not irrational and did not amount to a phobia. Finding a lodger and the installation of an alarm solved the problem. In both these cases behavioural assessment helped arrive at solution even though the solution itself may appear to be common sense.

The following topics cause particular concern in dealing with the older patient:

- Retirement
- Dementia
- Physical ill health and Medication
- Bereavement
- Anxiety and Depression
- Sleep
- Problems Associated with Carers
- Sexual Dysfunction
- Alcohol and Drugs

Retirement

Retirement has changed with work practices and life span changes, so that it can be a much longer and less predictable in terms of time, experience and anticipation. Like redundancy, retirement can be approached in the spirit of changing a job rather than leaving one. Unlike redundancy retirement is still often pleasurable and planned.

Plans for retirement can be considered and made some time before the due date. In the normal course of events this will bring about the necessary cognitive and behavioural changes to adapt to the transition. Where anxiety and depression occur the same areas of change may be looked at and help given to analyse, problem solve and make decisions. These areas include:

(1) *Moving or staying* – and if a move is contemplated, the advantages and disadvantages in terms of housing, services including medicine, cost and access to relatives.

(2) *A general financial prediction* including pensions and other sources, costs and savings at home, car ownership, leisure costs, cost of living and inflation. Referral to citizens advice bureau for help and information on benefits.

(3) *The social effects* in the losing or possibly gaining of friends and everyday contacts in the neighbourhood. The opportunity for increased dependency of or on relatives.

(4) The opportunities for *recreation, sports and unfulfilled ambitions* to be realised.

(5) Some *specific exercises* like the swopping of roles between partners, for example, on household chores and how to cope with more time together in the home.

(6) The availability of *special investments and concessions* like cheap travel for retired people.

(7) The importance of *making wills* and their provisions.

(8) Facing up to *loss of status* and the possibilities of voluntary or part time work as an intermediate step to full retirement.

This might all seem somewhat far removed from the role of cognitive behaviour therapist, but will be useful as a framework for intervention where long term worry and indecision is creating anxiety. This planning can be approached following an information gathering and problem solving format. Thought diaries are used too pinpoint specific areas of worry and to modify negative cognitions about themselves and the future. In an area or practice with substantial numbers of people on the verge of retirement, a group to discuss these topics can be run at the practice with outside specialists being brought in to speak on relevant subjects.

Loss of Status

It is possible for some people to maintain their feelings of worth through personal activities, hobbies and voluntary work. For others who derive status solely from work or through their role as parent or housekeeper, the diminished responsibility may create problems. Preventative work as above can be effective and reduce the risk of depression. Some patients present with stress and insomnia due to physical and mental exhaustion from trying to continue with activities even though they are no longer rewarding. This often stems from the thought that it is 'too late' to embark on new enterprises along with a fear that giving up some occupations is 'one foot in the grave'. Help can be given to review the thoughts and assumptions lying behind these statements, to monitor activities for mastery and pleasure and to look at other opportunities such as time with grandchildren or university of the third age, exercise or the more creative past times, writing or painting.

Dementia

The term dementia applied to a group of diseases that cause progressive global deterioration in the functioning of the brain.

With the ever increasing ageing population, dementia is going to be a major problem facing families in the 21st century. Current estimates put the incidence at 20 per cent of people in the UK over eighty and 6 per cent over sixty-five as affected (Social Services Inspectorate 1996). The dementias are characterised by intellectual, memory and behavioural problems. Alzheimer's is the principal category of dementia, others are associated with cerebrovascular disease and there are also several less common groups and a few potentially reversible ones caused by conditions such hypothyroidism and benign intracerebral tumours. It should be recognised that many of the elderly are from different racial and cultural backgrounds which may raise special issues for assessment and the cognitive and behavioural help given to both patient and carer (Pollitt 1996).

Assessment

This needs to be ongoing since dementia is progressive. The areas to be investigated in assessment include:

Loss of memory – this is of course one of the cardinal features. Loss of recent memory is usually most marked at first. This causes most problems to carers. Requests may be endlessly repeated (sometimes by telephone), everyday items are mislaid and anecdotes endlessly repeated as if for the first time.

Language impairment – aphasia particularly nominal aphasia may be one of the early signs and almost always develops later.

Apraxia – loss of control over fine movements may combine with arthritis to present problems of self care (including opening medicine bottles).

Agnosia – is the failure to recognise familiar objects. This may be hurtful with, for example, old friends or dangerous with, for example, traffic or fire.

Dysgraphia – may provide problems in signing cheques or documents.

Personality changes – may contribute to carer's distress: 'she is not the mother I knew'.

Disinhibition – involving anger, soiling or inappropriate sexual behaviour can be even more distressing and devastating.

Delusions and severe mood fluctuations – these may occur in the Dementia patient.

Insight – is often intact early on to an extent which is distressing to the patient. It usually diminishes later.

Physical deterioration – this is progressive. Incontinence has a major impact on carers and should always be monitored carefully so help can be provided at once.

Diaries may be helpful in sorting out the extent and nature of the problems and, if feasible for the sufferer in the early stages, may be therapeutic as a memory aid. Carer's diaries can be valuable but it is important to remember that carers may be very stressed and being asked to keep a diary may be the last straw.

Interventions

These need to be given on an evolutionary basis, tailored to meet the needs of the individual and carer at each stage. The dividing line between what is acceptable and what is regarded as abnormal depends a lot on terminology and social and cultural interpretation. Therefore it is important to look at change as well as current behaviour.

Treatment remains symptomatic with modifications aimed at minimising distress from the behavioural, cognitive and emotional sequelae. Treatment of the patient may also serve to reduce the severe emotional, physical and financial strains on the carers. About 80 per cent of the care for dementia patients is provided by the immediate family, and the coping resources and commitment of these carers is crucial and must be carefully and sensitively assessed.

Evidence from research shows that demented elderly people are still able to learn, but compared with non-demented patients they may need even greater consistency in implementing a programme for longer periods of time to maintain new behaviour, or reduce inappropriate behaviour. For example, calling out for the commode at inappropriate times may be reduced by offering the commode after all meals and drinks, and on each occasion explaining when the person last went and when they will be offered the chance to go again. This should be coupled with establishing an appropriate method of calling for assistance in an emergency.

On the whole more particularly behavioural programmes should be used with the more demented person, both for the sake of clarity and because of the reduced cognitive capacity. However, it is important not to overlook depression particularly in the early stages and some cognitive techniques combined with medication may make a positive impact.

Memory lapses can be dangerous and lead to accidents. Large notices can be put up as reminders as well as lists, alarms, appropriately timed telephone prompts and alarm clocks.

Sleep difficulties may be altered by ensuring stimulus control. Sleep should be reserved as far as possible for bed and for after supper, following a consistent bedtime routine. Sleep should preferably be in a different room from daytime activities (see also Chapter Five). If naps or rests are taken in the day they may be time limited and the patient may be led to expect and prepare for less sleep at night. The sleepless patient may find it easier and be less burdensome if bedtime hours are limited. Where possible increased activities, outings and exercise will improve the periods of relaxation and sleep.

Stimulation during the day can be increased and confusion decreased by using principles of reality orientation in an informal way at home. This means that, during all contact with the person, constant reminders are given about who he is, about the time and about the place. Patients should be encouraged to look after themselves where possible, even if they take a long time, for example with dressing and toiletting. Calendars, clocks and newspaper headlines or pictures are useful to help keep the person's attention, and encourage them to be aware of what is going on in their environment. The success of these measures depends heavily on the resources, enthusiasm, skill and of course existence of the carers.

It will often be the caring relatives who come to the doctor for advice. If difficulties can be foreseen as a result of regular checks with relatives, a preventative approach can be adopted. In this case minor problems are dealt with immediately and general strategies can be adopted to keep the elderly person as alert, stimulated and in touch with reality as is humanly possible.

Sleep Disorder, Anxiety and Depression, Sexual Dysfunction

These topics are covered elsewhere in the book but a few comments may be helpful for carrying out the assessment in elderly patients.

Surprisingly the great majority of elderly people do not complain of poor sleep and adapt to the fact that the continuity, depth and duration of sleep declines with age. Those that do complain should be treated sympathetically and an examination made of lifestyle including their sleeping timetable and culture, depressed mood, anxiety or fear.

Medication, nutrition and alcohol consumption should be investigated. Poor nutrition often precipitating a degree of hypothermia and low blood sugar is detrimental to sleep and health in general.

Anxiety and depression are common as in other age groups but are more often assumed to be acceptable states for elderly people, especially those with chronic physical ill health or social isolation. Another myth which circulated until relatively recently was that the problems of the older age patients were not amenable to psychotherapy. Thankfully this view has been dispelled and such patients may be assessed in the usual way. The onset and triggers for anxiety and depression are particularly important in depression occurring for the first time late in the persons life. In these cases the therapist can build on previous coping ideas which have served the person well over the years and may have only just broken down or reached capacity due to a recent bereavement or other critical factor.

There is considerable variation in the age at which people become sexually inactive. It should not be presumed that discussion and help on this topic are inappropriate. An elderly woman asked for help as she and her husband had not had sex for six months since he had been made redundant and subsequently retired. She attributed this to a period of high stress in their lives during which they had got out of the habit of making love. In fact the graded behavioural tasks of sensate focus were enough to sort out the problem involving two brief consultations at the surgery. Some brief sex therapy may also be required after a period of depression or physical illness. It may also be necessary to help to adapt love making to physical limitations. This can save the need to refer to a psychosexual clinic which would most likely never be accepted.

Carers

The psychological toll on carers has been alluded to in the section on dementia. The vast majority of people suffering the effects of strokes, Alzheimer's disease, chronic confusional states and chronic physical illness are cared for by relatives in the community. The carers, often elderly themselves, regularly consult the primary care team suffering from stress, anxiety and exhaustion. The constant demands on the carer which they cannot always meet, leaves them at best guilty and feeling they are failing in their wishes and duties and at worst murderous. The passive coper appears to suffer more than the active involved one, even if the physical burdens are higher for the latter (Matson 1994).

A content analysis of the type of worries brought to counselling by family caregivers revealed seven categories including: meeting the dependants needs; concern over the caregiver–recipient relationship; need to improve coping skills, feelings of guilt and inadequacy and planning for the future (Smith, Smith and Toseland 1991).

Research has shown that the ways in which carers cope is associated with the degree of their stress and depression. Coping being defined as 'the cognitive and behavioural efforts to manage psychological stress or demands which are appraised as taxing or exceeding the resources' (Lazarus 1993).

Stress can be reduced for carers in some of the following ways:

(1) Exploring with carers how to monitor the demands in different areas of their life and evaluate them in order to decide on priorities. This might involve some compromise between easing the burden of the carer and maintaining or improving the quality of life of the dependant. Although they are not necessarily incompatible. The goal might be to avoid or to obtain an institutional placement or to increase the amount of respite care.

(2) To teach the Timetabling skills in order to save physical and emotional energy.

(3) To obtain and delegate to outside help, such as specialist groups or citizens advice bureau.

(4) To join support groups for practical and emotional support.

(5) To keep a thought record to access negative thoughts of guilt, failure and worry about the future in order to modify some of these cognitions.

(6) To teach problem solving.

(7) To adjust to changing circumstances over time. Help may be needed to assess the changes.

(8) To include time for a variety of personal activities for which timetabling and the acceptance of an outside carer may be necessary even for an hour or two a week.

Often the carer is 'on duty' twenty-four hours a day, seven days a week and are too exhausted to accept the idea of help which involves any changes to their routine. This 'yes but' reaction should not be attributed to non-compliance and a very gently graded programme of change perhaps starting with the provision of respite care for the elderly patient, may be all the carer can accept at first.

Research shows that passivity is highly correlated with depression, avoidance and anxiety, so a more proactive approach to caring will increase the sense of control and well-being. By the creative use of timetabling, problem solving, cognitive restructuring and tactical coping it may be possible to find ways of balancing the needs of carer and dependent for mutual benefit.

Usually several members of the primary health care team are involved and a concerted effort by the district nurse, health visitor and GP may be needed to solve problems and set appropriate goals. Good communication within the team is particularly important in these cases. In addition it may be worthwhile to consult specialist services early if the locality is adequately served with psychogeriatricians, community psychiatric nurses and specialist clinical psychologists.

Alcohol and Drugs

Alcohol properly controlled can be a useful pleasure and a social lubricant in later, as well as earlier life, but the lonely elderly person can easily slide into excess alcohol intake which may go unnoticed, cause global deterioration of function and is in any case extremely hard to treat. It is important to be on the look-out for this problem to detect and if possible prevent it early.

Drugs which are abused in old age are usually prescribed and probably most GPs have some elderly patients who they know full well are taking an undesirable cocktail of drugs through the patients will and habit and the doctor's tacit acceptance. In these cases damage limitation helped by a little motivational interviewing (see Chapter Eight) may be all that is possible. Necessary prescribed drugs should, of course, be kept to a justified minimum. There are a number of simple techniques which are particularly helpful with the elderly patient who may find remembering to follow medication instructions particularly difficult:

(1) When remembering to take medicines, a container where the day's dose can be put into compartments marked 'breakfast', 'lunch', 'tea' and 'before bed' by the patient or a carer is extremely useful. These are now widely obtainable from pharmacies.

(2) The doctor should try to give instructions to a relative or friend as well as the patient.

(3) It is important to make sure the patient can take the form of medicine prescribed; that they can open containers or swallow pills.

(4) Patients should be encouraged to destroy or, preferably, return old medicines – many elderly patients' medicine cupboards contain truly horrifying quantities of unused drugs.

References

Lazarus, R. (1993) 'Coping theory and research: past, present and future.' *Psychosomatic Medicine 55*, 234–247.

Matson, L. (1994) 'Coping, caring and stress. A study of stroke carers and carers of older confused people.' *British Journal of Clinical Psychology 33*, 333–344.

Pollitt, P. (1996) 'Dementia in old age: an anthropological perspective.' *Psychological Medicine 26*, 1061–1074.

Smith, G., Smith, M. and Toseland, R. (1991) 'Problems identified by family caregivers in counselling.' *Gerontology 31*, 1, 15–19.

Social Services Inspectorate Report (1996). *Assessing Older People with Dementia Living in the Community*. Wetherby: SSI Publication. Department of Health.

Recommended for Further Reading:

Hanley, I. and Hodge, J. (eds) (1984) *Psychological Approaches to the Care of the Elderly*. London: Croom Helm.

Wood, R.T. (1996) *Handbook of Clinical Psychology in Ageing*. Chichester: Wiley.

Patient Booklet:

Forgetfulness and Dementia. Published by Family Doctor Publications (see General appendix for details).

Useful Addresses and Contacts:

Mind and Mortality Organisation. (For counsellors and psychologists working with the bereaved.)

Contact Dr. Murray Parkes, High Marl, 21 South Road, Chorleywood, Herts. WD3 5AS.

Cruse – contact through local telephone directory.

Age Concern – contact through local telephone directory.

General Appendix

Patient Leaflets and Booklets

Some of these leaflets have been described after their appropriate chapters but it seemed useful to describe the complete series from which they are derived in this Appendix.

British Association for Behavioural and Cognitive Psychotherapies Series

Titles:

   Anxiety and Panic Attacks
   Schizophrenia
   General Health Problems
   Post Traumatic Stress Disorder
   Agoraphobia
   Learning Disability
   Depression
   Obsessive Compulsive Disorder

These leaflets provide a general description of each type of problem together with an outline of the cognitive behavioural management. There is a brief outline of the general features of CBT. They may be obtained from: BABCP, Harrow Psychological Health Services, Harrow, Middlesex HA1 3JV. Tel: 0181 869 2326 Fax: 0181 977 1017.

Royal College of Psychiatrists Series

Titles:

   Depression
   Post Natal Depression
   Anorexia and Bulimia
   Anxiety and Phobias
   Bereavement

Surviving Adolescence
Sleep Problems

These are published as a service to The Royal College of psychiatrists by Dista Products. They are available free from Dista Representatives. Given their joint origin their is naturally more emphasis on drug treatments but they do give a brief description of the psychological treatments available.

Oxford Clinical Psychology Series

Titles:

Bulimia Nervosa £2
Obsessive–Compulsive Disorder £2
Understanding Panic £2
Depression £2
How to Relax £3
Managing Anxiety: a user's manual £5.50
Managing Anxiety (Mainly behavioural) £2.50
Controlling Anxiety (Mainly cognitive) £2.50
Managing Social Anxiety £2.50
Understanding Trauma £5

These are a series of extremely valuable quite detailed patient manuals derived from those actually in use for research and clinical work at the Psychology Department, Warneford Hospital, Headington, Oxford, OX3 7JX. Orders to the Booklets Secretary must be with payment according to the prices given above.

Understanding Health Series

Titles:

Understanding Depression
Understanding Drug Abuse

These are two leaflets dealing with relevant topics from within a large general medical series. They are published by Hawker Publications but sponsored by different drug firms who supply them free via their representatives. They are really general introductions to the topics; the Depression leaflet has little appeal or relevance but the Drug abuse one might be of help to, for example, parents of worried teenagers or new partners of users.

Family Doctor Series

Titles:

> **Stress**
> **Forgetfulness and Dementia**
> **Eating Disorders**

These are also booklets from a much larger general medical series which cover topics relevant to this book. They are well and clearly written by acknowledged authorities. Retail price £2.49. Bulk orders in blocks of five with twenty total as a minimum order from Family Doctor Publications, 14 Princeton Court, Felsham Road, London SW15 1AZ. Tel: 0181 780 5020 Fax: 0181 780 5155.

Getting a Good Night's Sleep?

A useful pamphlet along the CB lines given in Chapter Six from the work of Colin Elspie reprinted from the BMJ ABC of Sleep Disorders. Free from Lorex Synthelabo representatives.

Subject Index

Author Index

Printed in the United Kingdom
by Lightning Source UK Ltd.
102307UKS00001B/45-70